A Level

Biology

The Revision Guide

Editors:

Becky May, Kate Redmond.

Contributors:

Gloria Barnett, Claire Charlton, Martin Chester, Barbara Green, Anna-Fe Guy, Dominic Hall, Gemma Hallam, Stephen Phillips, Claire Reed, Katherine Reed, Adrian Schmit, Emma Singleton, Sharon Watson.

Proofreaders:

Ben Aldiss, Vanessa Aris, James Foster, Tom Trust.

Published by Coordination Group Publications Ltd.

This book is suitable for:

OCR, AQA A, AQA B and Edexcel.

There are notes at the tops of double pages to tell you if there's a bit you can ignore for your syllabus.

ISBN: 1 84146 975 0
Groovy website: www.cgpbooks.co.uk
Jolly bits of clipart from CorelDRAW
Printed by Elanders Hindson, Newcastle upon Tyne.

Contents

Cell Organisation

Woohoo — cells. Not the most original way to start a biology book, but riveting nonetheless. We're all made of cells, so you can't knock 'em really.

There are **Two Types** of Cell —
Prokaryotic and *Eukaryotic*

Prokaryotic cells are simpler than eukaryotic cells. Prokaryotes include bacteria and blue-green algae. Eukaryotic cells are more complex, and include all animal and plant cells. The next few pages cover eukaryotic cells.

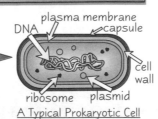
A Typical Prokaryotic Cell

DNA · plasma membrane · capsule · cell wall · ribosome · plasmid

PROKARYOTES	EUKARYOTES
Extremely small cells (0.5-3.0 μm diameter)	Larger cells (20-40 μm diameter)
No nucleus — DNA free in cytoplasm	Nucleus present
Cell wall made of a polysaccharide, but not cellulose or chitin	Cellulose cell wall (in plants and algae) or chitin cell wall (in fungi)
Few organelles	Many organelles
Small ribosomes	Larger ribosomes
Example: *E. coli* bacterium	Example: Human liver cell

Some Cells are **Adapted** for **Specific Functions**

Most eukaryotic cells in multi-cellular organisms are adapted to do a particular job. 'Fraid you need to know some examples.

1) The **alveolar epithelium cells** line the alveoli in the **lungs**. They're adapted to allow gases to pass through them easily. They're thin, with not much cytoplasm.

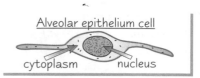
Alveolar epithelium cell
cytoplasm · nucleus

2) **Epithelium cells** in the **small intestine** are adapted to absorb food efficiently. The walls of the small intestine have lots of finger-like projections called **villi** to increase surface area — and the cells on the surface of the villi have their own **microvilli** to increase surface area even more.

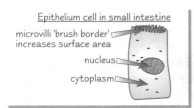
Epithelium cell in small intestine
microvilli 'brush border' increases surface area
nucleus
cytoplasm

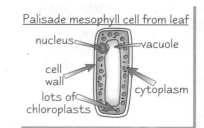
Palisade mesophyll cell from leaf
nucleus · vacuole · cell wall · lots of chloroplasts · cytoplasm

3) **Palisade mesophyll cells** in leaves do most of the photosynthesis. They contain **many chloroplasts**, so they can absorb as much sunlight as possible.

Similar Cells are Organised into **Tissues**

A single-celled organism performs all its life functions in its one cell. **Multi-cellular organisms** (like us) are more complicated — different cells do different jobs, so cells have to be **organised** into different groups. Similar cells are grouped together into **tissues**:

Squamous epithelium is a **single layer** of **flat cells** lining a surface. It's pretty common in the body. The cells lining the **alveoli** are squamous epithelium cells.

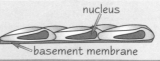
nucleus
basement membrane

Epithelium means a tissue that forms a covering or a lining.

Ciliated epithelium has moving hair-like structures called **cilia** on it. It's found on surfaces where things need to be moved — in the trachea for instance, where the cilia waft mucus along.

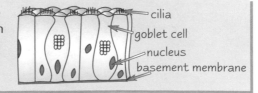
cilia · goblet cell · nucleus · basement membrane

Tissues aren't always made up of one type of cell. Some tissues include different types of cell working together.

To complicate things, you don't have epithelia in plants. The covering tissue is called **epidermis** instead.

Xylem is a plant tissue with two jobs — it **transports water** around the plant, and it **supports** the plant. The cells are mostly **dead and hollow** with no end walls (so they are like tubes) and they have **thick walls** for strength.

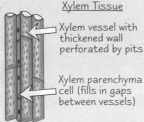
Xylem Tissue
Xylem vessel with thickened wall perforated by pits
Xylem parenchyma cell (fills in gaps between vessels)

Phloem tissue carries sugars around the plant. It's also arranged in tubes. Each cell has end walls with **holes** in them, so that sap can move easily through them. These end walls are called **sieve plates**.

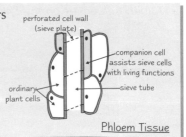
perforated cell wall (sieve plate)
companion cell assists sieve cells with living functions
sieve tube
ordinary plant cells
Phloem Tissue

Cell Organisation

Tissues are Organised into Organs

An **organ** is a group of tissues that work together to perform a particular function.

The **leaf** is an example of a plant organ.
It's made up of the following tissues:

1) **Lower epidermis** — contains stomata (holes) to let carbon dioxide and oxygen in and out.

2) **Spongy mesophyll** — full of spaces to let gases circulate.

3) **Palisade mesophyll** — most photosynthesis takes place here (see p2).

4) **Xylem** — carries water to the leaf.

5) **Phloem** — carries sugars away from leaf.

6) **Upper epidermis** — covered in a waterproof waxy cuticle to reduce water loss.

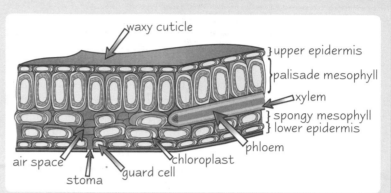

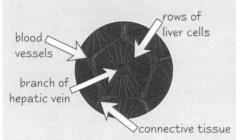

The **liver** is an example of an animal organ.
1) **Liver cells** are the main tissue.
2) There are blood vessels containing blood to provide food and oxygen for the liver cells. Blood is a tissue (yes, really).
3) **Connective tissue** holds the organ together.

Blood vessels aren't a tissue, though. They contain several tissues (epithelium, muscle etc.), so they're actually organs.

Plan Diagrams show Tissue Types in Organs

This is a **plan diagram** of a section of a leaf. Only **tissues** are shown on plan diagrams, **not cells**.

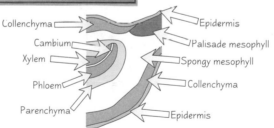

Practice Questions

Q1 What is the definition of a tissue?

Q2 Name one place in the human body where you would find ciliated epithelium.

Q3 What is the main function of the upper epidermis in a leaf?

Q4 State one way in which the epithelial cells of the small intestine are adapted for their function.

Exam Questions

Q1 Give three examples of epithelial cells found in mammals and, for each, explain how their structure suits them to their function. [9 marks]

Q2 Explain how each of the tissues in a leaf is adapted to allow the leaf to perform its function. [12 marks]

Cells — tiny lillle blobs with important jobs to do...

OK, so you've read the first topic and now it's the moment you've been waiting for — yep, it's time to get learning those facts. Make sure you learn the examples of tissues and organs and how cells are adapted to their jobs — examiners love examples. And make sure you know the differences between eukaryotic and prokaryotic cells. And brush your hair — you look like a mess.

Electron and Light Microscopy

You can't get away from microscopes in biology. So you need to learn this page, otherwise all those colourful splodges will remain meaningless for ever more.

Magnification is Size, Resolution is Detail

1) **Magnification** is how much bigger the image is than the specimen. It's calculated as: $\frac{\text{length of drawing or photograph}}{\text{length of specimen object}}$

2) **Resolution** is how detailed the image is. More specifically, it's how well a microscope distinguishes between two points that are close together. If a microscope lens can't separate two objects, then increasing the magnification won't help.

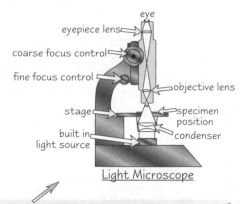

Light Microscope

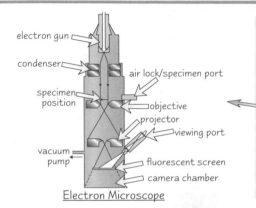

Electron Microscope

Light microscopes have a **lower resolution** than electron microscopes. Decreasing the wavelength of the light increases resolution, but even then a light microscope can only distinguish points 0.2 micrometres (µm) apart.

Electron microscopes use **electrons** instead of light to form an image, and focus them with an electromagnet. You can't see electrons, so the image has to be formed on a fluorescent screen. Electrons have a much **shorter wavelength** than light, and can resolve things down to 0.5 nanometres (0.0005 µm) — so electron microscopes provide better resolution and **more detailed images**.

Light Microscopes Show Cell Structure

If you just want to see the **general structure of a cell**, then light microscopes are fine. But even the best light microscopes can't see most of the organelles in the cell. You can see the larger organelles, like the nucleus, but none of the internal details.

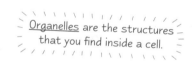

Organelles are the structures that you find inside a cell.

Liver cells seen under a light microscope:

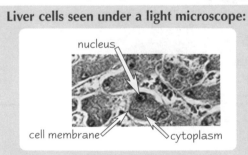

General animal cell as if seen with a light microscope

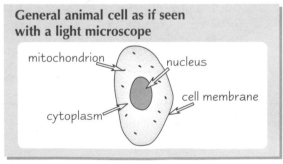

Electron Microscopes Show Organelles

There's not much in a cell that an electron microscope can't see. You can see the **organelles** and the **internal structure** of most of them. Most of what's known about cell structure has been discovered by electron microscope studies. The diagram to the right shows what you can see in an animal cell under an electron microscope. Very pretty indeed.

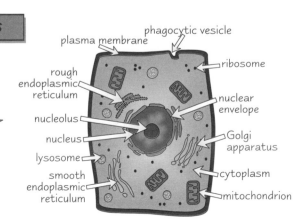

Electron and Light Microscopy

Comparing Light and Electron Microscopy

LIGHT MICROSCOPE	ELECTRON MICROSCOPE
Resolution down to 0.2 μm	Resolution down to 0.5 nm
Living tissue can be examined	Processing kills living cells
Colours can be seen	Natural colours can't be seen
Mobile	Can't be moved around
Relatively cheap	Very expensive

A micrometre (μm) is a thousandth of a millimetre. A nanometre (nm) is a thousandth of a micrometre. That's tiny.

Electron microscopes are ace, but scientists still use light microscopes as well, because they have some advantages.

Skip this section if you're doing OCR A or Edexcel.

Differential Centrifugation Sorts Organelles

To separate a particular organelle from all the others you use a technique called **differential centrifugation** (also called **ultracentrifugation**).

Isotonic means equal concentration. The concentration is equal to the concentration of the fluids in the organelles.

1) First, the cells are '**homogenised**' (mashed up) in **ice-cold isotonic buffer solution**. The **low temperature** prevents protein-digesting enzymes **digesting** the organelles. The **buffer** keeps the **pH constant** and the **isotonic solution** stops the organelles taking in lots of water via **osmosis** and bursting.

2) The cell fragments are poured into a **tube**. The tube is put into a **centrifuge** (with the **bottom** of the tube facing **outwards**, so heavy stuff gets flung outwards and ends up at the bottom of the tube), and is spun at a **low speed**. **Cell debris**, like the cells walls in plant cells, gets flung to the bottom of the tube by the centrifuge. It forms a thick sediment at the bottom, which is called a **pellet**. The rest of the organelles stay suspended in the **supernatant** (the fluid above the sediment).

3) The supernatant is **drained off**, poured into **another tube**, and spun in the centrifuge at a **higher speed**. The heavier organelles like the nuclei form a pellet at the bottom of the tube. The supernatant containing the rest of the organelles is drained off and spun in the centrifuge at an even higher speed.

4) This process is repeated at higher and higher speeds, until all the organelles are **separated out**. Each time, the pellets at the bottom of the tube are made up of lighter and lighter organelles.

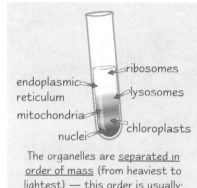

The organelles are <u>separated in order of mass</u> (from heaviest to lightest) — this order is usually: nuclei, then chloroplasts, then mitochondria, then lysosomes, then endoplasmic reticulum, and finally ribosomes.

Practice Questions

Q1 Why do electron microscopes have a better resolution than light microscopes?

Q2 What is used to focus an electron microscope?

Q3 Name two organelles that can be seen by light microscopes, and two that can't be seen.

Q4 State the name of the process that's used to separate organelles.

Q5 Explain what the term "isotonic" means.

Exam Questions

Q1 Explain the advantages and disadvantages of using an electron microscope rather than a light microscope to study cells. [6 marks]

Q2 Describe how cells are prepared for differential centrifugation. [5 marks]

Learn to use a microscope — everything will become clearer...

You need to know the differences between light and electron microscopes, and the advantages and disadvantages of using each one. Differential centrifugation might have possibly one of the most poncy names in biology (and that's saying something) — but you've still got to learn all about it, otherwise you can say bye bye to easy marks.

Functions of Organelles

Organelles are all the tiny bits and bobs inside a cell that you can only see in detail with an electron microscope. It's cool to think that all these weird and wonderful things live inside our tiny cells.

Cells Contain Organelles

An organelle is a structure found inside a cell — each organelle has a specific function. Most organelles are surrounded by membranes, which sometimes causes confusion — don't make the mistake of thinking that a diagram of an organelle is a diagram of a whole cell. They're not cells — they're **parts of** cells, see.

ORGANELLE	DIAGRAM	DESCRIPTION	FUNCTION
Cell wall	plasma membrane / cell wall / cytoplasm	A rigid structure that surrounds **plant cells**. It's made mainly of the carbohydrate **cellulose**.	**Supports** plant cells.
Plasma membrane	plasma membrane / cytoplasm	The membrane found on the surface of **animal cells** and just inside the cell wall of **plant cells**. It's made mainly of **protein** and **lipids**.	**Regulates the movement** of substances into and out of the cell. It also has **receptor molecules** on it, which allow it to respond to chemicals like hormones.
Nucleus	nuclear membrane / nucleolus / nuclear pore / chromatin	A large organelle surrounded by a **nuclear membrane**, which contains many **pores**. The nucleus contains **chromatin** and often a structure called the **nucleolus**.	The **chromatin** contains the genetic material (DNA) which **controls the cell's activities**. The pores allow substances (e.g. RNA) to move between the nucleus and the cytoplasm. The **nucleolus** makes **RNA**.
Lysosome		A **round organelle** surrounded by a **membrane**, with no clear internal structure.	Contains **digestive enzymes**. These are kept separate from the cytoplasm by the surrounding membrane, but can be used to **digest invading cells** or to **destroy the cell** when it needs to be replaced.
Ribosome	small subunit / large subunit	A **very small organelle** either floating free in the cytoplasm or attached to rough edoplasmic reticulum.	The **site** where **proteins** are made.
Rough Endoplasmic Reticulum (RER)	ribosome / fluid	A system of membranes enclosing a fluid-filled space. The surface is **covered with ribosomes**.	**Transports proteins** which have been made in the ribosomes.
Smooth Endoplasmic Reticulum		Similar to rough endoplasmic reticulum, but with no **ribosomes**.	**Transports lipids** around the cell.
Golgi Apparatus	vesicle	A group of smooth endoplasmic reticulum consisting of a series of **flattened sacs**. Vesicles are often seen at the edges of the sacs.	It **packages** substances that are produced by the cell, mainly proteins and glycoproteins. It also **makes lysosomes**.
Microtubule		Very small, hollow **cylinders**, made from the substance **tubulin**.	Act as a **guide** for **moving organelles** in the cell.

Functions of Organelles

ORGANELLE	DIAGRAM	DESCRIPTION	FUNCTION
Vesicle		A small **fluid-filled** sac in the cytoplasm, surrounded by a membrane.	**Transports substances** to and from the outside of the cell via the plasma membrane. Some are formed by the Golgi apparatus, while others (**pinocytic** or **phagocytic** vesicles) are formed at the cell surface.
Mitochondrion		They are usually oval. They have a **double membrane** — the inner one is folded to form structures called **cristae**. Inside is the **matrix**, which contains enzymes involved in respiration (but, sadly, no Keanu Reeves).	The **site of respiration**, where **ATP** is produced. They are found in large numbers in cells that are very active and require a lot of energy.
Chloroplast		A small, **flattened** structure found in **plant cells**. It's surrounded by a **double membrane**, and also has membranes inside called **thylakoid membranes**. These membranes are stacked up in some parts of the chloroplast to form **grana**. Grana are linked together by lamellae — thin, flat pieces of thylakoid membrane.	The **site** where **photosynthesis** takes place. The light-dependent reaction of photosynthesis happens in the **grana**, and the light-independent reaction of photosynthesis happens in the **stroma**.
Centriole		Small, **hollow cylinders**, containing a ring of microtubules, seen in **animal cells** during cell division.	Involved with the **separation of chromosomes** during cell division
Cilia		Small, **hair-like structures** found on the surface membrane of some **animal cells**. In cross section, they have an outer membrane and a ring of 9 pairs of **microtubules** inside, with a single pair of microtubules in the middle.	The microtubules allow the cilia to **move**. This movement is used by the cell to **move substances along the cell surface**.

Practice Questions

Q1　Name two organelles found only in plant cells.

Q2　Name two organelles found only in animal cells.

Q3　Explain the differences between rough and smooth endoplasmic reticulum.

Exam questions

Q1　The presence and number of specific organelles can give an indication of a cell's function. Give THREE examples of this, naming the organelles concerned and stating their function.　[9 marks]

Q2　a)　Identify these two organelles seen in an electron micrograph, from the descriptions given below.

    (i)　A sausage-shaped organelle surrounded by a double membrane. The inner membrane is folded and projects into the inner space, which is filled with a grainy material.

    (ii)　A collection of flattened membrane 'bags' arranged roughly parallel to one another. Small circular structures are seen at the edges of these 'bags'.　[2 marks]

  b)　State the function of the two organelles that you have identified.　[2 marks]

Organs and organelles — 'his and her' biology terms

Organelle is a very pretty-sounding name for all those blobs. But under a microscope some of them are actually quite fetching — well I think so anyway, but then my mate finds woodlice fetching, so there's no accounting for taste. Anyway, you need to know the names and functions of all the organelles and also what they look like under the microscope.

Biochemical Tests for Molecules

Skip this page if you're doing Edexcel.

Here's a bit of light relief for you — two pages all about how you test for different food groups.
There's nothing very complicated, you just need to remember a few chemical names and some colour changes.

Use the **Benedict's Test** for **Sugars**

The Benedict's test identifies **reducing sugars**. These are sugars that can donate electrons to other molecules — they include **all monosaccharides** and **some disaccharides**, e.g. maltose. When added to reducing sugars and heated, the **blue Benedict's reagent** gradually turns **brick red** due to the formation of a **red precipitate**.

> The colour changes from:
>
> **blue** — **green** — **yellow** — **orange** — **brick red**.

The higher the concentration of reducing sugar, the further the colour change goes — you can use this to **compare** the amount of reducing sugar in different solutions. A more accurate way of doing this is to **filter** the solution and **weigh the precipitate**.

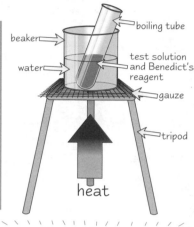

To test for **non-reducing sugars** like sucrose, which is a disaccharide (two monosaccharides joined together), you first have to break them down chemically into monosaccharides. You do this by boiling the test solution with **dilute hydrochloric acid** and then neutralising it with sodium hydrogen carbonate before doing the Benedict's test.

See p.10 for more on monosaccharides and disaccharides.

Use the **Iodine Test** for **Starch**

Make sure you always talk about iodine in potassium iodide solution, not just iodine.

In this test, you don't have to make a **solution** from the substance you want to test — you can use **solids** too. Dead easy — just add **iodine dissolved in potassium iodide solution** to the test sample. If there's starch present, the sample changes from **browny-orange** to a dark, **blue-black** colour.

Use the **Biuret Test** for **Proteins**

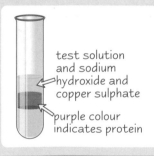

test solution and sodium hydroxide and copper sulphate

purple colour indicates protein

There are **two stages** to this test.
1) The test solution needs to be **alkaline**, so first you add a few drops of **2M sodium hydroxide**.
2) Then you add some **0.5% copper (II) sulphate solution**. If a **purple layer** forms, there's protein in it. If it stays **blue**, there isn't. The colours are pale, so you need to look carefully.

Use the **Emulsion Test** for **Lipids**

Shake the test substance with **ethanol** for about a minute, then pour the solution into water. Any lipid will show up as a **milky emulsion**. The more lipid there is, the more noticeable the milky colour will be.

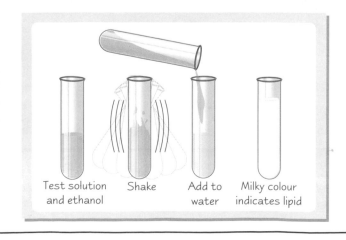

Test solution and ethanol   Shake   Add to water   Milky colour indicates lipid

Biochemical Tests for Molecules

Skip this section if you're doing OCR or Edexcel.

Chromatography *Separates Out Molecules*

If you have a mixture of biological chemicals in a sample that you want
to test, you can separate them using the technique of **chromatography**.

1) You put a spot of the test solution onto a strip of special
chromatography paper, then dip the end of the strip into a **solvent**.

2) As the solvent spreads up the paper, the different chemicals
move with it, but at **different rates**, so they separate out.

3) You can identify what the chemicals are,
using their **Rf values** (see diagram below).

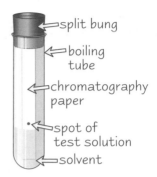

split bung
boiling tube
chromatography paper
spot of test solution
solvent

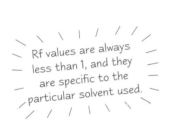

Rf values are always
less than 1, and they
are specific to the
particular solvent used.

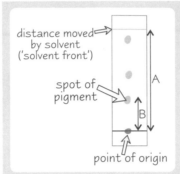

distance moved by solvent
('solvent front')
spot of pigment
A
B
point of origin

$$\text{Rf value of pigment} = \frac{B}{A}$$

$$= \frac{\text{distance travelled by spot}}{\text{distance travelled by solvent}}$$

Sometimes, the solvent doesn't completely separate out all the chemicals. In this case you need
to use **two way chromatography**, which uses a second solvent to complete the separation.

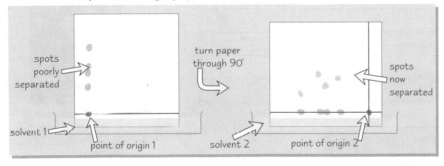

spots poorly separated
turn paper through 90°
spots now separated
solvent 1
point of origin 1
solvent 2
point of origin 2

Some chemicals, like amino acids,
aren't coloured, which makes it hard
to identify them using
chromatography. There are various
ways you can colour them, though
(e.g. adding ninhydrin).

Practice Questions

Q1 How can you work out the different concentrations of reducing sugars in two solutions?

Q2 Describe how you would test a solution for starch. What result would you expect if:
a) starch was present;   b) starch was not present?

Q3 How is an 'Rf value' of a chemical calculated?

Q4 When would you use 'two-way' chromatography?

Exam Questions

Q1 You are given an unknown solution to test for different biochemical groups.
Describe the tests you would carry out and how you would analyse the results.   [14 marks]

Q2 Describe how you would separate and identify the different pigments
in a leaf extract by means of chromatography.   [7 marks]

The Anger Test — Annoy the test subject. If it goes red, anger is present...

*The days of GCSEs might have gone forever, but with this page you can almost feel like you're back there in the mists of
time, when biology was easy and you fancied someone out of S-Club 7. Aah. Well, you'd better make the most of it and
get these tests learnt — 'cos things get trickier than a world-class magician later on...*

Carbohydrates

All carbohydrates contain only carbon, hydrogen and oxygen. Carbohydrates are dead important chemicals — for a start they're the main energy supply in living organisms and some of them, like cellulose, have an important structural role.

Carbohydrates are Made from **Monosaccharides**

All carbohydrates are made from sugar molecules. A single sugar molecule is called a **monosaccharide**. Examples include glucose, fructose, ribose, deoxyribose and galactose.

There are two types of glucose — **alpha** (α) and **beta** (β) glucose. You need to know how their molecules are arranged slightly differently. This has important effects on their **properties** and **functions** (see p.11).

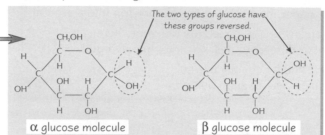

The two types of glucose have these groups reversed.

α glucose molecule   β glucose molecule

Remember, <u>beta</u> glucose has the H on the <u>bottom</u> as you look at the structural diagram.

You also need to know the difference between pentose sugars and hexose sugars. **Pentose sugars** are monosaccharides that have **five carbon atoms** in their molecule. **Hexose sugars** are monosaccharides with **six** carbons in their molecules.

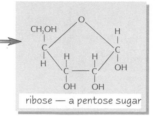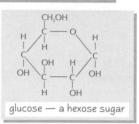

ribose — a pentose sugar   glucose — a hexose sugar

Disaccharides are **Two Monosaccharides** Joined Together

Disaccharides are sugars made from two monosaccharide sugar molecules stuck together. Examples are:

DISACCHARIDE	MONOSACCHARIDES IT'S MADE UP OF
maltose	glucose + glucose
sucrose	glucose + fructose
lactose	glucose + galactose

Extensive scientific research revealed an irreversible bond joining sugars to Pollyanna's gob.

Glycosidic Bonds Join Sugars Together

Sugars are held together by **glycosidic bonds**. When the sugars join, a molecule of water is squeezed out. This is called a **condensation reaction**.

If you're asked to show a condensation reaction in an exam, don't forget to put the water molecule in as a product.

These simplified diagrams only show the parts of the molecule which are involved in the reaction.

monosaccharide   monosaccharide   glycosidic bond   disaccharide

H_2O is removed

Hydrolysis Breaks Sugars Apart

When sugars are separated, the condensation reaction goes into **reverse**. This is called a **hydrolysis reaction** — a water molecule reacts with the glycosidic bond and breaks it apart.

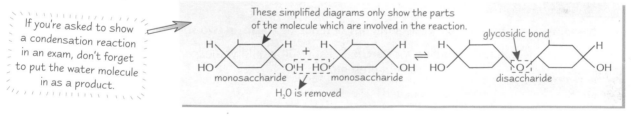

disaccharide   monosaccharide   monosaccharide

H_2O reacts with glycosidic bond

It's all in the name — "hydro" is to do with water, and "lysis" means breaking up.

Condensation and hydrolysis reactions are dead important in biology. **Proteins and lipids** are put together and broken up by them as well. So you definitely need to understand how they work.

SECTION TWO — BIOLOGICAL MOLECULES

Carbohydrates

Polysaccharides are Loads of Sugars Joined Together

Polysaccharides are molecules which are made up of **loads of sugar molecules** stuck together. The ones you need to know about are:

1) **starch** — the main storage material in plants;

2) **glycogen** — the main storage material in animals;

3) **cellulose** — the major component of cell walls in plants.

Examiners like to ask about the link between the structures of polysaccharides and their functions.

① Starch is made up of **two** other polysaccharides of **alpha-glucose**:

*   **Amylose** is a long, **unbranched chain** of alpha-glucose. The angles of the glycosidic bonds give it a **coiled structure**, almost like a cylinder. Its **compact**, coiled structure makes it really **good for storage**.

*   **Amylopectin** is a long, **branched chain** of alpha-glucose. Its **side branches** make it particularly good for the storage of glucose — the enzymes that break down the molecule can get at the glycosidic bonds easily, to break them and release the glucose.

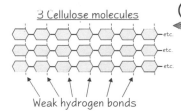
Amylopectin

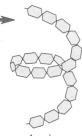
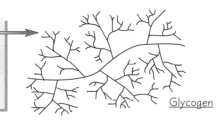
Amylose

② Glycogen is a polysaccharide of **alpha-glucose**. Its structure is very similar to amylopectin, except that it has **loads** more **side branches** coming off it. It's a very **compact** molecule found in animal liver and muscle cells. Loads of branches mean that stored glucose can be released quickly, which is **important for energy release** in animals.

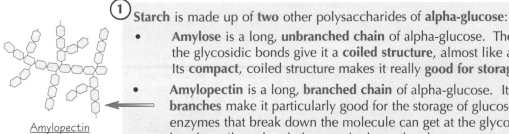
Glycogen

3 Cellulose molecules

③ Cellulose is made of long, unbranched chains of **beta-glucose**. The bonds between beta sugars are **straight**, so the chains are straight. The chains are linked together by **hydrogen bonds** (see p.15) to form strong fibres called **microfibrils**. The strong fibres mean cellulose can provide **structural support** for cells. Another feature is that the **enzymes** that break the glycosidic bonds in starch can't reach the glycosidic bonds in cellulose, so those enzymes **can't break down cellulose**.

Weak hydrogen bonds

Practice Questions

Q1   State the difference between a pentose and a hexose sugar.

Q2   What is the name given to the type of bond that holds sugar molecules together?

Q3   Explain the term "condensation reaction".

Q4   Name the two different types of molecule that are combined together in a starch molecule.

Q5   Name three polysaccharides and give the function of each one.

Q6   Cellulose is made from beta glucose. How does this help with its function as a structural polysaccharide?

Exam Questions

Q1   Describe how glycosidic bonds in carbohydrates are formed and broken in living organisms.   [7 marks]

Q2   Compare and contrast the structures of glycogen and cellulose, showing how each molecule's structure is linked to its function.   [10 marks]

Who's a pretty polysaccharide, then...

If you learn these basics it makes it easier to learn some of the more complicated stuff later on — 'cos carbohydrates crop up all over the place in biology. Remember that condensation and hydrolysis reactions are the reverse of each other — and don't forget that starch is composed of two polysaccharides. So many reminders, so little space …

Lipids

Lipids are fats, oils and waxes — they are all made up of carbon, hydrogen and oxygen, and they're all insoluble in water. Ever seen a candle dissolve in water? No — exactly.

Lipids are Fats, Oils and Waxes — they're Useful

1) Lipids contain a lot of **energy per gram**, so they make useful **medium** or **long-term energy stores**. But they can't be broken down very quickly, so organisms use carbohydrates for **short-term storage**.

2) Lipids stored under the skin in **mammals** act as **insulation**. Skin loses heat from blood vessels, but the fatty tissue under the skin doesn't have an extensive blood supply, so it conserves heat.

Many aquatic animals that live in cold climates (e.g. whales) have a thick layer of fat called 'blubber' under their skin to protect them from the cold and to help keep them afloat.

3) In **marine mammals** (e.g. whales, seals) lipids provide **buoyancy**, because the density of lipids is lower than that of muscle and bone.

4) Lipids under the skin and around the internal organs also provide **physical protection**, acting as a **cushion** against blows.

5) Lipids can act as a **waterproofing** layer — for example in the **waxy cuticle** on the surface of leaves and in the **exoskeleton** of insects. Lipids don't mix well with water, so water can't get through a lipid layer very easily.

Most Fats and Oils are Triglycerides

Most lipids are composed of compounds called triglycerides. Triglycerides are composed of one molecule of **glycerol** with **three fatty acids** attached to it.

All **fatty acids** consist of the same basic structure, but the **hydrocarbon tail varies**. The tail is shown in the diagram with the letter 'R'.

Fatty acid molecules have long 'tails' made of **hydrocarbons**. The tails are '**hydrophobic**' (they repel water molecules). These tails make lipids insoluble in water. When put in water, fat and oil molecules **clump together** in globules to reduce the surface area in contact with water.

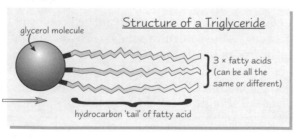

Structure of a Triglyceride

glycerol molecule

3 × fatty acids (can be all the same or different)

hydrocarbon 'tail' of fatty acid

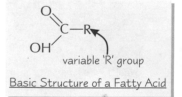

variable 'R' group

Basic Structure of a Fatty Acid

Triglycerides are Formed by Condensation Reactions

Like carbohydrates, lipids are formed by **condensation reactions** and broken up by **hydrolysis reactions**.

The diagram below shows a **fatty acid** joining to a **glycerol molecule**, forming an **ester bond**. A molecule of water is also formed — it's a **condensation reaction**. This process happens twice more, to form a **triglyceride**. The **reverse** happens in **hydrolysis** — a molecule of water is added to each ester bond to break it apart, and the triglyceride splits up into three fatty acids and one glycerol molecule.

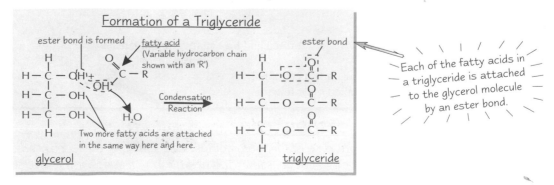

Formation of a Triglyceride

ester bond is formed

fatty acid (Variable hydrocarbon chain shown with an 'R')

ester bond

Condensation Reaction

H_2O

Two more fatty acids are attached in the same way here and here.

glycerol

triglyceride

Each of the fatty acids in a triglyceride is attached to the glycerol molecule by an ester bond.

Lipids

Lipids can be Saturated or Unsaturated

There are two kinds of lipids — **saturated** lipids and **unsaturated** lipids. **Saturated** lipids are mainly **animal fats** and **unsaturated** lipids are found mostly in **plants** (unsaturated lipids are called **oils**). The difference between these two types of lipids is in their **hydrocarbon tails**.

1) Saturated fats **don't** have any **double bonds** between their carbon atoms — every bond has a **hydrogen** atom attached. The lipid is 'saturated' with hydrogen.

2) Unsaturated fats **do** have double bonds between carbon atoms. If they have **two or more** of them, the fat is called **polyunsaturated** fat.

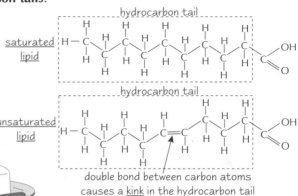

double bond between carbon atoms causes a <u>kink</u> in the hydrocarbon tail

Unsaturated fats melt at lower temperatures than saturated ones. When used in margarine or butter spreads, it makes them easier to use 'straight from the fridge'.

Phospholipids are a Special Type of Lipid

The lipids found in **cell membranes** aren't triglycerides — they're **phospholipids**. The difference is small but important:

1) In phospholipids, a **phosphate group** replaces one of the fatty acid molecules.

2) The phosphate group is **ionised**, which makes it **attract water** molecules.

3) So part of the phospholipid molecule is **hydrophilic** (attracts water) while the rest (the fatty acid tails) is **hydrophobic** (repels water). This is important in the cell membrane (see p.24 to find out why).

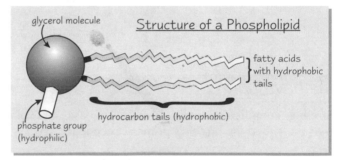

Structure of a Phospholipid

glycerol molecule

fatty acids with hydrophobic tails

hydrocarbon tails (hydrophobic)

phosphate group (hydrophilic)

Practice Questions

Q1 Why is it wrong to call lipids 'fats'?

Q2 Why are lipids insoluble in water?

Q3 What's the name given to the type of bond that joins fatty acids to glycerol in a lipid molecule?

Q4 Explain the difference between a triglyceride and a phospholipid.

Exam Questions

Q1 State five functions of lipids in animals. For each, explain the feature of lipids that allows them to perform this function. [10 marks]

Q2 Describe the chemical reactions involved in the assembly and break down of triglycerides in living organisms. [8 marks]

Q3 Describe the differences between a triglyceride and a phospholipid, and explain how these differences affect the properties of the molecule. [8 marks]

What did the seal say to the upset whale? — Quit blubbering...

Truly awful joke — I hang my head in shame. You don't get far in life without extensive lard knowledge, so learn all the details on this page good and proper. Lipids pop up in other sections, so make sure you know the basics about how their structure gives them some quite groovy properties. Right, all this lipids talk is making me hungry — chips time...

Proteins

There are hundreds of different proteins — all of them contain carbon, hydrogen, oxygen and nitrogen. They are the most abundant organic molecules in cells, making up 50% or more of a cell's dry mass — now that's just plain greedy.

Proteins are Made from Long Chains of Amino Acids

All proteins are made up of amino acids joined together. All amino acids have a **carboxyl group** (-COOH) and an **amino group** (-NH$_2$) attached to a carbon atom.

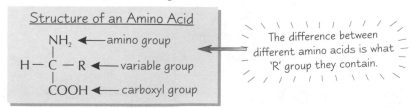

Structure of an Amino Acid

NH$_2$ ◄—— amino group

H — C — R ◄—— variable group

COOH ◄—— carboxyl group

The difference between different amino acids is what 'R' group they contain.

Proteins are Formed by...you guessed it...Condensation Reactions

Just like carbohydrates and lipids, the parts of a protein are put together by **condensation** reactions and broken apart by **hydrolysis** reactions. The bonds that are formed between amino acids are called **peptide bonds**.

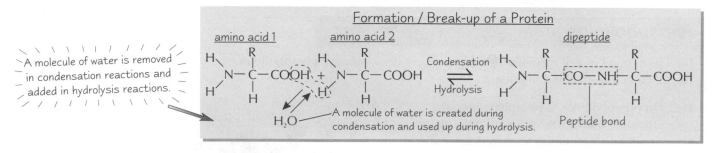

Formation / Break-up of a Protein

A molecule of water is removed in condensation reactions and added in hydrolysis reactions.

amino acid 1   amino acid 2   Condensation / Hydrolysis   dipeptide

H$_2$O — A molecule of water is created during condensation and used up during hydrolysis.

Peptide bond

Proteins have up to Four Structures

Proteins are **big, complicated** molecules. They're easier to explain if you describe their structure in four 'levels'. These levels are called the protein's **primary, secondary, tertiary** and **quaternary** structures.

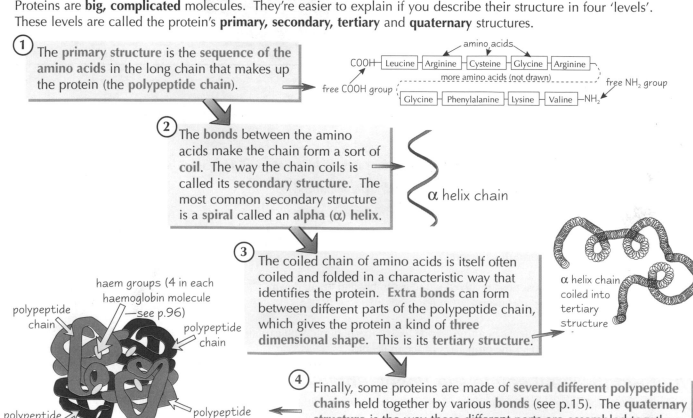

① The **primary structure** is the **sequence of the amino acids** in the long chain that makes up the protein (the **polypeptide chain**).

amino acids

COOH — Leucine — Arginine — Cysteine — Glycine — Arginine

free COOH group   more amino acids (not drawn)   free NH$_2$ group

Glycine — Phenylalanine — Lysine — Valine —NH$_2$

② The **bonds** between the amino acids make the chain form a sort of **coil**. The way the chain coils is called its **secondary structure**. The most common secondary structure is a **spiral** called an **alpha (α) helix**.

α helix chain

③ The coiled chain of amino acids is itself often coiled and folded in a characteristic way that identifies the protein. **Extra bonds** can form between different parts of the polypeptide chain, which gives the protein a kind of **three dimensional shape**. This is its **tertiary structure**.

α helix chain coiled into tertiary structure

haem groups (4 in each haemoglobin molecule —see p.96)

polypeptide chain

polypeptide chain

polypeptide chain

polypeptide chain

A haemoglobin molecule

④ Finally, some proteins are made of **several different polypeptide chains** held together by various **bonds** (see p.15). The **quaternary structure** is the way these different parts are assembled together.

Proteins

Different Bonds Hold Proteins Together

Various types of bond hold protein molecules in shape.

Hydrogen bonds are weak bonds formed between a positively charged atom or group and a negatively charged atom or group.

1) **Hydrogen bonds** hold together the **secondary** structure of a protein. For example, in an alpha helix, a hydrogen bond forms between the **C=O** group of one amino acid and the **N-H** group of **another amino acid**, four amino acids along the polypeptide chain. Hydrogen bonds also help hold the tertiary structure of a protein together.

2) The **tertiary** structure of a protein is also held together by **weak ionic bonds**. These are weak attractions between a negatively charged part of one molecule and a positively charged part of another.

3) Whenever two molecules of the amino acid cysteine come close together, the sulphur in one cysteine bonds to the sulphur in the other cysteine. This is called a **disulphide bond**. It's part of the tertiary structure of a protein.

4) When water-repelling **hydrophobic** groups are close together in the protein, they tend to **clump closely together**. These **hydrophobic bonds** are important in making the protein **fold up** into its final structure.

Protein Shape Relates to its Function

You need to learn a few **examples** of how proteins are **adapted for their jobs**.

Globular proteins are round and compact. They're soluble so they are easily transported around by the blood.

Collagen is a protein that forms **supportive tissue** in animals, so it needs to be strong.

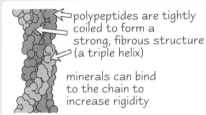

polypeptides are tightly coiled to form a strong, fibrous structure (a triple helix)

minerals can bind to the chain to increase rigidity

Enzymes are proteins — each enzyme has a specific shape, with an **active site** that locks onto the substrate molecule. See p.18 for more on enzymes and substrates.

Haemoglobin is a **globular protein** that absorbs oxygen (see diagram on p.14). Its structure is curled up, so **hydrophilic** ('water-attracting') side chains are on the **outside** of the molecule and **hydrophobic** ('water-repelling') side chains face **inwards**. This makes them soluble in water and good for transport in the blood.

Insulin is a hormone that reduces blood glucose levels.

it's a 'globular protein' — so it's good for transport

disulphide bonds hold the molecule in shape

it's a small molecule — so it's easily transported and absorbed by cells

Practice Questions

Q1 Name the four elements that are found in all proteins.

Q2 What are the common features of all amino acid molecules?

Q3 What is the name given to the bond that holds amino acids together in proteins?

Q4 What are the four types of bond that hold a protein molecule in shape?

Exam Questions

Q1 Describe the structure of a protein, explaining the terms primary, secondary, tertiary and quaternary structure. No details are required of the chemical nature of the bonds. [10 marks]

Q2 Describe the structure of the collagen molecule, and explain how this structure relates to its function in the body. [6 marks]

The name's Bond — Peptide Bond...

Quite a lot to learn on these pages — proteins are annoyingly complicated. Not happy with one, or even two, structures — they've got four of the things, and you need to learn 'em all. Condensation and hydrolysis reactions are back by popular demand and you need to learn all the different bonds too.

Water and Inorganic Ions

Skip these pages if you're doing AQA A.

Life can't exist without water — in fact boring, everyday water is one
of the most important substances on the planet. Funny old world.

Water is Vital to Living Organisms

Water makes up about 80% of cell contents — it has loads of important **functions**, inside and outside cells.

1) Water is a **metabolic reactant**. That means it's needed for loads of important **chemical reactions**, like photosynthesis and hydrolysis reactions (remember them...).

2) Water is a **solvent** — which means it can dissolve many substances. Most biological reactions take place **in solution**, so water's solvent properties are vital.

3) Water **transports** substances. The fact that it's a **liquid** and a solvent makes it easy for water to transport all sorts of materials around plants and animals, like glucose and oxygen.

4) Water helps with **temperature control**. When water **evaporates**, it uses up heat from the surface that it's on. This cools the surface and helps lower the temperature.

Water Molecules have a Simple Structure

The **structure of a water molecule** helps to explain many of its **properties**.
Examiners like asking you to relate structure to properties, so make sure you're clear on this.

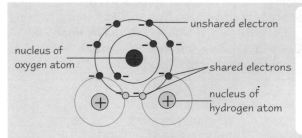

Water is **one atom of oxygen** joined to **two atoms of hydrogen** by **shared electrons**. Because the shared hydrogen electrons are pulled close to the oxygen atom, the other side of each hydrogen atom is left with a **slight positive charge**. The unshared electrons on the oxygen atom give it a **slight negative charge**. That means water is a **polar** molecule — it has negative charge on one side and positive charge on the other.

The **negatively charged oxygen atoms** of water **attract** the **positively charged hydrogen atoms** of other water molecules. This attraction is called **hydrogen bonding** and it gives water some of its special properties.

1) **Cohesion** — water molecules tend to stick together. This property enables water to flow.

2) **Surface tension** — water behaves as though it has a 'skin'. That's why some small invertebrates (like pond-skaters) can walk on water. It wouldn't happen if the molecules weren't held together.

3) **High specific heat capacity** — specific heat capacity is the **energy required** to raise the temperature of 1 gram of a compound by 1°C. Water has a high specific heat capacity — it takes a lot of energy to heat it up. This is useful for aquatic organisms, as it stops rapid temperature changes.

4) **High latent heat of evaporation** — it takes a lot of heat to evaporate water, so it's great for cooling things.

Ice Floats — Which is Useful

Another weird property of water that's useful in nature is that it reaches its **maximum density** at about **4°C**. This means that ice is **less dense** than the water around it, so it **floats**. This acts as an **insulation** for the water below — so the sea or a lake won't freeze solid, which allows organisms under the ice to survive.

Water and Inorganic Ions

Water's *Polarity* Makes it a *Good Solvent*

Because water is **polar**, it's a **good solvent** for other polar molecules. **Ionic** substances like salt, and **organic** molecules that have an **ionised group** will dissolve in water. The **positive** end of a water molecule will be attracted to a **negative ion** and the negative end of a water molecule will be attracted to a **positive ion**. The ion gets **totally surrounded** by water molecules — in other words, it **dissolves**.

> Remember — a molecule is polar if it has a negatively charged bit and a positively charged bit. This is also called "uneven charge distribution."

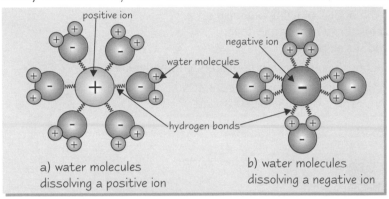

a) water molecules dissolving a positive ion

b) water molecules dissolving a negative ion

Chemical reactions take place much more easily in solution, because the dissolved ions are more **free to move around** and react than if they were held tightly together in a solid. Once dissolved, the solute can **easily be transported** by the water.

OCR ONLY

Inorganic Ions are Important for *Metabolism*

Many **inorganic ions** that can dissolve in water are important in metabolism. Ions are **charged particles** — inorganic ions are those that **don't contain carbon**. Some of the most important inorganic ions and their uses are shown below:

ION	IMPORTANT USE
Calcium (Ca^{2+})	Important in the formation of bone.
Sodium (Na^+)	Involved in nerve transmission.
Potassium (K^+)	Involved in activating enzymes.
Magnesium (Mg^{2+})	Contained in chlorophyll.
Chloride (Cl^-)	Used to produce hydrochloric acid in the stomach.
Nitrate (NO_3^-)	Needed for the synthesis of proteins by plants.
Phosphate (PO_4^{3-})	Needed for the formation of ATP.

Practice Questions

Q1   State four uses of water in living organisms.

Q2   What is a 'polar molecule'?

Q3   Explain why the fact that ice floats on water is useful to living organisms.

Q4   State two reasons why water is useful as a solvent in living systems.

Q5   What is phosphate needed for?

Exam Questions

Q1   Relate the structure of the water molecule to its uses in living organisms.   [12 marks]

Q2   Plants deprived of the mineral magnesium tend to be unhealthy and their leaves are yellow,
whilst those deprived of nitrogen have stunted growth. Suggest reasons for these observations.   [7 marks]

Psssssssssssssssssssssssssssssssssssssssssss — *need the loo yet?*

Water is pretty darn useful really. It looks so, well, dull— but in fact it's scientifically amazing, and essential for all kinds of jobs — like maintaining aquatic temperatures, transporting things and enabling reactions. You need to learn all its properties and uses, plus the uses of inorganic ions. Right, I'm off — when you gotta go, you gotta go.

Action of Enzymes

*Enzymes crop up loads in biology — they're really useful 'cos they make reactions work more quickly. So, whether you feel the need for some speed or not, read on — because you **really** need to know this basic stuff about enzymes.*

Enzymes are Biological Catalysts

Enzymes speed up chemical reactions by acting as **biological catalysts**.

> A catalyst is a substance that speeds up a chemical reaction without being used up in the reaction itself.

1) They catalyse every **metabolic reaction** in the bodies of living organisms. Even your **phenotype** (physical appearance) is down to enzymes that catalyse the reactions that cause growth and development.

2) Enzymes are **globular proteins** (see p.15) although some have **non-protein components** too.

3) Every enzyme has an area called its **active site**. This is the part that connects the enzyme to the substance it interacts with, which is called the **substrate**.

Enzymes Reduce Activation Energy

In a chemical reaction, a certain amount of energy needs to be supplied to the chemicals before the reaction will start. This is called the **activation energy** — it's often provided as **heat**. Enzymes **reduce** the amount of activation energy that's needed, often making reactions happen at a **lower temperature** than they could without an enzyme. This **speeds** up the **rate of reaction**.

When a substrate fits into the enzyme's active site it forms an **enzyme-substrate complex**:

1) If two substrate molecules need to be **joined**, attaching to the enzyme holds them **close together**, **reducing** any **repulsion** between the molecules so they can bond more easily.

2) If the enzyme is catalysing a **breakdown reaction**, fitting into the active site puts a **strain** on bonds in the substrate, so the substrate molecule **breaks up** more easily.

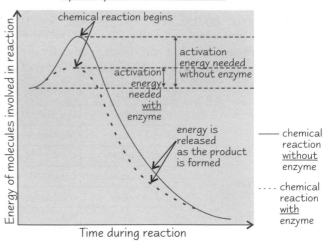

Graph Showing How Enzymes Speed up the Rate of Reaction

The 'Lock and Key' Model is a Good Start...

Enzymes are a bit picky. They only work with **specific substrates** — usually only one. This is because, for the enzyme to work, the substrate has to **fit** into the **active site**. If the substrate's shape doesn't match the active site's shape, then the reaction won't be catalysed. This is called the **'lock and key'** model.

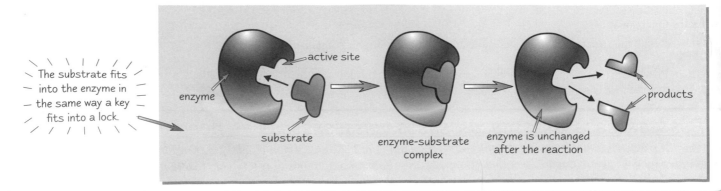

The substrate fits into the enzyme in the same way a key fits into a lock.

Action of Enzymes

...but the 'Induced Fit' Model is a Better Theory

Scientists now believe that the lock and key model doesn't tell the whole story. The enzyme and substrate do have to fit together in the first place, but then it seems that the **enzyme-substrate complex changes shape** slightly to complete the fit. This **locks** the substrate even more tightly to the enzyme. This is called the '**induced fit**' model. It helps explain why enzymes are so **specific** and only bond to one particular substrate. The substrate doesn't only have to be the right shape to fit the active site, it has to make the active site **change shape** in the right way as well.

The 'Luminous Tights' model was popular in the 1980s but has since been found to be grossly inappropriate.

Skip this section if you're doing AQA A, AQA B or Edexcel.

You can Measure the Rate of an Enzyme-Controlled Reaction

There are two ways of measuring how well an enzyme's working:

1) You can **measure how fast the product of the reaction appears**. The diagram below shows how to measure this with the enzyme, **catalase**. Catalase is found in many living organisms — it catalyses the **breakdown** of **hydrogen peroxide** into **water** and **oxygen**. It's easy to collect the oxygen produced and measure **how fast** it's given off.

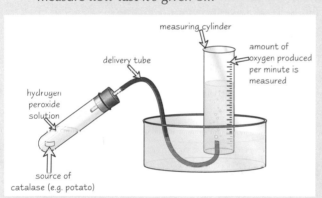

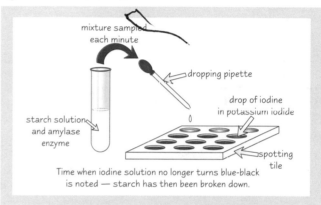

Time when iodine solution no longer turns blue-black is noted — starch has then been broken down.

2) Sometimes, it is easier to measure the **disappearance of the substrate** rather than the appearance of the product. For example, **amylase** enzyme catalyses the breakdown of starch to maltose. Starch is easier to detect than maltose, so it's easier to time the disappearance of the starch. The diagram shows the method.

Practice Questions

Q1 Define the term "catalyst".

Q2 What is the name given to the amount of energy needed to start a reaction?

Q3 What is an "enzyme-substrate complex"?

Q4 Explain why enzymes are specific (i.e. only work with a single or a small group of substrates).

Q5 State the two things you can measure to establish the rate of an enzyme-controlled reaction.

Exam questions

Q1 Explain the differences between the 'lock and key' model of enzyme action, and the 'induced fit' model. [8 marks]

Q2 Catalase is an enzyme that catalyses the breakdown of hydrogen peroxide into oxygen and water. Explain how you could measure the rate of this reaction, using potato as the source of enzyme. [4 marks]

But why is the enzyme-substrate complex?

OK, nothing too tricky here. The main thing to remember is that every enzyme has a specific shape, so it only works with specific substrates that fit the shape. The induced fit model is the new, trendy theory to explain this — the lock and key model is, like, so last year. Everyone who's anyone knows that.

Factors that Affect Enzyme Activity

Just when you thought you'd seen the last of enzymes, here they are again to brighten up your day one more time. This time it's all about the conditions that enzymes work best in.

Temperature *has a* Big Influence *on Enzyme Activity*

Like any chemical reaction, the rate of an enzyme-controlled reaction increases when the temperature's raised. More heat means more **kinetic energy**, so molecules move faster. This makes the enzyme more likely to **collide** with the substrate. But, if the temperature increases beyond a certain point, the **reaction stops**. This is because the rise in temperature also makes the enzyme's particles **vibrate**:

1) If the temperature goes above a certain level, this vibration **breaks** some of the **bonds** that hold the enzyme in shape.

2) The **active site changes shape** and the enzyme and substrate **no longer fit together**.

3) At this point, the enzyme is **denatured** — it no longer functions as a catalyst.

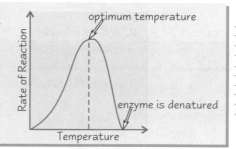

Every enzyme has an optimum temperature. In humans it's around 37°C but some enzymes, like those used in biological washing powders, can work well at 60°C.

pH *Also Affects Enzyme Activity*

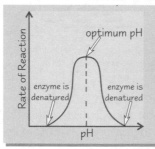

All enzymes have an **optimum pH value**. Most work best at neutral pH 7, but there are exceptions. **Pepsin**, for example, works best at acidic pH 2, which suits it to its role as a stomach enzyme. Above and below the optimum pH, the H+ and OH- ions found in acids and alkalis can mess up the **ionic bonds** that hold the enzyme's tertiary structure in place. This makes the active site change shape, so the enzyme is **denatured**.

Enzyme Concentration *Affects the Rate of Reaction*

1) The **more enzyme molecules** there are in a solution, the more likely a substrate molecule is to **collide** with one. So increasing the concentration of the enzyme increases the rate of reaction.

2) But if the amount of substrate is limited, there comes a point when there's more than enough enzyme to deal with all the available substrate, so adding more enzyme has **no further effect**.

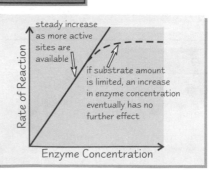

Substrate Concentration *Affects the Rate of Reaction* Up To a Point

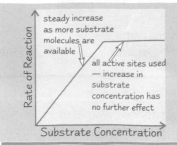

Substrate concentration affects the rate of reaction up to a certain point. The higher the substrate concentration, the faster the reaction, but only up until a **'saturation' point**. After that, there's so many substrate molecules that the enzymes have about as much as they can cope with, and adding more **makes no difference**.

Factors that Affect Enzyme Activity

Enzyme Activity can be Inhibited

Enzyme activity can be prevented by **enzyme inhibitors** — molecules that **bind to the enzyme** that they inhibit. Inhibition can be **competitive** (active site directed) or **non-competitive** (non-active site directed).

1) **Competitive inhibitors** have a **similar shape to the substrate**. They compete with the substrate to bond to the active site, but no reaction follows. Instead they **block** the active site, so **no substrate** can **fit** in it. How much inhibition happens depends on the **relative concentrations** of inhibitor and substrate — if there's a lot of the inhibitor, it'll take up all the active sites and stop any substrate from getting to the enzyme.

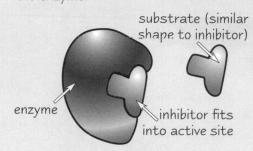

substrate (similar shape to inhibitor)

enzyme

inhibitor fits into active site

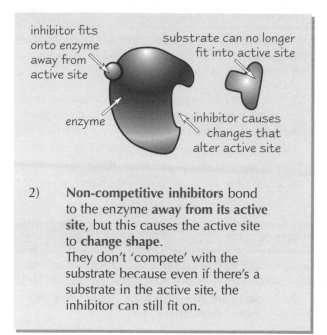

inhibitor fits onto enzyme away from active site

substrate can no longer fit into active site

enzyme

inhibitor causes changes that alter active site

2) **Non-competitive inhibitors** bond to the enzyme **away from its active site**, but this causes the active site to **change shape**. They don't 'compete' with the substrate because even if there's a substrate in the active site, the inhibitor can still fit on.

Competitive and non-competitive inhibitors can be **reversible** or **non-reversible**. This mainly depends on the **strength of the bond** between the enzyme and the inhibitor.

1) If it's a **strong, covalent bond** then the inhibitor can't be removed easily and the inhibition is **irreversible**.
2) If it's a **weaker hydrogen bond** or a weak, **intermolecular ionic bond**, then the inhibitor can be removed and the inhibition is **reversible**.

Practice Questions

Q1   Why do high temperatures denature enzymes?

Q2   Explain why increasing the concentration of an enzyme doesn't always increase the rate of reaction.

Q3   What is the difference between a competitive and a non-competitive enzyme inhibitor?

Q4   What is the difference between a reversible and an irreversible enzyme inhibitor?

Exam questions

Q1   When doing an experiment on enzymes, explain why it is necessary to control
the temperature and pH of the solutions involved.   [8 marks]

Q2   When a small amount of chemical X is added to a mixture of an enzyme and its substrate,
the formation of reaction products is reduced. Increasing the amount of X in the solution
causes further reduction in products. State, with reasons, the likely nature of chemical X.   [4 marks]

Don't be shy — lose your inhibitions and learn these pages...

It's not easy being an enzyme. They're just trying to get on with their jobs, but the whole world seems to be against them sometimes. High temperature, wrong pH, inhibitors — they're all out to get them. Sad though it is, make sure you know every word. Learn how different factors affect enzyme activity, and be able to describe the different types of inhibitors.

Industrial Production of Useful Enzymes

Skip these pages if you're doing OCR or AQA B.

Enzymes' special properties mean that they are used loads in biotechnology (biotechnology is the use of microorganisms to make useful products). Because enzymes are just so darn important, many of them are mass-produced industrially.

Extracellular enzymes are used in Biotechnology

Enzymes that work **inside cells** are **intracellular enzymes**. Ones that **pass out** of cells are **extracellular enzymes** — these are used more often in **biotechnology** for two main reasons:

1) They're **easier to isolate** than intracellular enzymes because you don't need to **break open** cells to get to them. Also, you don't need to **separate** them from all the other stuff inside a cell — they're usually secreted from the cell on their own.

2) They're **more stable** than intracellular enzymes, which are often only stable within the cell environment.

Many **micro-organisms** (e.g. some bacteria and fungi) secrete **extracellular enzymes** onto their food to digest it (see p.54). Because of this, bacteria are often used to **commercially produce** large quantities of **useful extracellular enzymes** that can then be used to create useful products.

> E.g. *Bacillus subtilis* bacteria are used for the commercial production of extracellular <u>protease enzymes</u>.

Enzymes are Produced Industrially by Fermentation

In biotechnology, **fermentation** is the process of **culturing** (growing) micro-organisms to produce **enzymes**, like proteases, pectinases and lactases.

1) The bacteria are grown in large, non-corrosive vessels called **fermenters**.

2) Inside the fermenter the nutrient medium, temperature, pH and oxygen levels are carefully **monitored**, to provide **optimum** conditions for the bacteria's growth. The faster the bacteria grow, the more enzyme will be produced.

3) The bacteria are grown under **aseptic conditions** to avoid contamination by other microorganisms. This involves:

- checking the **starter culture** of bacteria is pure — removing any unwanted microorganisms;
- sterilising the **fermenter** with steam before use;
- sterilising the **nutrient medium** in the fermenter before the bacteria are added;
- sterilising the **air** supplied to the fermenter.

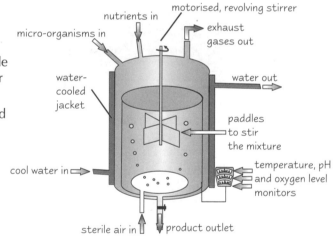

4) A process called **downstream processing** is then used to **extract** and **purify** of the enzyme, turning it from bacteria-and-enzyme slush into pure, dry, powdered enzyme.

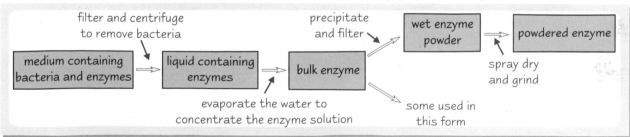

Proteases are Found in Washing Powders

Biological washing powders and liquids contain enzymes to help them **remove stains**.

1) **Proteases** digest (**hydrolyse**) proteins in milk, egg and blood.
2) **Lipases** digest fats.
3) **Cellulases** are sometimes added to get rid of the fluff that dulls the colour of worn fabrics.

> Enzymes added to detergents must work well at pH 9-11, and must be <u>thermostable</u> (stable in heat) so they'll work in hot water.

Industrial Production of Useful Enzymes

The Food Processing Industry uses Pectin

1) **Pectins** are found in and between plant cell walls. They form **gels** and make the juice thicker in ripe fruit.
2) If powdered **pectinase** enzymes are added to **crushed fruit** the amount of juice that can be extracted increases.
3) Extracted juice can have a **cloudy** appearance — adding pectinase enzymes **clears** it.

Biosensors use Enzymes to Detect Specific Chemicals

Enzymes' properties mean they're used in **biosensors** and many **medical analytical tests**.

Enzymes are useful because:

1) They're **specific** (they only bind to one test substance), which makes them **reliable.**
2) They're very **sensitive** and react with **low concentrations** of substrate.
3) They **work quickly**.

A simple test for **diabetes mellitus** uses a **reagent strip** which detects glucose in urine. The plastic strip has a coloured square at one end. The square contains **3 reagents**:

- **glucose oxidase**, an enzyme which catalyses the reaction

  | glucose + oxygen + water $\Longrightarrow$ gluconic acid + hydrogen peroxide |

- **pink dye** which changes colour when it's oxidised by hydrogen peroxide
- **peroxidase**, an enzyme which catalyses the oxidation of the dye

  | hydrogen peroxide + pink dye $\Longrightarrow$ blue dye + water |

The strip is dipped into a sample of urine — if it turns **blue**, glucose is present.

Immobilised Enzymes have many Advantages

Immobilised enzymes are attached to or **trapped** in a non-reactive, insoluble material, like a **fibrous polymer mesh**.

1) The enzymes aren't mixed in with the product so it's easy to recover them and **re-use** them. This keeps **production costs** down.
2) The product isn't **contaminated** by the enzyme.
3) Immobilised enzymes are more **pH-** and **heat-stable**.
   E.g. The **dairy industry** uses **immobilised lactase** to convert the lactose in milk into galactose and glucose.

enzyme entrapped in a fibrous polymer mesh

reactants in   product out

Immobilised enzyme operating within fibrous mesh

Practice Questions

Q1   What is the difference between intracellular and extracellular enzymes?

Q2   Name three conditions inside a fermenter that are monitored and controlled during the fermentation process.

Q3   What do manufacturers add to the detergent in biological washing powders?

Q4   Which type of enzyme is used to make fruit juice look clearer?

Exam questions

Q1   a) Explain why extracellular rather than intracellular enzymes are usually used in commercial processes.   [3 marks]

b) Explain why it is important to prevent microbial contamination during fermentation.   [2 marks]

Q2   a) What is an immobilised enzyme?   [2 marks]

b) Explain two advantages of using immobilised enzymes.   [2 marks]

Come in Mr. Enzyme, I've been Ex'Pectin you

Enzymes are grrreat — if they didn't exist we'd all have smeary stains down the fronts of our clothes. OK, so we'd also all be dead, but you have to get your priorities right — dirty clothes won't get you far in life. One of the greatest lessons my mum taught me was that it's hard to make new friends, find romance and get a job if you've got food all down your clothes.

The Cell Membrane Structure

Two pages all about cell membranes and what they're made of. Try and contain your excitement when you read about the fluid mosaic structure — there have been some nasty cases of extreme over-excitement in the past.

Membranes Control What Passes Through Them

Cells and many of the **organelles** inside them are surrounded by **membranes**.
Membranes have a **range of functions**:

1) **Membranes around organelles** divide the cell up into **different compartments** to make the different **functions more efficient** — e.g. the substances needed for **respiration** (like enzymes) are kept together inside **mitochondria**.

2) Membranes control **which substances enter and leave** a cell or organelle.

3) Membranes **recognise** specific chemical substances and other cells.

Cell Membranes have a 'Fluid Mosaic' Structure

The **structure** of all **membranes** is basically the same. They are composed of **lipids** (mainly phospholipids), **proteins** and **carbohydrates** (usually attached to proteins or lipids).

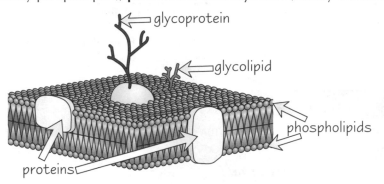

glycoprotein

glycolipid

phospholipids

proteins

In 1972, the **fluid mosaic model** was suggested to describe the arrangement of molecules in the membrane. In the model, **phospholipid molecules** form a continuous, double layer (**bilayer**). This layer is 'fluid' because the phospholipids are constantly moving. **Protein molecules** are scattered through the layer, like tiles in a **mosaic**.

Detailed 3D pictures of cell membranes support the fluid mosaic model. Also, experiments with cell fusion show that proteins move about in the membrane, which means that the membrane is fluid.

Phospholipids Can Form Bilayers

Phospholipids consist of a **glycerol molecule** plus **two molecules** of **fatty acid** and a **phosphate group** (see p.13).

1) The phosphate / glycerol head is **hydrophilic** — it attracts water.
The **fatty acid tails** are **hydrophobic** — they repel water.

2) In **aqueous (water-based) solutions** phospholipids automatically arrange themselves into a **double layer** so that the **hydrophobic tails** pack together **inside the layer** away from the water, and the **hydrophilic heads** face **outwards** into the aqueous solutions.

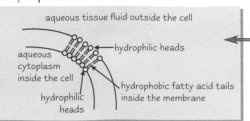

aqueous tissue fluid outside the cell

hydrophilic heads

aqueous cytoplasm inside the cell

hydrophobic fatty acid tails inside the membrane

hydrophilic heads

Water soluble molecules (e.g. glucose) can't pass through the fatty, hydrophobic interior of the membrane.

OCR ONLY

Cholesterol Gives the Membrane More Stability

1) **Cholesterol** belongs to a group of lipids called **steroids**. It's present in all cell membranes except those of bacteria. It can make up to 25% of the lipids in **animal cell membranes** but isn't found so much in plant membranes.

2) Having cholesterol molecules between phospholipid molecules makes the membrane **less fluid** and **more stable**.

The Cell Membrane Structure

Glycolipids and Glycoproteins Contain Polysaccharides

1) **Glycolipids** are lipids that have **combined with polysaccharides**. They're found in the **outer layer** of cell membranes. Their exact role isn't known but they may be involved in **cell recognition**.

2) **Glycoproteins** (also found in the **outer layer**) are proteins with **attached polysaccharides** of short, branched **chains of monosaccharides**. Glycoproteins have a variety of specific shapes due to the **different branching patterns** of the monosaccharides. These allow different cells to recognise each other. For example, some glycoproteins are **antigens** — they're recognised by **white blood cells**, which starts an immune response (see p.82 for more on this).

> Remember — polysaccharides are made up of chains of single sugar molecules, (monosaccharides).

Intrinsic and Extrinsic Proteins Have Different Functions in the Membrane

1) **Intrinsic** proteins **completely span** the membrane from inside to outside.

2) **Extrinsic** proteins only **partly** span the membrane — they're stuck in either the **outer** phospholipid layer or the **inner** phospholipid layer.

3) Intrinsic and extrinsic proteins have **different functions** — usually, intrinsic proteins are for **transport** and extrinsic proteins are **receptors**.

4) **Intrinsic channel proteins** form a tiny **gap** in the membrane to allow water soluble molecules and ions through by diffusion.

5) **Intrinsic carrier proteins** carry water soluble molecules and ions through the membrane by **active transport** and **facilitated diffusion** (see p.28).

6) **Extrinsic** proteins recognise and bind on to **specific molecules** (e.g. hormones).

7) **Enzymes** can be embedded in the inner membrane of a cell or organelle — e.g. ATPase in the inner membrane of mitochondria.

8) Proteins in the membrane also help **strengthen** the membrane. There are **hydrogen bonds** between the proteins and the hydrophilic heads of the phospholipids.

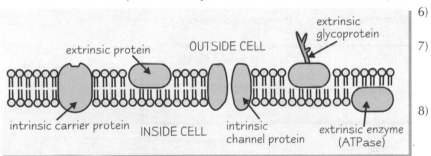

Practice Questions

Q1 Give three functions of cell membranes.

Q2 Which types of molecules are carbohydrate molecules usually attached to?

Q3 Which part of a phospholipid molecule is hydrophobic?

Q4 Name three molecules, other than phospholipids and proteins, that are present in animal cell membranes.

Exam Questions

Q1 a) How does a phospholipid differ from a triglyceride? [1 mark]
b) Describe the role of phospholipids in controlling the passage of water soluble molecules through the cell membrane. [2 marks]

Q2 The diagram represents a section of a cell surface membrane.

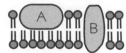

a) Name A and B. [2 marks]
b) Explain how the tertiary structure of a protein molecule allows it to act as a receptor molecule. [2 marks]

Membranes actually <u>are</u> all around...

The cell membrane is a complex structure — but then it has to be, 'cos it's the line of defence between a cell's contents and all the big bad molecules outside. Don't confuse the cell membrane with the cell wall (found in plant cells). The cell membrane controls what substances enter and leave the cell whereas the cell wall provides structural support.

Transport Across the Cell Membrane

There are four methods of transport across a cell membrane. You need to learn all four — diffusion, osmosis, facilitated diffusion and active transport. It's a big topic, which is why there are four whole pages dedicated to it.

Diffusion *is the* Passive Movement *of* Particles

1) If there's a **high concentration** of particles (molecules or ions) in one area of a liquid or gas, then these particles will gradually move and **spread out** into areas of **lower concentration**. Eventually, the particles will be **evenly distributed** throughout the liquid or gas. This movement is called diffusion.

2) Diffusion is described as a **passive process** because **no energy** is needed for it to happen.

3) Diffusion can happen **across cell membranes**, as long as the particles can **move freely** through the membrane. For example, water, oxygen and carbon dioxide molecules are small enough to pass easily through pores in the membrane.

The Speed of Diffusion *Depends on* Several Factors

1) The **concentration gradient** is the path between an area of higher concentration and an area of lower concentration. Particles diffuse **faster** when there is a **high concentration gradient** (a big difference in concentration between the two areas).

2) The **shorter** the **distance** the particles have to travel, the **faster** the rate of diffusion.

3) **Small molecules** move faster than large molecules, so they **diffuse faster**.

4) At **high temperatures** particles have more **kinetic** (movement) energy, so they **diffuse more quickly**.

5) The larger the **surface area** of the cell membrane, the faster the rate of diffusion.

The rate at which a substance diffuses can be worked out using **Fick's law**:

$$\text{rate of diffusion} \ \alpha \ \frac{\text{surface area} \times \text{difference in concentration}}{\text{thickness of membrane}}$$

α means "is proportional to"

Osmosis *is a Particular Kind of Diffusion*

1) Osmosis is when **water molecules** diffuse through a **partially permeable membrane** from an area of **higher water potential** (i.e. higher concentration of water molecules) to an area of **lower water potential**.

2) A **partially permeable membrane** allows some molecules through it, but not all. Water molecules are small and can diffuse through easily but large solute molecules can't.

3) Water molecules will diffuse **both ways** through the membrane — but the **net movement** will be to the side with a **lower concentration of water molecules**.

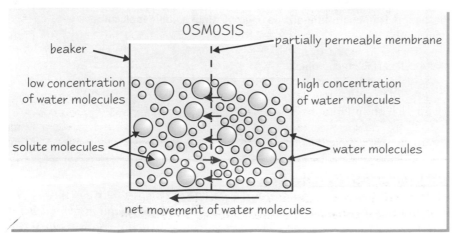

OSMOSIS

beaker — partially permeable membrane

low concentration of water molecules — high concentration of water molecules

solute molecules — water molecules

net movement of water molecules

Partially permeable membranes can be useful at sea.

D'oh   Phew

Transport Across the Cell Membrane

Water Potential is the Ability of Water Molecules to Move

1) **Water potential** is the potential (likelihood) of water molecules to diffuse out of a solution.

> Water molecules are **more likely** to diffuse out of solutions with a **higher concentration** of water molecules. These solutions have a **high water potential**.
>
> Water molecules are **less likely** to diffuse out of solutions with a **lower concentration** of water molecules — these have a **low water potential**.

2) Water potential is represented by the symbol ψ. It's measured in **kilopascals** (kPa).

3) **Pure water** has the **highest water potential** and is given the value of **zero kilopascals**. All solutions have a **lower** water potential than pure water, so their water potentials are always **negative**.

4) Water molecules **diffuse** from areas with a **higher water potential** to areas with a **lower water potential**.

You can Calculate the Water Potential Inside Cells

The water potential in a cell depends on **two factors**.
You can use these factors to calculate water potential. Clever.

1) **SOLUTE POTENTIAL** (ψ_s)

The amount of **solute molecules** in a solution affects its water potential. Solute molecules form **weak, chemical bonds** with water molecules and slow down their movement.
The amount by which solute molecules **reduce** the water potential of a solution is called its **solute potential**.

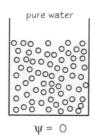
pure water
$\psi = 0$

dilute sugar solution
$\psi = -200$ kPa

concentrated sugar solution
$\psi = -800$ kPa

Water molecules bound to solute molecule

2) **PRESSURE POTENTIAL** (ψ_p)

In cells the water potential is affected by the **cell membrane** (and the cell wall in plants). These **exert pressure inwards** on the cell, in effect squeezing water molecules out the cell. This pressure is called **pressure potential**.

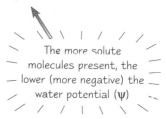
The more solute molecules present, the lower (more negative) the water potential (ψ)

$$\text{water potential } (\psi) = \text{solute potential} (\psi_s) + \text{pressure potential} (\psi_p)$$

Solutions can be Isotonic, Hypotonic or Hypertonic

Isotonic, **hypotonic** and **hypertonic** are terms that describe how the **solute potentials** of solutions **compare** with each other.

Solutions which have the **same solute potential** are **isotonic**. Their water potentials are therefore the same, so if they're separated by a partially permeable membrane, there is **no net movement** of water between the two.	A **hypotonic** solution has a **lower solute potential**, and therefore a **higher water potential**, than another solution. So there would be a net movement of water **from** the hypotonic solution to the other solution through a partially permeable membrane.	A **hypertonic** solution has a **higher solute potential** and **lower water potential** than another solution. The net movement of water across a partially permeable membrane would be **into** the hypertonic solution.

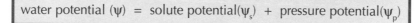

Ginantonic solution — my gran's favourite...

*A good way to describe **osmosis** is that it's the diffusion of water molecules through a partially permeable membrane from an area of **higher water potential** to an area of **lower water potential**. Water potential is a tricky idea — but it impresses the examiners, so try and get your head round it.*

Transport Across The Cell Membrane

Cells are Affected by the Water Potential of the Surrounding Solution

You need to learn the diagrams below for what happens to plant and animal cells when they're put into solutions of different concentrations. Flick back a page to see how it's linked to water potential.

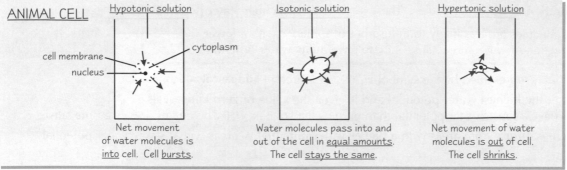

ANIMAL CELL

Hypotonic solution — Net movement of water molecules is into cell. Cell bursts.

Isotonic solution — Water molecules pass into and out of the cell in equal amounts. The cell stays the same.

Hypertonic solution — Net movement of water molecules is out of cell. The cell shrinks.

PLANT CELL

Turgid cells are important for keeping the plant upright and held firmly in the ground.

Hypotonic solution — Net movement of water is into cell. The vacuole swells. The vacuole and cytoplasm push against the cell wall — the cell is turgid (swollen).

Isotonic solution — Water molecules move into and out of the cell in equal amounts. The cell stays the same.

Hypertonic solution — Net movement of water is out of the cell. The cell is flaccid (soft). The cytoplasm shrinks and the membrane pulls away from the cell wall. This is called plasmolysis.

Facilitated Diffusion uses Carrier Proteins and Channel Proteins

Some **larger molecules** (e.g. amino acids, glucose) and **charged atoms** (e.g. sodium ions) can't diffuse through the phospholipid bilayer of the cell membrane themselves. Instead they diffuse through **carrier proteins** or **channel proteins** in the cell membrane. This is called **facilitated diffusion**.

1) Channel proteins form **pores** through the membrane for charged particles to diffuse through.

2) Carrier proteins **change shape** to move large molecules into and out of the cell:

The carrier proteins in the cell membrane have **specific shapes** — so specific carrier proteins can only facilitate the diffusion of specific molecules. Facilitated diffusion can only move particles along a **concentration gradient**, from a higher to a lower concentration. It **doesn't** use any **energy**.

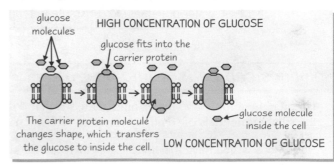

glucose molecules

HIGH CONCENTRATION OF GLUCOSE

glucose fits into the carrier protein

The carrier protein molecule changes shape, which transfers the glucose to inside the cell.

glucose molecule inside the cell

LOW CONCENTRATION OF GLUCOSE

Active Transport Moves Substances Against a Concentration Gradient

1) Active transport uses **energy** to move **molecules** and **ions** across cell membranes, **against** a **concentration gradient**.

2) Molecules attach to **specific carrier proteins** (sometimes called 'pumps') in the **cell membrane**, then **molecules of ATP** (adenosine triphosphate) provide the energy to change the shape of the protein and move the molecules across the membrane.

OCR ONLY

An example of active transport is the uptake of **mineral ions** into plant root hairs. Plant **root hair cells** stick out into the soil, giving a **large surface area** for absorbing water and minerals from the soil. Their **cell membranes** include **carrier proteins** for the active transport of mineral ions into the plant. The cells also have lots of **mitochondria** to provide the **energy** for active transport.

Transport Across The Cell Membrane

Skip these two sections if you're doing AQA B.

Materials can be **Taken into** Cells by **Endocytosis**

Endocytosis is when a cell takes in substances by surrounding them with a section of the cell membrane to form a small vacuole called a **vesicle**.

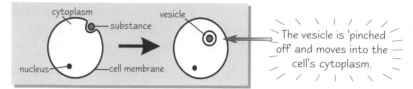

The vesicle is 'pinched off' and moves into the cell's cytoplasm.

There are 2 types of endocytosis:

1) **Phagocytosis** is when solid particles or whole cells are brought into the cell. The contents of the vesicle are **digested** by **enzymes** secreted from **lysosomes**. Molecules and ions then **diffuse** out of the vesicle into the cell's **cytoplasm**.

2) **Pinocytosis** is similar to phagocytosis — but **liquid** is taken into the cell.

Materials can be **Removed from** Cells by **Exocytosis**

Materials are **secreted out** of cells by **exocytosis**.

1) **Substances produced by the cell** move through the **endoplasmic reticulum** to the **Golgi body**.

2) **Vesicles** pinch off from the sacs of the Golgi body and move towards the cell membrane. They **merge** with the **cell membrane** and **release** their contents outside of the cell.

3) Digestive enzymes, hormones, mucus and milk are secreted by **exocytosis**.

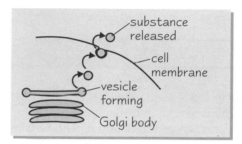

Practice Questions

Q1   What is meant by the term "concentration gradient"?

Q2   What is a partially permeable membrane?

Q3   Define water potential.

Q4   Active transport and facilitated diffusion both involve carrier proteins.   Which one needs energy?

Q5   Give two examples of substances secreted by exocytosis.

Exam Questions

Q1   The effect of temperature on the rate of diffusion of sodium ions was investigated. Pieces of potato, of equal surface area, were placed in distilled water at different temperatures. After 20 minutes the concentration of sodium ions in the water was measured and the results used to plot this graph.

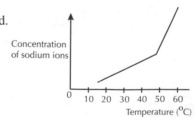

Explain the increase in the rate of diffusion between 20°C and 40°C.

[2 marks]

Q2   a)   In terms of water potential, explain how water moves from the soil into a root hair cell.

[3 marks]

b)   Explain how the special features of root hair cells increase the active uptake of ions.

[3 marks]

A little less conversation, a little more exocytosis, baby...

Phew, the end of a mammoth topic on transport through the cell membrane — so now you can move on and forget it ever happened. Just kidding (I should be doing stand-up, no really) — now you need to go back over it and check you know the details. Learn the differences between similar terms, like hypertonic and hypotonic, and phagocytosis and pinocytosis.

Structure of DNA and The Genetic Code

*These pages are about the structure of DNA (**deoxy**ribonucleic acid) and RNA (plain ol' ribonucleic acid), plus a little thing called the genetic code, which is kinda important to us living things. (OK, spot the major understatement here.)*

DNA and RNA are Very Similar Molecules

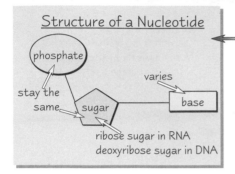

Structure of a Nucleotide

phosphate

stay the same   sugar   varies   base

ribose sugar in RNA
deoxyribose sugar in DNA

Although DNA is called __deoxy__ribonucleic acid, it still contains oxygen.

DNA and RNA are **nucleic acids** — made up of lots of **nucleotides** joined together. Nucleotides are units made from a **pentose sugar** (with 5 carbon atoms), a **phosphate** group and a **base** (containing nitrogen and carbon).

The sugar in **DNA** nucleotides is a **deoxyribose** sugar — in **RNA** nucleotides it's a **ribose** sugar. Within DNA and RNA, the sugar and the phosphate are the same for all the nucleotides. The only bit that's different between them is the **base**. There are five possible bases and they're split into two groups:

	NAME	BASIC STRUCTURE	BASE	found in DNA	found in RNA
1)	Purine bases	2 rings of atoms	adenine	✓	✓
			guanine	✓	✓
2)	Pyrimidine bases	single ring of atoms	cytosine	✓	✓
			thymine	✓	✗
			uracil	✗	✓

DNA and RNA are Polymers of Mononucleotides

Mononucleotides (single nucleotides) join together by a **condensation reaction** between the **phosphate** of one group and the **sugar** molecule of another. As in all condensation reactions, **water** is a by-product.

DNA is made of **two strands of nucleotides**. RNA has just the one strand. In DNA, the strands spiral together to form a **double helix**. The strands are held together by **hydrogen bonds** between the bases.

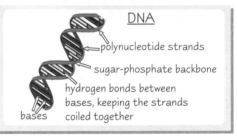

DNA

polynucleotide strands

sugar-phosphate backbone

hydrogen bonds between bases, keeping the strands coiled together

bases

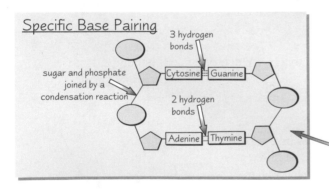

Specific Base Pairing

3 hydrogen bonds

sugar and phosphate joined by a condensation reaction

Cytosine ≣ Guanine

2 hydrogen bonds

Adenine ꞊ Thymine

Each base can only join with one particular partner — this is called **specific base pairing**.

1)   In DNA **adenine** always pairs with **thymine** (**A - T**) and **guanine** always pairs with **cytosine** (**G - C**).

2)   It's the same in RNA, but **thymine**'s replaced by **uracil** (so it's **A - U** and **G - C**).

2 hydrogen bonds form between __adenine__ and __thymine__.
3 hydrogen bonds form between __guanine__ and __cytosine__.

DNA's Structure Makes it Good at its Job

1)   The job of DNA is to carry **genetic information**. A DNA molecule is very, very **long** and is **coiled** up very tightly, so a lot of genetic information can fit into a **small space** in the cell nucleus.

2)   Its **paired structure** means it can **copy itself** — this is called **self-replication** (see p.32). It's important for cell division and for passing on genetic information to the next generation.

AQA A ONLY

In the 1950s, scientists proved that DNA is involved in transmitting genetic information by studying how viruses replicate inside bacterial cells. By labelling the viral DNA with a radioactive substance that could be tracked, the scientists observed that the viruses injected their DNA into cells. The DNA then replicated inside the cells. The new viruses were genetically identical to the original virus, showing that genetic information had been passed on.

Structure of DNA and The Genetic Code

DNA Contains the Basis of the Genetic Code

Genes are sections of DNA that code for a specific **sequence of amino acids** that forms a particular **protein**. The way that DNA codes for proteins is called the **genetic code**.

1) Genes code for specific amino acids with sequences of three bases, called **base triplets**. Different sequences of bases code for different amino acids. For example AGA codes for serine and CAG codes for valine.

2) There are **64** possible **base triplet combinations**. There are only about **20** amino acids in human proteins so there are some base triplets to spare. These aren't wasted though: ⟹

- some amino acids use more than one base triplet.
- some base triplets act as 'punctuation' to stop and start production of an amino acid sequence. These create **stop codons** and **start codons** (see p.34).

The Genetic Code is Non-Overlapping and Degenerate

1) In the genetic code, each base triplet is read in sequence, separate from the triplet before it and after it. Base triplets **don't share** their bases — so the code is described as **non-overlapping**.

2) The genetic code in DNA is also described as **degenerate**. This is because there are **more triplet codes** than there are amino acids. Some **amino acids** are coded for by **more than one base triplet**, e.g. Tyrosine can be coded for by TAT or TAC.

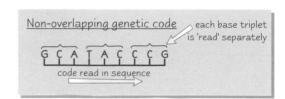

Non-overlapping genetic code — each base triplet is 'read' separately

G C A T A C C C G

code read in sequence

3) There are sections of DNA that **don't code** for amino acids — these lengths of DNA are called **introns** (all the bits that do form part of the genetic code are called **exons**). Introns are removed from DNA during protein synthesis. Their purpose isn't known for sure.

Genes can Exist in More than One Form — called Alleles

A gene can exist in more than one form. The different forms are called **alleles** — they code for **different types** of the **same characteristic**. For example, one gene codes for eye colour, but it comes in two forms — one allele codes for the colour **blue** and another allele codes for **brown**. The two alleles have **slightly different base sequences**.

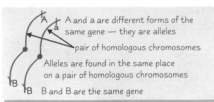

A and a are different forms of the same gene — they are alleles

pair of homologous chromosomes

Alleles are found in the same place on a pair of homologous chromosomes

B and B are the same gene

Our DNA is stored in **chromosomes** in the nucleus of cells. These chromosomes are paired into matching pairs (**homologous pairs**) during cell division (see p.36). Alleles coding for the same characteristic will be found at the **same position** on each chromosome in a homologous pair.

AQA B ONLY

Practice Questions

Q1 What three things are nucleotides made from?

Q2 Which base pairs join together in a DNA molecule?

Q3 What type of bonds join the bases together?

Q4 What is an intron?

Exam Questions

Q1 Explain how the structure of DNA is related to its function. [2 marks]

Q2 Describe, using diagrams where appropriate, how nucleotides join together and how two single strands of DNA become joined. [5 marks]

Give me a D, give me an N, give me an A! What do you get? — very confused…

You need to know the basic structure of DNA and RNA and also how DNA's structure makes it good at its job. Then there's the genetic code to get to grips with — hmmm, rather you than me, but it **basically** comes down to the sequence of **bases**. I'm afraid there's nowt else you can do except buckle down, pull your socks up and get all them facts learnt.

DNA Self-Replication and RNA

Here comes some truly essential stuff — DNA replication is the real nitty-gritty of biology. So eyes down for some serious fact-learning. I'm afraid it's all horribly complicated — all I can do is keep apologising. Sorry.

DNA can Copy Itself — Self-Replication

DNA has to be able to **copy itself** before **cell division** can take place, which is essential for growth and development and reproduction — pretty important stuff.

1) **Specific base pairing** means that each type of base in DNA only pairs up with one other type of base — **A** with **T**, **C** with **G**. When a molecule of **DNA splits**, the **unpaired bases** on each strand can match up with complementary bases on **free-floating nucleotides** in the cytoplasm, making an **exact copy** of the DNA on the other strand. This happens with the help of enzymes. The result is **two molecules** of DNA **identical** to the **original molecule** of DNA:

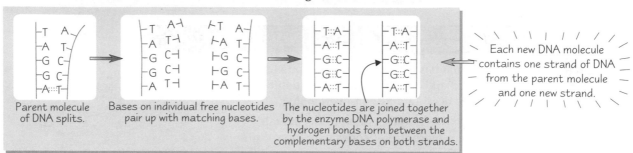

Parent molecule of DNA splits.

Bases on individual free nucleotides pair up with matching bases.

The nucleotides are joined together by the enzyme DNA polymerase and hydrogen bonds form between the complementary bases on both strands.

Each new DNA molecule contains one strand of DNA from the parent molecule and one new strand.

2) This type of copying is called **semi-conservative replication** — because **half** of the new strands of DNA are from the **original** piece of DNA.

OCR ONLY

You can **Prove** that **Semi-Conservative Replication** Happens

You can prove that DNA replicates itself semi-conservatively by using two **isotopes** of **nitrogen** (DNA contains nitrogen) — heavy nitrogen ^{15}N and light nitrogen ^{14}N.

1) Two samples of bacteria are grown — one in a nutrient broth containing **light** nitrogen, and one in a broth with **heavy** nitrogen. As the **bacteria reproduce**, they **take up nitrogen** from the broth to help make nucleotides for new DNA. So the nitrogen gradually becomes part of the bacteria's DNA.

2) A **sample of DNA** is taken from each batch of bacteria, and spun in a **centrifuge**. The DNA from the **heavy** nitrogen bacteria settles **lower** down the **centrifuge tube** than the DNA from the light nitrogen bacteria — because it's **heavier**.

3) Then the bacteria grown in the heavy nitrogen broth are **taken out** and put in a broth containing only **light nitrogen**. The bacteria are left for **one round of DNA replication**, and then **another DNA sample** is taken out and spun in the centrifuge.

4) This DNA sample settles out **between** where the light nitrogen DNA settled out and where the heavy nitrogen DNA settled out.

5) This means that the DNA in the sample contains a **mixture** of heavy and light nitrogen. The bacteria have **replicated semi-conservatively** in the light nitrogen. So the new bacterial DNA molecules contain **one strand** of the **old DNA** containing **heavy** nitrogen and **one strand** of **new DNA** containing **light** nitrogen.

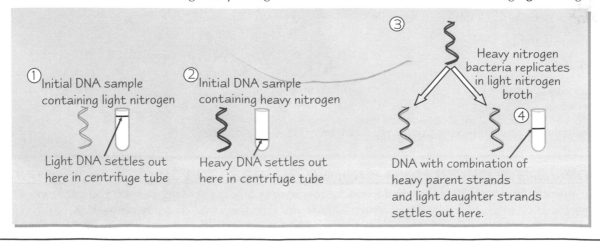

① Initial DNA sample containing light nitrogen

Light DNA settles out here in centrifuge tube

② Initial DNA sample containing heavy nitrogen

Heavy DNA settles out here in centrifuge tube

③ Heavy nitrogen bacteria replicates in light nitrogen broth

④ DNA with combination of heavy parent strands and light daughter strands settles out here.

DNA Self-Replication and RNA

There are Three Types of RNA

There are **three types** of RNA, and all are involved in **making proteins** (see over the page for more on this — bet you can't wait).

Messenger RNA (mRNA)

1) **mRNA is a single polynucleotide strand** that's formed in the **nucleus**.

2) The important thing to know about it is that it's formed by using a section of a **single strand of DNA** as a **template**. **Specific base pairing** means that mRNA ends up being an exact **reverse copy** of the DNA template section (see the piccy on the right to make sense of this).

3) You also need to know that the **3 bases in mRNA** that pair up with a base triplet on the DNA strand are called a **codon**. Codons are dead important for making proteins (see p.34), so **remember this word**. Make sure you realise that a codon has the **opposite bases** to a base triplet (except the base **T** is replaced by **U** in **RNA**).

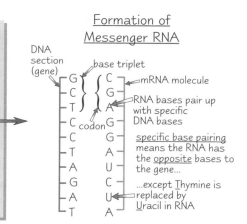

Formation of Messenger RNA

DNA section (gene) — base triplet — mRNA molecule

RNA bases pair up with specific DNA bases

codon

specific base pairing means the RNA has the opposite bases to the gene...

...except Thymine is replaced by Uracil in RNA

Transfer RNA

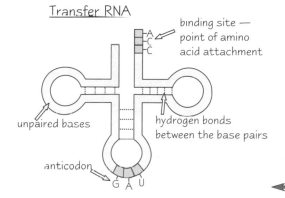

binding site — point of amino acid attachment

unpaired bases

hydrogen bonds between the base pairs

anticodon

Transfer RNA (tRNA)

1) **tRNA is a single polynucleotide strand** that's folded into a **clover shaped molecule**.

2) Each tRNA molecule has a **binding site** at one end, where a specific **amino acid** attaches itself to the bases there.

3) Each tRNA molecule also has a specific sequence of **three bases** at one end of it, called an **anticodon**.

4) The significance of binding sites and anticodons are all revealed over the page. But you need to know **where they are found** on a tRNA molecule, so learn the diagram on the left off by heart.

Ribosomal RNA (rRNA)

1) rRNA is made up of polynucleotide strands that are folded and attached to proteins to make things called **ribosomes** (see p.6).

2) Ribosomes are the site where proteins are made — and that's what the next page is all about...

Practice Questions

Q1   What is the name used to describe the type of replication in DNA?

Q2   What three types of RNA are there?

Q3   What is the name of the group of three bases on mRNA that correspond to a base triplet on DNA?

Q4   What shape does a chain of tRNA fold itself into?

Exam questions

Q1   Describe and explain the semi-conservative method of DNA replication.

[6 marks]

My genes are degenerate — there's a hole in the back pocket... (I'll get my code)

Quite a few terms to learn here — you're on the inescapable road to science geekville I'm afraid, and it's a road lined with crazy diagrams and strange words. DNA self-replication is sooo important — so make sure you understand what's going on. You need to learn the structure of the three types of RNA — it'll help you understand protein synthesis, on the next page.

Protein Synthesis

You've learnt about the genetic code and types of RNA — now you can learn all about its role in making proteins. This stuff is biology at its most clever, and it's probably going on inside you right now. Weird.

Protein synthesis (making proteins) happens in **two stages** — **transcription** and **translation**. It involves both DNA and RNA.

First Stage — *Transcription* Occurs in the *Nucleus*

In **transcription** a 'negative copy' of a **gene** is made. This copy is called **mRNA**.

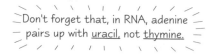

Don't forget that, in RNA, adenine pairs up with <u>uracil</u>, not <u>thymine.</u>

1) A gene (a section of DNA) in the DNA molecule **uncoils** and the hydrogen bonds between the two strands in that section break, separating the strands.

2) One of the strands is then used as the **template** for transcription — it's called the 'sense strand'.

3) Free **RNA nucleotides** in the nucleus line up alongside the template strand. Once the RNA nucleotides have **paired up** with their **complementary bases** on the DNA strand they're joined together by the enzyme **RNA polymerase**.

4) The strand that's formed is **mRNA**.

5) It then moves out of the nucleus through a nuclear pore, and attaches to a **ribosome** in the cytoplasm, where the next stage of protein synthesis takes place.

6) When enough mRNA has been produced, the uncoiled strands of DNA re-form the hydrogen bonds and **coil back into a double helix**, unaltered.

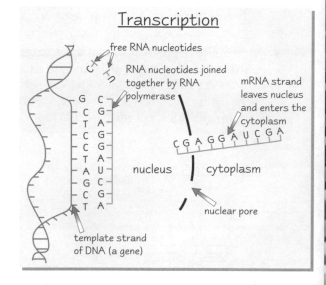

Transcription

free RNA nucleotides

RNA nucleotides joined together by RNA polymerase

mRNA strand leaves nucleus and enters the cytoplasm

nucleus   cytoplasm

nuclear pore

template strand of DNA (a gene)

Second Stage — *Translation* Occurs in a *Ribosome*

In **translation**, **amino acids** are stuck together to make a **protein**, following the order of amino acids coded for on the mRNA strand.

1) The **mRNA strand** has travelled to a ribosome in the cytoplasm, and attached itself.

2) All 20 **amino acids** needed to make human proteins are in the cytoplasm. tRNA molecules attach to the amino acids and transport them to the ribosome.

3) In the ribosome, a tRNA molecule binds to the start of the mRNA strand. This tRNA molecule has the **complementary anticodon** to the **first codon** on the mRNA strand, and attaches by **base pairing**. Then a second tRNA molecule attaches itself to the **next codon** on the mRNA strand in the **same way**.

4) The two amino acids attached to the tRNA molecules are joined together with a **peptide bond** (using ATP and an enzyme).

5) The first tRNA molecule then **moves away** from the ribosome, leaving its amino acid behind. The mRNA then **moves across** the ribosome by one codon and a third tRNA molecule binds to the **next codon** that enters the ribosome.

6) This process continues until there's a **stop codon** on the mRNA strand that doesn't code for any amino acid. You're left with a line of amino acids joined by peptide bonds. This is a **polypeptide chain** — the **primary structure** of a protein. The polypeptide chain moves away from the ribosome and translation is complete.

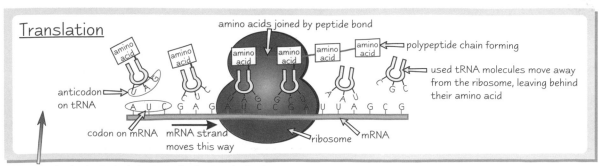

Translation

amino acids joined by peptide bond

polypeptide chain forming

used tRNA molecules move away from the ribosome, leaving behind their amino acid

anticodon on tRNA

codon on mRNA   mRNA strand moves this way

ribosome   mRNA

So, in protein synthesis, the <u>sequence of codons</u> on the mRNA strand determines the <u>sequence of amino acids</u> that makes up the primary structure of the protein.

When translation is complete, the polypeptide chain folds itself into its <u>secondary</u> and <u>tertiary</u> structure, and a <u>protein</u> is formed (see p.14).

Protein Synthesis

The **Structure of Enzymes** is **Determined** by **Protein Synthesis**

1) All **enzymes** are **proteins**, which are sequences of amino acids.

2) The amino acid sequences are determined by the base sequence in DNA, so **DNA** determines the **structure of enzymes**.

3) Enzymes speed up all our **metabolic pathways** (see p.18). They have a big influence over how our **genes** are **expressed physically**, by controlling chemical reactions required for growth and development. This physical expression of the gene contributes to the organism's **phenotype** (what the organism looks like).

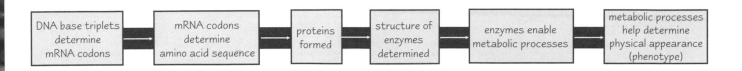

The **Human Genome Project** has Identified **all** Human Genes

EDEXCEL ONLY

The **Human Genome Project** is an international project that aimed to **map** where every human gene is found on our chromosomes. This goal was achieved — and is one of the most amazing scientific achievements ever. To extend the project, scientists are now trying to work out **what each gene codes for**. Knowing where a particular gene is found helps scientists learn to understand how they might be **damaged** or how **mutations** on some genes can lead to illness or disorders. It also makes it easier to replace faulty genes. You see, biology wasn't just invented to make your lives miserable — it's actually quite useful. See p.71 for more on the Human Genome Project.

Practice Questions

Q1 What are the two main stages in protein synthesis?

Q2 Which base is not present in RNA?

Q3 Write the RNA sequence which would be complementary to the following DNA sequence. AATTGCGCCCG

Q4 Where does transcription take place?

Q5 Where does translation take place?

Exam questions

Q1 Explain the terms codon and anticodon. [2 marks]

Q2 Describe the process of protein synthesis. [10 marks]

mRNA codons join to tRNA anticodons?! — I need a translation please...

When you first go through protein synthesis it might make approximately no sense, but I promise its bark is worse than its bite. All those strange words disguise what is really quite a straightforward process — and the diagrams are dead handy for getting to grips with it. Keep drawing them yourself, 'til you can reproduce them perfectly.

The Cell Cycle and Mitosis

I don't like cell division. There, I've said it. It's unfair of me, because if it wasn't for cell division I'd still only be one cell big. It's all those diagrams that look like worms nailed to bits of string that put me off.

A **Chromosome** is a **Single Strand** of DNA Wrapped Round **Histone Proteins**

Each chromosome is a thread-like structure made up of **one long molecule** of **DNA**. The DNA is wound round **histone proteins**, which support the DNA. It's coiled up very tightly to make a nice, **compact** chromosome.

The DNA molecule is divided into sections. Each section carries the code to make a particular <u>polypeptide</u> (protein). These sections are called <u>genes</u> (see bottom of p.32), and each chromosome can carry loads of genes.

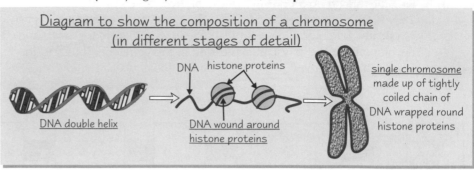

Diagram to show the composition of a chromosome
(in different stages of detail)

DNA   histone proteins

DNA double helix

DNA wound around histone proteins

single chromosome made up of tightly coiled chain of DNA wrapped round histone proteins

AQA A ONLY

You can **stain chromosomes** so you can see them under a **microscope**. E.g., to see the chromosomes in **onion cells**, a small piece of onion is put in a half-and-half mixture of **ethanoic acid** and **alcohol**, and left for 10 minutes. Then it's rinsed with water and put in a **hydrochloric acid** solution and warmed for 5 minutes, which separates all the cells from each other. Then the onion sample is again rinsed off with water and put on a slide with a dye called **ethanoic orcein**. This stains the chromosomes. Then a coverslip is put on and gently squashed down to squish the cells into a **thin layer**, which makes the cells and chromosomes easy to see.

A **Karyotype** Shows **All** the **Chromosomes** from **One Cell**

A **karyotype** is a **drawing** made from a photo of all the **chromosomes** in a cell. All the chromosomes are matched and put into **pairs** in order of decreasing size. Pairs of matching chromosomes are called **homologous chromosomes**. In a homologous pair both chromosomes are the same shape and size and have the **same genes** in the same location. One chromosome in each homologous pair comes from the female parent, and the other from the male parent.

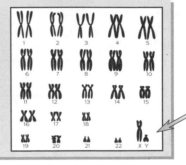

Human cells have 23 pairs of chromosomes, but only 22 pairs are homologous — the 23rd pair consists of the sex chromosomes (X and Y in men, and X and X in women).

Human cells contain 46 single chromosomes in total — this is called the **diploid number** (**2n**). Different species have different diploid numbers. **Gametes** (sex cells) contain **half** the diploid number of chromosomes — called the **haploid number** (**n**). See p.40 for why this happens.

Mitosis is the **Cell Division** Used in **Asexual Reproduction**

Cells increase in number by **cell division**. There are two types of cell division — **mitosis** and **meiosis**. **Mitosis** produces daughter cells that are **genetically identical** to the parent cell. It's used in **asexual reproduction**. It's also needed for the **growth** of multicellular organisms (like us) and for **repairing** damaged tissues.

Cells from multi-cellular organisms have a clear **cell cycle** that starts when they are produced by cell division, and ends with them dividing themselves to produce more identical cells. The cell cycle consists of a period of cell division called **mitosis** (M phase) and a period in between divisions called **interphase**. Interphase is sub-divided into 3 separate growth stages. These are called G_1, **S** and G_2. Each stage involves specific cell activities:

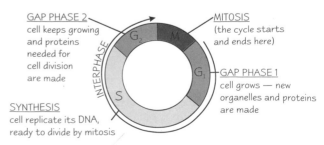

GAP PHASE 2
cell keeps growing and proteins needed for cell division are made

MITOSIS
(the cycle starts and ends here)

GAP PHASE 1
cell grows — new organelles and proteins are made

INTERPHASE

SYNTHESIS
cell replicate its DNA, ready to divide by mitosis

The Cell Cycle and Mitosis

Mitosis has Four Main Stages

Mitosis is really one **continuous process**, but it's described as a series of **division stages** — prophase, metaphase, anaphase and telophase. **Interphase** comes before the division stages — it's when cells grow and prepare to divide by replicating their DNA.

1) **Prophase** — The chromosomes **condense**, getting shorter and fatter. Tiny bundles of protein called **centrioles** start moving to opposite ends of the cell, forming a network of protein fibres across it called the **spindle**. The nuclear membrane breaks down and chromosomes lie free in the cytoplasm.

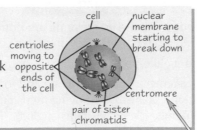

cell
nuclear membrane starting to break down
centrioles moving to opposite ends of the cell
centromere
pair of sister chromatids

Mitosis can be a moving time.

2) **Metaphase** — The chromosomes (each with two chromatids) line up along the middle of the cell and become attached to the spindle by their centromere.

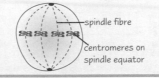

spindle fibre
centromeres on spindle equator

As mitosis begins, the chromosomes are made of two strands joined in the middle by a <u>centromere</u>. The separate strands are called <u>chromatids</u>. There are two strands because each chromosome has already made an <u>identical copy</u> of itself during the <u>synthesis phase</u> of the cell cycle. When mitosis is over, the chromatids end up as one-strand chromosomes in the new daughter cells.

3) **Anaphase** — The centromeres attaching the chromatids to the spindles divide, separating each pair of sister chromatids. The spindles contract, pulling chromatids to opposite poles, centromere first.

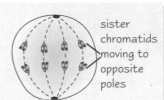

sister chromatids moving to opposite poles

4) **Telophase** — The chromatids reach the **opposite poles** on the spindle. They uncoil and become long and thin again. They're now called **chromosomes** again. A **nuclear membrane** forms around each group of chromosomes, so there are now **two nuclei**. The **cytoplasm divides** and there are now **two daughter cells** which are **identical** to the original cell. Mitosis is finished and each daughter cell starts the **interphase** part of the cell cycle to get ready for the next round of mitosis.

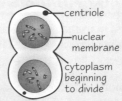

centriole
nuclear membrane
cytoplasm beginning to divide

Practice Questions

Q1 What is a chromosome made up of?

Q2 Explain why the chromosome becomes visible as two chromatids at the end of prophase.

Q3 What is cell division by mitosis used for?

Exam Questions

Q1 The diagrams show cells at different stages of mitosis.

Z — Cell A — X
Cell B
Cell C
Y

a) For each of the cells A, B and C state the stage of mitosis, giving a reason for your answer. [6 marks]
b) Name the structures labelled X, Y and Z in cell A. [3 marks]

Q2 During which stages of the cell cycle would the following events take place?
a) DNA replication. [2 marks]
b) Formation of spindle fibres. [2 marks]

Doctor, I'm getting short and fat — don't worry, it's just a phase.

Quite a lot to learn in this topic — but it's all dead important stuff so no slacking. All cells undergo mitosis — it's how they multiply and how organisms like us grow and develop. Remember that chromosomes are in fact usually made up of two sister chromatids joined by a centromere. Aaw, nice to know family values are important to genetic material too.

Cloning, Mutation and Cancer

Skip these pages if you're doing AQA A.

Clones sound quite exciting — until you realise your average potato is a clone. Mutations are just mistakes in the sequence of nucleotide bases in DNA, but they can have a big effect on a whole organism, including giving it cancer.

Asexual Reproduction *Produces* Clones

Asexual reproduction needs only **one** parent. The offspring are normally **genetically identical** to this parent and are called **clones**. Asexual reproduction in plants can be natural or artificial:

1) **Tubers** grow naturally on plants like potatoes, and give clones when planted.

2) Some plant cells (called **meristems**) are able to divide and form all the cells needed to create a new plant. So humans can **artificially clone** plants by removing meristems and cultivating them in rooting powder and compost to create new plants, identical to the original. This is **vegetative propagation**.

3) Artificial cloning from tiny plant specimens (**explants**) is called **micropropagation**:

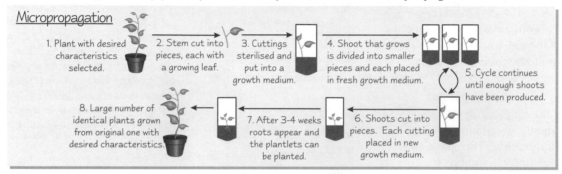

Micropropagation

1. Plant with desired characteristics selected.
2. Stem cut into pieces, each with a growing leaf.
3. Cuttings sterilised and put into a growth medium.
4. Shoot that grows is divided into smaller pieces and each placed in fresh growth medium.
5. Cycle continues until enough shoots have been produced.
6. Shoots cut into pieces. Each cutting placed in new growth medium.
7. After 3-4 weeks roots appear and the plantlets can be planted.
8. Large number of identical plants grown from original one with desired characteristics.

Cloning Animals *is Possible but* More Complicated

The first mammal clone was **Dolly the sheep**. She was made when the **nucleus** of a **mammary cell** from one ewe was placed into the **ovum** of another ewe, which had had its nucleus removed. This new cell was transferred into the uterus of a different ewe to develop.

Another method is used to clone animals with desirable features, like cows with **high milk yields**. Eggs from the best cow are fertilised in a petri dish with sperm from the best bull — this is called **in-vitro fertilisation**. The fertilised egg divides, giving a ball of genetically identical cells, which develop into an **embryo**. The young embryo can be **split** into separate cells — each cell grows into a new embryo that's genetically identical to the original one. These embryos are then transplanted into **surrogate** cows to develop.

sheep A
donor cell from udder
unfertilised egg
sheep B
enucleated egg
nucleus removed
nucleus from sheep A is fused with the enucleated egg from sheep B
the developing embryo is placed into the uterus of a surrogate sheep
cloned sheep "Dolly"

Mutations *Alter the* Sequence of DNA

Mutations are changes in the base sequence of an organism's **DNA**. A gene codes for a particular protein. If the sequence of bases in a gene changes, a **different protein** is produced. There are three main types of **gene mutation**:

1) **Addition** — extra base included, e.g.

| Normal base sequence— CCG ATG ACC ATT |
| After mutation — CCG AT**A** GAC CAT |

Addition means the <u>whole sequence of bases</u> after the mutation is out by one base. All the codons after the mutation are different, and code for different amino acids. The resulting protein won't have the right 3D structure, so it won't work at all.

2) **Substitution** — wrong base included, e.g.

| Normal base sequence— CCG ATG ACC ATT |
| After mutation — CC**T** ATG ACC ATT |

Only <u>one codon is affected</u> by substitution. More than one codon can code for an amino acid, so if the new codon codes for the same amino acid as the old one, the sequence of amino acids will remain the same and the resulting protein won't change. But if the new codon codes for a different amino acid, a new, non-functioning protein will be formed.

3) **Deletion** — base missed out, e.g.

| Normal base sequence— CCG AT**G** ACC ATT |
| After mutation — CCG ATA CCA TT |

Deletion means the whole sequence of bases is out by one, just like with an addition mutation. This is also called a <u>frame-shift</u>, by the way.

Cloning, Mutation and Cancer

Gene Mutations can Block Metabolic Pathways and Cause Cancer

Gene mutations can mean that the protein produced isn't the protein that the gene normally codes for. Remember that all **enzymes** are **proteins**. If there's a mutation in the gene that codes for an enzyme, then that enzyme won't **fold up** properly, its **active site** will be the wrong shape and it **won't work**. Enzymes **catalyse** biological reactions, so **faulty enzymes** mean that the reaction they're supposed to catalyse **won't happen** properly. When these reactions are vitally important for the metabolism of the cell, the mutation in a gene for an enzyme is **seriously bad news**.

Our metabolism is all the chemical reactions that take place in our cells to keep us alive. These reactions usually happen in a series of small reactions, rather than one big one. The series of reactions are called metabolic pathways.

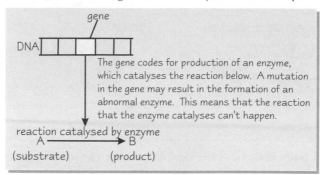

The gene codes for production of an enzyme, which catalyses the reaction below. A mutation in the gene may result in the formation of an abnormal enzyme. This means that the reaction that the enzyme catalyses can't happen.

reaction catalysed by enzyme
A ⟶ B
(substrate)   (product)

Cancer is also caused by gene mutation. **Cell division** is controlled by genes, you see. Normally, when a cell has divided enough times to make **enough new cells**, it stops. If there's a mutation in the gene that controls cell division, the cells **grow out of control**. They **keep on dividing** to make more and more cells — which form a **tumour**. Tumours can be broken up and **carried** around the body in **blood**, getting lodged in different parts of the body. They keep on **growing uncontrollably**, squashing the normal tissues around them.

Mutations happen naturally by chance. But there are some substances, called **carcinogens**, that increase the chance of a normal cell becoming a cancer cell — like **tobacco smoke**, **radiation**, **ultraviolet light** from the **Sun** and **x-rays**.

Genes that have mutated to cause cancer are called oncogenes.

Practice Questions

Q1   What is meant by asexual reproduction?

Q2   Explain how animals with desirable characteristics can be cloned.

Q3   What is a mutation, and how can it affect protein structure?

Q4   Give two examples of carcinogens.

Exam Questions

Q1   Sickle cell anaemia is a genetic disease resulting from a gene mutation.

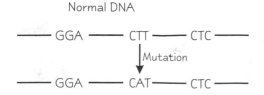

Normal DNA

— GGA — CTT — CTC —
↓ Mutation
— GGA — CAT — CTC —

a) From information in the diagram, what type of mutation causes sickle cell anaemia?   [1 mark]

b) Explain how this change in base has affected the protein formed.   [3 marks]

Q2   Phenylketonuria (PKU) is a disorder in humans, whereby the amino acid phenylalanine can't be broken down to tyrosine. Give a possible cause for this disorder.   [2 marks]

Clones and mutations are mad scientist territory — don't try this at home...

If this page sounds like gibberish to you, don't panic. It's probably just that you're still not comfortable with some earlier stuff. If you're feeling unsure about bases, codons, and how these translate into amino acids and proteins, go back a bit and have another look at the section on DNA and RNA (pages 30-35).

Meiosis and Sexual Reproduction

*More cell division — lovely jubbly. Meiosis is the cell division used in sexual reproduction. It consists of two divisions, not one. The **second division** is exactly the same as mitosis, which is handy.*

DNA From One Generation is Passed to the Next by Gametes

1) **Gametes** are the **sperm** cells in males and the **ova** (egg cells) in females. They join together at **fertilisation** to form a **zygote**, which divides and develops into a **new organism**.

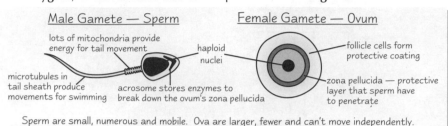

Male Gamete — Sperm

lots of mitochondria provide energy for tail movement

haploid nuclei

microtubules in tail sheath produce movements for swimming

acrosome stores enzymes to break down the ovum's zona pellucida

Female Gamete — Ovum

follicle cells form protective coating

zona pellucida — protective layer that sperm have to penetrate

Sperm are small, numerous and mobile. Ova are larger, fewer and can't move independently.

2) Normal **body cells** have the **diploid number** (**2n**) of chromosomes — meaning each cell contains **two** of each chromosome, one from the mum and one from the dad.

3) **Gametes** have a **haploid** (**n**) number of chromosomes — there's only one copy of each chromosome.

4) At **fertilisation**, a **haploid sperm** fuses with a **haploid egg**, making a cell with the normal diploid number of chromosomes. Half these chromosomes are from the father (the sperm) and half are from the mother (the egg).

Meiosis Halves the Chromosome Number

1) **Meiosis** is a type of cell division. It's essential for **sexual reproduction**. Cells that divide by meiosis are **diploid** to start with, but the cells that result from meiosis are **haploid**. Without meiosis, you'd get **double** the number of chromosomes in each generation, when the gametes fused.

2) Meiosis happens in the **reproductive organs**. In humans it's in the **testes** for males and the **ovaries** for females. In plants it's in the **anthers** and **ovules**.

3) Unlike mitosis, there are **two divisions**. This **halves** the chromosome number.

diploid cell with 2n chromosomes

MEIOSIS I

two cells with the haploid number of chromosomes (n)

MEIOSIS II

four haploid cells with chromosomes in the right form for fusion

The two divisions in meiosis are called **meiosis I** and **II**.
Each division has 4 stages, just like mitosis — **prophase**, **metaphase**, **anaphase** and **telophase**.

1) In **Meiosis I** the **homologous pairs** of **chromosomes** are separated, which **halves** the number of chromosomes in the daughter cells.

2) **Meiosis II** is like mitosis — it separates the **pairs of chromatids** that make up each chromosome.

3) Unlike mitosis, which results in two genetically identical diploid cells, meiosis results in **four haploid cells** (gametes) that **are genetically different** from each other.

Chromatids Cross-Over During Prophase in Meiosis I

Crossing-over helps make cells from meiosis **non-identical**.

At the start of the prophase in meiosis I (called **prophase I**), **homologous pairs** of chromosomes come together and pair up to form a **bivalent**. The chromatids twist around each other and fragments of **non-sister chromatids** (chromatids belonging to different chromosomes) swap over. The place where they swap over is called the **chiasma** (plural = **chiasmata**).

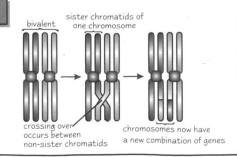

bivalent

sister chromatids of one chromosome

crossing over occurs between non-sister chromatids

chromosomes now have a new combination of genes

Meiosis and Sexual Reproduction

Skip this section if you're doing OCR, AQA A or AQA B.

Meiosis is the Key to Genetic Variation

There are two main events during meiosis that lead to **genetic variation**:

1) The four daughter cells formed from meiosis have completely different combinations of **chromosomes**. This is because of **random segregation** of chromosomes in meiosis I, and of the chromatids in meiosis II.

2) The **crossing-over** of chromatids in the prophase of meiosis I (**prophase I**) means that each of the **four daughter cells** formed from meiosis contain chromatids with **different genes**:

In <u>meiosis I</u>, homologous pairs of <u>chromosomes</u> line up then separate to opposite ends of the cell, and the cell splits in two. The chromosomes can split up any which way:

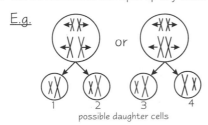

So you get a <u>random combination</u> of chromosomes in the daughter cells. In <u>meiosis II</u>, the <u>chromatids</u> line up and separate to opposite ends of the cell. They can split up any which way too.

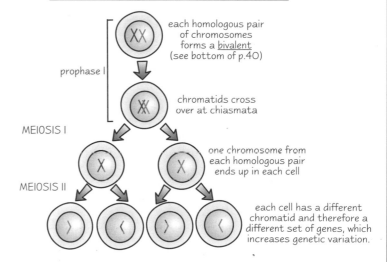

each homologous pair of chromosomes forms a <u>bivalent</u> (see bottom of p.40)

chromatids cross over at chiasmata

one chromosome from each homologous pair ends up in each cell

each cell has a different chromatid and therefore a different set of genes, which increases genetic variation.

Practice Questions

Q1 Explain what is meant by the terms haploid and diploid.

Q2 Give two adaptations of sperm that allow them to perform their function.

Q3 How many divisions are there in meiosis?

Q4 In which organs in a human would meiosis take place?

Exam Question

Q1 The diagram shows stages of meiosis in a human ovary. Each circle represents a cell.

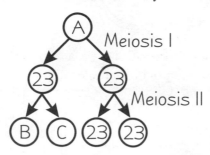

a) How many chromosomes would be found in cells A, B and C? [3 marks]

b) Explain why it's important for gametes to have half the number of chromosomes as normal body cells. [2 marks]

Reproduction isn't as exciting as some people would have you believe...

*For some reason, this stuff can take a while to go in (insert own joke). But that's no excuse to just sit there staring frantically at the page and muttering "I don't get it," over and over again. Use the diagrams to help you understand — they look evil, but they really help. The key thing is to understand what happens to the **number of chromosomes** in meiosis.*

Reproduction in Humans

Skip these pages if you're doing OCR, AQA A, or AQA B.

Yay, it's those diagrams you used to snigger at in Year 7. No time for immature behaviour now though, because you've got to learn about how these systems produce the gametes that make babies. Not a laughing matter. (Tee hee.)

Ova are Produced in the Ovaries of Female Mammals

The female reproductive system produces and develops **ova** (the female gametes), and delivers them to the uterus through the fallopian tubes. It also protects and nourishes the developing **embryo** in the uterus.

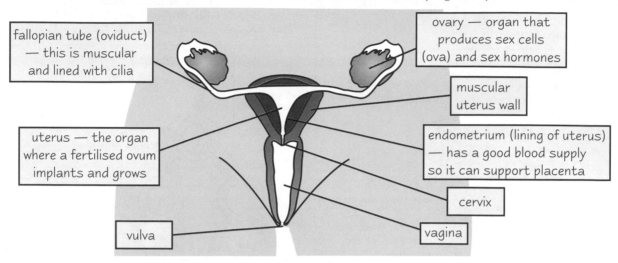

fallopian tube (oviduct) — this is muscular and lined with cilia

ovary — organ that produces sex cells (ova) and sex hormones

muscular uterus wall

uterus — the organ where a fertilised ovum implants and grows

endometrium (lining of uterus) — has a good blood supply so it can support placenta

cervix

vulva

vagina

The female reproductive system also produces the female **hormones** that control the menstrual cycle (see p.44 for more on this).

Sperm are Produced in the Testes of Male Mammals

The role of the male reproductive system is to produce the male gametes (sperm) and transfer these into the woman's vagina during sexual intercourse.

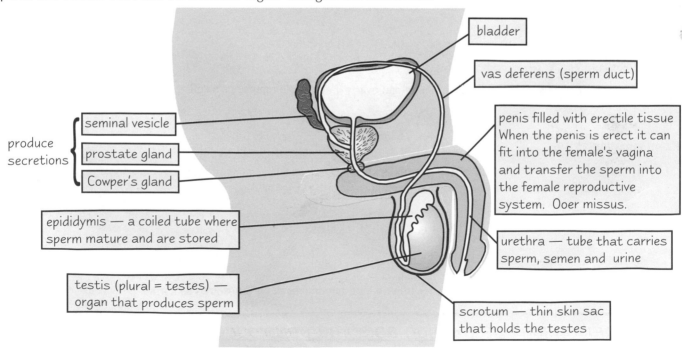

bladder

vas deferens (sperm duct)

produce secretions

seminal vesicle

prostate gland

Cowper's gland

penis filled with erectile tissue When the penis is erect it can fit into the female's vagina and transfer the sperm into the female reproductive system. Ooer missus.

epididymis — a coiled tube where sperm mature and are stored

urethra — tube that carries sperm, semen and urine

testis (plural = testes) — organ that produces sperm

scrotum — thin skin sac that holds the testes

The testes also produce the male hormone, **testosterone**.

Reproduction in Humans

The Process that Makes Ova is Called Oogenesis

Oogenesis begins when the female's still a foetus. Yes, female foetuses begin to make eggs while they're still in the uterus. Odd, I say. Odd.

1) In the foetus, the cells around the outside of the ovaries divide by mitosis to make **oogonia**.

2) The oogonia move towards the middle of the ovary and become **primary oocytes**.

3) These primary oocytes become surrounded by **follicle cells** and are then known as **primary follicles**. When a girl is born, she has millions of these primary follicles, but only some of them develop fully.

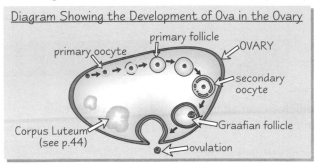

Diagram Showing the Development of Ova in the Ovary

primary oocyte
primary follicle
OVARY
secondary oocyte
Corpus Luteum (see p.44)
Graafian follicle
ovulation

4) At puberty, sex hormones like **FSH** stimulate the primary follicles to divide by meiosis to produce **secondary oocytes** (these are the **ova** that you learn about at GCSE).

5) Each month, one of these secondary oocytes develops inside a **Graafian (mature) follicle**. The follicle travels to the surface of the ovary and bursts, which releases the secondary oocyte into the **fallopian tube**, ready for **fertilisation**. This is called **ovulation**.

The Process that Makes Sperm is Spermatogenesis

Sperm are produced in the walls of **seminiferous tubules** in the **testes** from **puberty onwards**. The process is called **spermatogenesis**.

1) Diploid (2n) cells in the **germinal epithelium** of the tubules divide by **mitosis** many times to give **spermatogonia**.

2) These grow into **primary spermatocytes**.

3) The primary spermatocytes then divide by meiosis to produce haploid (n) **secondary spermatocytes**.

4) The secondary spermatocytes divide once more, to produce **spermatids**. These eventually mature into **sperm**.

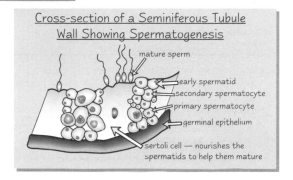

Cross-section of a Seminiferous Tubule Wall Showing Spermatogenesis

mature sperm
early spermatid
secondary spermatocyte
primary spermatocyte
germinal epithelium
sertoli cell — nourishes the spermatids to help them mature

Practice Questions

Q1 Give two functions of the female reproductive system.

Q2 What is the male sex hormone and where is it produced?

Q3 Draw a flowchart to show the stages of oogenesis.

Q4 Where do the secondary spermatocytes mature into sperm?

Exam Question

Q1 a) Eggs are produced in the ovaries by a process known as oogenesis. The diagram below shows how a follicle develops in the ovary. Explain what is happening at Y and Z. [2 marks]

Y
Z

b) Explain how an oocyte reaches the site where fertilisation occurs from where it was produced in the ovary. [3 marks]

Ooooogenesis — putting the 'oooh' into reproduction...

Learn everything on the 'in-yer-face' diagrams — especially all the terms that are new to you, like vas deferens, and epididymis. Don't be put off by oogenesis and spermatogenesis — they're not that complicated really, it's just that the cells go through loads of different stages as they develop, which unfortunately you need to know the names of.

Hormones and the Menstrual Cycle

Skip these pages if you're doing OCR or AQA B.

There's a lot covered on this page — the menstrual cycle, implantation of the fertilised ovum, the placenta during pregnancy, birth, lactation... Normally all that stuff takes at least nine months, and doesn't include farm animals either.

The **Human Menstrual Cycle** is Controlled by **Hormones**

The human menstrual cycle lasts about **28 days**. It involves development of a follicle in the ovary, release of an ovum, and **thickening** of the **uterus lining** so a fertilised ovum can **implant**. If there's no fertilisation, the lining breaks down and exits through the vagina. This is **menstruation**, which marks the end of one cycle and the start of another.

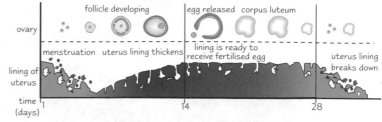

The menstrual cycle is controlled by four hormones — **Follicle-Stimulating Hormone** (FSH), **Luteinising Hormone** (LH), **oestrogen** and **progesterone**. They are either produced in the pituitary gland or in the ovaries:

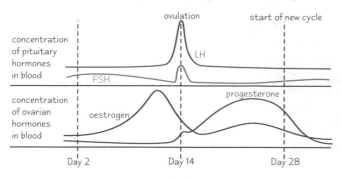

Hormones released by the pituitary —

1) **FSH** is released into the bloodstream at the **start** of the cycle and carried to the ovaries. It stimulates the development of one or more follicles, which stimulates the secretion of oestrogen.

2) **LH** is released into the bloodstream around **day 12**. It causes release of the ovum (**ovulation**). When the egg bursts out it leaves its primary follicle behind. LH helps the follicle turn into a **corpus luteum**, which is needed later.

Hormones released by the ovaries —

1) **Oestrogen** is produced by the **developing follicle**. It causes the **lining** of the uterus to **thicken**. It also **inhibits** release of FSH. This stops any more follicles maturing. A peak in oestrogen production starts a surge in FSH and LH production, which causes ovulation.

2) **Progesterone** is released by the **corpus luteum** after ovulation. Progesterone keeps the lining thick, ready for implantation if fertilisation occurs. It also inhibits release of FSH and LH. If no embryo implants, the corpus luteum dies, so progesterone production stops and FSH inhibition stops. This means the cycle starts again, with development of a new follicle.

The ovum is released around day 14 of the menstrual cycle, and must be fertilised within 24 hours. If sexual intercourse leads to fertilisation, the fertilised egg moves to the uterus where it implants in the wall. This takes up to 3 days.

The **Placenta** is the **Link** Between **Mum** and **Baby**

The placenta allows the **mother's blood** to flow close to the **foetus's blood**, without them mixing. This stops harmful substances from the mother's blood mixing with the baby's blood, but means that useful substances can **diffuse** between the two blood supplies.

1) The placenta takes over from the corpus luteum, secreting the hormones **progesterone** and **oestrogen**.

2) Oxygen and products of digestion **diffuse** across it from the mother's blood to the foetus's.

3) **Waste products** like carbon dioxide and urea diffuse from the foetus's blood to the mother's.

4) It stops disease-causing **bacteria** getting across from mum to foetus. But some viruses, and **toxins** like alcohol, nicotine and drugs, can still cross.

5) Some **antibodies** can diffuse across, giving the foetus **temporary immunity**.

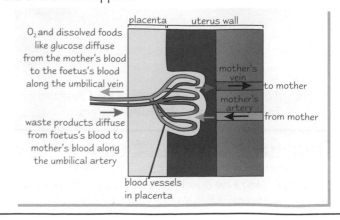

Hormones and the Menstrual Cycle

Oxytocin and Prolactin Control Birth and Lactation

Birth — **Oxytocin** is a hormone released by the **pituitary gland**. Its main role is to stimulate the smooth muscle in the uterus wall to contract. As more and more is released, the frequency and force of contractions increases. The contractions force the baby through the cervix and out through the vagina.

Lactation — At birth, the **pituitary** releases the hormone **prolactin**. This stimulates the breasts to produce milk. **Oxytocin** causes release of milk from the breasts when the baby sucks on the nipple.

AQA A ONLY

Hormones Can be Used to Control Reproduction

Hormones can be used in loads of different ways to affect reproduction of humans and animals. Learn these examples.

1) **Contraceptives** — There are different types of contraceptive pill.

   The **combined pill** contains both **oestrogen** and **progesterone**. It inhibits secretion of **FSH**. No follicles can mature, so no ovulation takes place.

   The **mini-pill** contains **progesterone only**. It also inhibits FSH production, but it's not as effective as the combined pill.

2) **Treating infertility** — Some women can't conceive due to low amounts of the hormone **FSH**. They can be given a drug, **Clomiphene**, to increase the amount of FSH secreted by the pituitary.

3) **Reproduction in farm animals** — FSH and LH are used to stimulate a large number of follicles to mature in the ovaries of animals with desirable features. After ovulation, these ova can be fertilised and the embryos transplanted into surrogates.

   A **progesterone-containing coil** can be inserted into an animal. When the coil is removed, the pituitary begins to produce **FSH** and ovulation happens soon after. This is used to **synchronise** breeding of animals, which saves on costs.

   Some people have moral and ethical issues with using hormones to mess with natural reproduction (see p.63).

4) **Increasing milk yield** — A hormone called **bovine somatotrophin** can be injected into cows to increase their milk yield.

Practice Questions

Q1   Which hormones in the menstrual cycle are released by the pituitary gland? Which are released by the ovaries?

Q2   Give three functions of the placenta.

Q3   Which hormone is responsible for the contractions during labour?

Q4   Give two uses of hormones in manipulating reproduction.

Exam Question

Q1   The combined pill is an oral contraceptive.

   a) Which hormones are present in this pill?   [2 marks]

   b) Explain how these hormones prevent pregnancy.   [3 marks]

   c) Women sometimes have problems in conceiving if too little FSH is released by the pituitary.
      They can be treated with the drug, Clomiphene, which increases the amount of FSH.
      Evaluate the use of such a drug in manipulating reproduction, outlining benefits and drawbacks.   [4 marks]

They used to call it 'the curse' — now I know why...

Lots of hormones. You need to know their names, where they come from, what they do... where their wives go shopping. Make sure you understand how the two diagrams of the menstrual cycle on p.44 link up to each other. It's a lot easier to work out what different hormones do and when if you see it on a diagram rather than written down.

Sexual Reproduction in Plants

Skip these pages if you're doing OCR, AQA A or AQA B.

Flowers are quite timid about sex. They have to rely on a passing bee or a handy gust of wind to break the ice. But once they get going, there's no keeping that pollen tube inside its grain. Saucy.

Pollination is the Transfer of Pollen Between Flowers

Pollination is transfer of pollen from an **anther** to a **stigma** of flowers of the **same species**. It's NOT the same as fertilisation — don't get these two confused. There are **two types** of pollination:

1) **Self-pollination** — pollen is transferred to the stigma of the **same flower**. This is possible because most flowers are **hermaphrodites** — they have both female **and** male sex organs.

2) **Cross-pollination** — pollen is transferred to the stigma of a **different flower** of the same species.

Cross-pollination leads to greater **genetic variation**, which makes it **preferable** to self-pollination (because variation is needed for **evolution** to take place). Plants have evolved ways to make sure cross-pollination is more likely to happen than self-pollination:

1) **Protandry** — Anthers mature before stigmas, so self-pollination can't occur, e.g. wood-sage.

2) **Protogyny** — Stigmas mature before the anthers, e.g. ribwort plantain.

3) **Dioecious** species — Some species have evolved so that they have either all male parts or all female parts, making self-pollination impossible, e.g. willow.

The design of a flower is related to the way it's pollinated. The table summarises the characteristic features of a typical wind-pollinated and insect-pollinated flower (see next page for more on this).

Conventional dating techniques don't work for flowers.

FEATURE	INSECT-POLLINATED	WIND-POLLINATED
Petals	Large, brightly coloured and shiny.	Inconspicuous, dull and small.
Sepals	Present beneath the petals.	Small or absent.
Stamen (male part)	Sturdy and found inside flower.	Flimsy, with large anthers and long filaments hanging out of flower.
Carpel (female part)	Sticky and enclosed within the flower.	Stigmas are long and feathery with a large surface area to trap pollen.
Pollen grains	Large and sticky.	Light and dry.
Scent	Present.	Absent.
Nectar	Produced by nectaries to attract insects.	None produced.

Most Flowers use either Wind or Insects for Sexual Reproduction

Flowers enable plants to reproduce sexually, but seeing as they can't move they need cunning ways of getting the male gametes (found in pollen) to the female bits of other flowers — no getting jiggy for them. So most use either insects or the wind to do this, and have certain adaptations depending on which method they use.

Insect-pollinated flowers have adaptations to attract insects, such as **brightly coloured petals** and a strong **scent**. Insects land on the flower and pollen grains get stuck to them. They then deposit the pollen onto other flowers they land on.

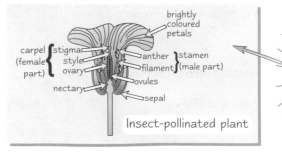

Insect-pollinated plant

The male gametes are found in the *pollen grains*. They're made in the *anther*. The female gametes are found in the *ovules*. They're made in the *ovary*.

Grasses are **wind-pollinated**. These don't need to attract insects, so they tend to be dull and unscented. Often they don't have petals, leaving the anthers and stigmas **exposed** to the wind. The wind blows pollen grains from the anther of one plant to the stigma of another plant.

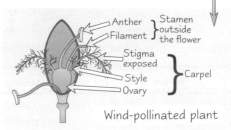

Wind-pollinated plant

Sexual Reproduction in Plants

Fertilisation *is the* Fusion *of Male and Female* Gametes

1) If a compatible pollen grain lands on the stigma of a flower, the grain absorbs water and splits open.

2) A **pollen tube** grows from it down the **style**. There are **three nuclei** in the pollen tube — one **tube nucleus** at the tube's **tip** and two **male gamete nuclei** behind it. The tube nucleus makes **digesting enzymes**. These are released by the tube so that they digest surrounding cells, making a **way through** for the pollen tube.

3) When the tube reaches the **ovary**, it grows through the **micropyle** (a tiny hole in the ovule wall) and into the **embryo sac** within the **ovule**.

4) In the embryo sac, the **tube nucleus disintegrates** and the tip of the pollen tube **bursts**, releasing the two male gamete nuclei. One male nucleus fuses with the **egg nucleus** to give a **diploid zygote**. This divides by mitosis to become the **embryo** of the seed.

5) The second male nucleus fuses with the **polar nuclei** at the centre of the **embryo sac**. This produces a **triploid nucleus**, which becomes a food store of the mature seed (called the **endosperm**).

6) So a **double fertilisation** has taken place (**two** male nuclei have fused with female nuclei). This only happens in flowering plants.

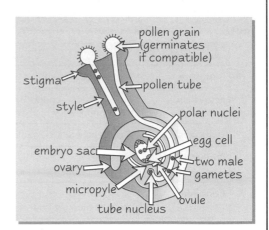

Practice Questions

Q1 What is the difference between self-pollination and cross-pollination?

Q2 How many nuclei are found in a pollen tube?

Q3 Where in a flower can gametes be found?

Q4 Describe four features of a wind-pollinated plant.

Exam Questions

Q1 a) The diagram below shows the events leading to fertilisation in a flowering plant. Label parts A-D. [4 marks]

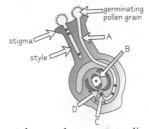

b) Explain why the pollen tube needs to secrete digestive enzymes. [2 marks]

Q2 The diagram shows a picture of a rye grass flower.

Give two features from the diagram that show it is wind-pollinated. [2 marks]

Sex by wind — and I thought flowers were romantic...

It's easier to remember features if you know why they're there. Flowers pollinated by wind need their anthers sticking out, so the pollen blows away, and their stigmas are feathery to catch pollen blowing past. Insect-pollinated flowers attract insects, which get covered in pollen and carry it to the next flower.

Energy Transfer Through an Ecosystem

Skip these pages if you're doing AQA A or AQA B.

Two nice, easy pages — loads of it's common sense and some stuff might already be familiar.
Just be careful when you're learning all the definitions, because some of the words mean very similar things.

There are **Twelve Main Definitions** You **Need To Know**

TERM	MEANING
Biosphere	The part of the Earth's surface and atmosphere inhabited by living things.
Ecosystem	An ecosystem supports life. Nutrients are recycled though an ecosystem, and energy flows through an ecosystem. E.g. a pond, a lawn, a wood. An ecosystem includes both the living and the non-living things there.
Habitat	A place where an organism lives, e.g. a wood pigeon's habitat is a wood.
Producer	Producers make their own food using an external energy source, e.g. light from the Sun. Plants are producers. Organisms that make their own food are also called **autotrophs**.
Consumer	Consumers eat other organisms for food and energy. Cows eat a **producer** (grass) so they're **primary** consumers. Humans then eat cows so they're **secondary** consumers.
Decomposer	Decomposers, e.g. bacteria and fungi, feed on dead organic matter.
Trophic level	A particular **feeding stage** in the food chain, e.g. producer, primary consumer, secondary consumer, etc.
Food chain	A sequence representing the way energy flows from one organism to another.
Community	**All** the organisms living in a particular ecosystem.
Population	A group of organisms of the **same species** living in the same place at the same time.
Food web	A diagram showing all the feeding relationships between the organisms of a **community**. It's made up of many interconnected food chains.
Niche	The role played by an organism in a community (like its behaviour, what it eats and what eats it). Each species has its own unique niche.

Energy Flows Through **Food Chains**

1) Each organism in a food chain is on a different **trophic level** — it can be a producer, a primary consumer, a secondary consumer, etc.

2) Food chains start with a **producer**.

3) The **primary consumer** eats the producer, and so on up the food chain.

4) Only about **10%** of the **energy** stored in the organisms at one trophic level passes to the organisms in the next level. Some energy is lost as **heat** from the organisms, and some is lost in their **waste**.

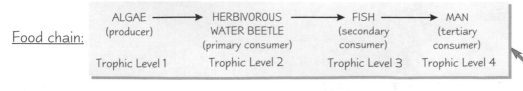

Food chain:

ALGAE (producer)	→	HERBIVOROUS WATER BEETLE (primary consumer)	→	FISH (secondary consumer)	→	MAN (tertiary consumer)
Trophic Level 1		Trophic Level 2		Trophic Level 3		Trophic Level 4

Food Webs are Made Up of Many **Inter-Linked Food Chains**

Most organisms don't eat just one thing — so food chains don't tell the full story. **Food webs** tell you more — for example, this one shows that algae are eaten by three different primary consumers, not just by the water beetle. Like food chains, food webs always start with producers and end with the top consumers.

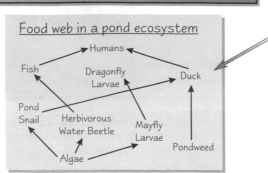

Food web in a pond ecosystem

~ The arrows always point *from* the organism being eaten *to* the organism that eats it. ~

Energy Transfer Through an Ecosystem

There are **Three Main Types** of **Ecological Pyramid**

In all these 'pyramids' the **width** of each block is proportional to the figure it's representing.

1) **Pyramids of numbers** show **how many organisms** there are at each trophic level. They're not always pyramid-shaped:

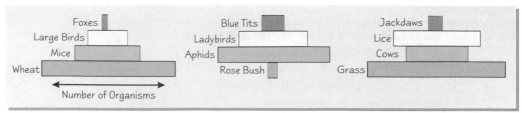

2) **Pyramids of biomass** show the **total dry mass** of the organisms (in **kg m^{-2}**) in each trophic level at a particular time. These are **almost always** pyramid-shaped:

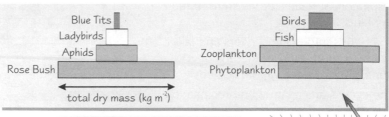

3) **Pyramids of energy** show how much energy (in kilojoules per squared metre per year — **KJ m^{-2} y^{-1}**) is passed on from one trophic level to the next. It's never all passed on, so they're **always pyramid-shaped**.

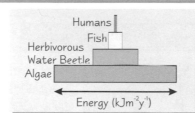

> If the producers don't live very long but reproduce loads, their dry mass at a particular time (called the <u>standing crop</u>) won't be very big — even if they support lots of consumers.

Productivity is About **How Much Food** Organisms **Produce**

1) The **productivity** of a producer is how efficiently it uses energy (e.g. light) to make new tissues — the better it makes tissue, the more food it makes for primary consumers and the more food there is in the ecosystem.

2) **Gross primary productivity** (GPP) is the **total amount** of energy absorbed by the producers **per unit area per year** and used to make new tissues. The units are **KJ m^{-2} y^{-1}**

3) The **net primary productivity** (NPP) is the **energy** that's **available** for the **next trophic level**.

4) So:

> **NPP = GPP – energy used in respiration or lost as waste by the producers.**

EDEXCEL ONLY

Practice Questions

Q1 What is an ecosystem?

Q2 What is meant by the term 'niche'?

Q3 Which type of ecological pyramid is always pyramid shaped?

Q4 What is the relationship between NPP and GPP?

> 'Arbitrary' just means that the units could be anything. It doesn't matter what they are, so you don't have to worry about them — which is nice.

Exam Questions

Q1 Pyramids of biomass are not always pyramid shaped. Explain why. [2 marks]

Q2 Approximately 1% of the sun's energy is incorporated into the producers. Only 10% of the energy in one trophic level passes to the organisms in the next trophic level. If 10,000 arbitrary units of energy are given out by the sun, how many of these arbitrary units will be incorporated into the secondary consumers? [3 marks]

Things eat each other — how do they make it so complicated?

A good question, but not one you've got time to ponder now. What you need to do is learn that list of 12 definitions. Some are obvious, like decomposers, but some are more tricky, like the difference between a population and a community. Don't try to understand the reasons behind the terms, it's a waste of energy. Just get them learnt.

Recycling Nutrients

Skip these pages if you're doing AQA A or AQA B.

There are 3 cycles you need to know about — water, carbon and nitrogen. The water cycle's pretty straightforward and the carbon's not too bad, but the nitrogen cycle's evil. But fear not — learn the diagrams and you'll be fine.

Water is Constantly Recycled

1) Water falls as **precipitation** (rain, hail, sleet or snow).

2) Some is used by organisms. This returns to the atmosphere by **evaporation** from respiratory surfaces, or via **transpiration** in plants.

3) Some runs into oceans, rivers and lakes. Water evaporates from these giving **atmospheric water vapour** (clouds).

4) The cycle starts again with precipitation from the clouds.

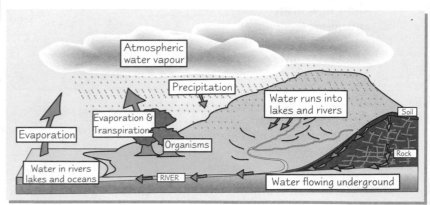

Carbon is Recycled in the Carbon Cycle

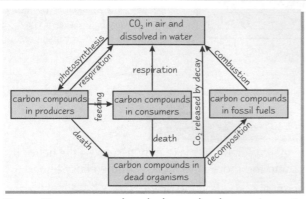

1) Carbon is found as **carbon dioxide gas** (CO_2) in the atmosphere and dissolved in water.

2) CO_2 from the atmosphere is absorbed by **green plants** and used for **photosynthesis** to make carbohydrates. Plants are known as **carbon sinks**, because lots of carbon is locked up in their tissues.

3) These carbohydrates **enter consumers** when they **feed** on the plants and on each other.

4) When organisms **respire**, CO_2 returns to the atmosphere.

5) **Burning fossil fuels** also returns CO_2 to the atmosphere.

6) **Decomposers** break down dead organic matter, releasing CO_2 back into the atmosphere.

7) Carbon follows another major recycling pathway in the **sea**. Marine organisms make **shells** using **carbonates**, which contain carbon. When they die, the shells fall to the ocean floor and eventually form **limestone rocks**. The carbon in these rocks returns to the atmosphere as CO_2 during **volcanic eruptions** or **weathering**.

Microorganisms are Important in the Nitrogen Cycle

Don't let the diagram on the next page scare you — it's not that bad once you start learning it. Honest. Basically, **all living things** need **nitrogen** to make molecules like **proteins**, **ATP** and **DNA**. Plants can only absorb nitrogen in the form of **ammonium** or **nitrate ions**, while **consumers** get their nitrogen by eating other organisms.

Here's a list of the facts to help you understand the diagram on page 51:

1) The **ammonium** and **nitrate ions** used by plants are in the soil because of **nitrogen fixation**. This is when **atmospheric nitrogen** is converted to ammonium or nitrate ions by **nitrogen fixing bacteria**. Nitrogen fixing bacteria can live freely in the soil (**e.g. *Azotobacter***) or **symbiotically** in the root nodules of leguminous plants (**e.g. *Rhizobium***).

2) Energy from **lightning** also helps turn atmospheric nitrogen into nitrates.

3) The industrial **Haber process** uses atmospheric nitrogen to make nitrate and ammonia fertilisers. Using these fertilisers increases the concentration of ammonium and nitrate ions in the soil.

4) **Decomposers** turn nitrogen-containing compounds in **dead organisms** into **ammonium ions**. These are then converted to **nitrite** by *Nitrosomonas* bacteria, and the nitrite's converted to **nitrate** by *Nitrobacter* bacteria. The ammonium to nitrate process is called **nitrification**.

5) **Denitrification** is when nitrates are turned back into atmospheric nitrogen by bacteria like *Thiobacillus* and *Pseudomonas*. This only happens in the absence of oxygen — e.g. in waterlogged soil (because these bacteria need **anaerobic** conditions).

Recycling Nutrients

The **Nitrogen Cycle Diagram** is Scary but **Important**

OK, here goes. All those arrows and boxes look alarming, but actually it's pretty straightforward, once you understand the processes that are going on. Link it up to the explanation on p.50 and it'll soon start to make sense.

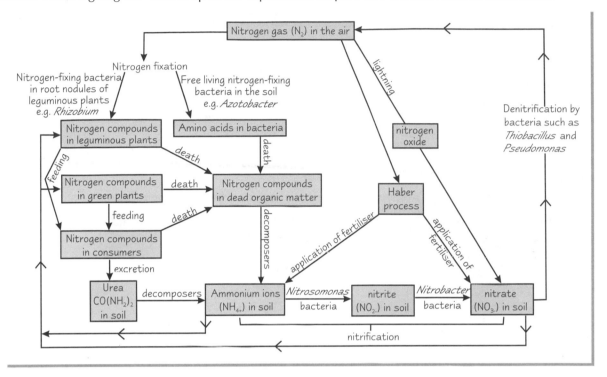

Human Activities Can **Disrupt** the Carbon and Nitrogen Cycles

1) When **fossil fuels** are burnt they release CO_2.

2) Increased levels of CO_2 in the atmosphere are linked to the **Greenhouse Effect**. CO_2 is good at **absorbing heat radiation**, so the more CO_2 in the atmosphere, the hotter it gets. If the Earth's temperature gets too high, it could cause **changes** in **weather patterns** — so there'd be droughts and floods.

3) **Plants** remove CO_2 from the atmosphere. So **deforestation** increases CO_2 levels. When trees are cut down to make room for farmland, they're often **burned**, which releases even more CO_2.

4) **Fertilisers** containing ammonium and nitrates are added to soils. Sometimes, they seep out into lakes and rivers. This causes **eutrophication**, which ends up in the mass death of organisms in the water (see p57 for more on eutrophication).

Practice Questions

Q1   Describe how water returns to the atmosphere in the water cycle.

Q2   Name three ways in which carbon is added to the atmosphere in the carbon cycle.

Q3   What role does lightning play in the nitrogen cycle?

Q4   In what form do plants absorb nitrogen from the soil?

Exam Questions

Q1   Give an account of the nitrogen cycle, highlighting the importance of microbes.   [10 marks]

Q2   Name two processes that increase atmospheric carbon dioxide in the normal carbon cycle.   [2 marks]

Look at the state of that nitrogen cycle — I want my mum...

It looks scary, I won't deny it. But once you start it's really not hard to learn. The best way to learn the cycles is to try and draw the diagrams (no peeking), see which bits you missed, then try again. When you've managed it perfectly three times in a row it's probably in your head for good, but come back to it now and again just to check.

Environmental Adaptations

Skip these pages if you're doing OCR, AQA A or AQA B.

Organisms have adaptations, which help them survive in their particular environments. Like, my tiny brain means I'm well adapted to write stupid introductions and top tips for you. Which I'm sure you're delighted about.

Organisms Can be Adapted to their Environment in Three Ways

Organisms are adapted to make the most of their **surroundings** in three different ways:

① Structural adaptations
— the **size and shape** of the organism, the structure of any **appendages** (e.g. limbs, tail, ears, etc.), whether it has fur, feathers, scales, etc. E.g. fish have fins and a streamlined body to help them swim in water.

② Physiological adaptations
— how the **cells**, **organs** and **organ systems** are made up. E.g. plants that live in places of high salinity have special cells of even higher salt concentration than their surroundings to allow water uptake by osmosis.

③ Behavioural adaptations
— how the organism **acts**. E.g. some animals hibernate in winter to avoid the low temperatures and lack of food.

Darwin's **theory of natural selection** explains how organisms become adapted to their environment.

Gene mutations arise by chance. Some of these mutations code for **characteristics** that improve an organism's chances of survival in a particular environment.

The organisms with the favourable characteristic are likely to **survive longer**, reproduce more, and pass their **genes** on to more offspring.

This means that more of the next generation **inherit** the favourable characteristic.

Over time, the whole species may gradually change its characteristics by this process of **natural selection**. Sometimes **new species** can arise.

Adaptations of Organisms Relate to Their Environment

Many plants have features to **prevent water loss** by transpiration. They're called **xeromorphic** adaptations. You find them in plants that live in warm, dry or windy habitats, which speed up **transpiration rate**. Examples include:

1) Thicker **waxy cuticles** on leaves and stems.

2) Leaves are reduced to **spines**. This decreases the number of stomata and lowers the surface area from which water can be lost. E.g. **cacti** have spines for leaves.

3) Leaves can **roll up** in especially dry conditions — e.g. **marram grass**. This reduces the surface area for losing water and traps moist air, slowing down transpiration.

<u>Marram Grass Leaf</u>

upper epidermis with thick waxy cuticle

lower epidermis

epidermal hairs trap humid air

leaf curled trapping humid air and lowering exposed surface area

Other plants live in areas where there's **lots of water**. These are called **hydrophytes**. Hydrophytes that are **fully submerged** in fresh water have adaptations like:

1) No cuticle or stomata.

2) Reduced **supporting tissue** to help them move with the water currents.

3) **Air bladders** to help them float nearer the surface where there's higher light intensity.

Animals also have external adaptations to help them survive. For example, **moles** live underground:

1) They have tiny eyes, because vision isn't so important underground.

2) Their forelimbs are designed to shovel the earth.

Other examples are otters, seals and dolphins, which have streamlined bodies to help them swim efficiently.

Environmental Adaptations

Invertebrates are Adapted to the Oxygen Level in their Environment

Oxygen is essential to organisms that carry out **aerobic respiration**. Oxygen levels differ between habitats:

1) There's generally **more oxygen** in **terrestrial** habitats than in aquatic ones.
2) There's **more oxygen** in **moving water** (e.g. a fast-flowing river) than stagnant water (e.g. the bottom of a pond), because the movement of the water incorporates air.

Invertebrates have **physiological** and **structural** adaptations to cope with the particular oxygen level in their environment. Oxygen enters some invertebrates by **diffusion** through the whole body surface. A large **surface area to volume ratio** is needed for this (see p.86). Invertebrates have different adaptations for improving oxygen diffusion into their bodies:

INVERTEBRATE	ADAPTATIONS FOR GETTING OXYGEN
Amoeba	**Single-celled** organism, so surface area to volume ratio is high.
Flatworms (platyhelminthes)	**Flattened body shape** increases surface area to volume ratio.
Annelids, e.g. leeches	As well as receiving oxygen through diffusion, they have a simple **circulatory system** to get it to all their internal cells. Their blood contains **haemoglobin** to increase the **oxygen carrying capacity**. Not all invertebrates have haemoglobin in their blood.
Tubifex worms, a type of aquatic **oligochaete**	They live at the bottom of rivers in **low oxygen concentrations**. • They bury their heads in the mud and leave their tails sticking up. • They then absorb oxygen through the surface of their **tail ends**, which **wave about** to move **oxygenated water** over them. • The blood **capillaries** in their tail ends are close to the surface, to make diffusion easier. • Their blood contains **haemoglobin**.
Lugworms	They have **external gills**, which allow more blood to flow close to the water so that gases can be exchanged more easily.

Other invertebrates are adapted by having **breathing tubes**, **tracheal systems** or **lungs** to obtain oxygen.

Practice Questions

Q1   What is meant by
      a) structural adaptations?
      b) physiological adaptations?
      c) behavioural adaptations?

Q2   Name three external xeromorphic adaptations.

Q3   What is a hydrophyte?

Exam Questions

Q1   Name one behavioural, one structural and one physiological adaptation to
      low oxygen concentration shown by a tubifex worm.   [3 marks]

Q2   The oxygen concentration was measured on the same day in three habitats — a fast-flowing river,
      a pond and a terrestrial environment. The three concentrations were $10 \text{ cm}^3\text{l}^{-1}$, $210 \text{ cm}^3\text{l}^{-1}$,
      and $5 \text{ cm}^3\text{l}^{-1}$. Match the most likely habitat to each oxygen concentration and explain your answer.   [5 marks]

Xeromorphic — an exciting word for a boring subject...

Actually that's unfair. It's taken millions of years for plants to evolve those adaptations, and here I am slagging them off. When I've managed to develop a thicker waxy cuticle on my leaves and stems, then I can comment, and not before. Oh, and learn this page. It may not be thrilling — but if you know it, it could earn you vital marks.

Modes of Nutrition

Skip these pages if you're doing OCR, AQA A or AQA B.

Mmmm food. Different organisms have different ways of feeding themselves — and some of them don't even use cutlery, for shame.

All Organisms are either Autotrophs or Heterotrophs

The first thing you need to know about nutrition is that **all organisms** are either **heterotrophs** or **autotrophs**.

① **Autotrophs** are **producers**. They make their own complex organic molecules from simple, inorganic ones, using an external energy source. **Photoautotrophs**, like green plants, use the light energy from the sun as their energy source. **Chemoautotrophs**, like some bacteria, use energy from chemical reactions to build up organic molecules.

② **Heterotrophs** are **consumers**. Heterotrophic organisms get nutrients from complex, organic molecules. These are digested into small, simple molecules, then built up again to make the molecules the organism needs. So whether they eat plants or animals, heterotrophs depend on **autotrophs** to build the molecules in the first place. Parasites, saprophytes (decomposers) and free-living animals are all heterotrophs.

Holozoic Organisms Digest Food Inside Their Bodies

Holozoic nutrition is where food is digested in a tube in the body — the **alimentary canal**. It happens in **five stages**:

Human nutrition is holozoic. Dude.

Ingestion	⟹	Food is taken into the body through the mouth.
Digestion	⟹	Large, insoluble molecules are converted to small, soluble ones in the gut.
Absorption	⟹	Smaller, soluble molecules are taken into the bloodstream from the gut.
Assimilation	⟹	Absorbed products of digestion are converted into complex molecules and used by the body.
Egestion	⟹	Undigested food is passed out of the body.

Saprophytes Digest Food Outside Their Bodies

Saprophytes feed on **dead organic matter** and **wastes** like faeces.

1) **Rhizopus** is a saprophytic **fungus**, which feeds on starch and other organic materials in plants.

2) Rhizopus fungi have thread-like cells called **hyphae** to penetrate the food.

3) **Enzymes** are released from the hyphae to digest the food surrounding them. Large insoluble molecules are broken down by the enzymes, giving smaller soluble products that are then absorbed into the hyphae cells.

Saprophytic Digestion

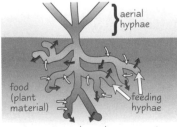

aerial hyphae

food (plant material)

feeding hyphae

➡ enzymes released
⇨ products of digestion absorbed

You can see extracellular saprophytic digestion by using the **starch agar assay**. The saprophytic fungi are grown on agar that contains starch. Then the starch agar is flooded with **iodine**, and turns blue-black (see p.8). But around areas of fungal growth there are **clear zones**. This is because the starch has been digested by the fungi.

Modes of Nutrition

Mutualism is where Both Partners Benefit

Mutualism is an association between organisms of **different species** where both partners benefit.

An example is between the nitrogen-fixing bacterium, *Rhizobium* (don't confuse with *Rhizopus* at the bottom of p.54) and a leguminous, flowering plant of the family *Papilionaceae*. *Rhizobium* gets into the roots of the plant through its root hairs and causes **root nodules** to develop. It multiplies inside these and **reduces** nitrogen to make **ammonium**. The plant gets a source of ammonium so it can grow, even in poor soils. In return, the *Rhizobium* gets sugars, vitamins and a sheltered habitat.

Another example is the relationship between **ruminants** like cattle and the **microbes** that live in their **rumen** (part of the stomach). The **ruminant** provides **food** and a **warm moist environment** for the microbes. The **microbes digest cellulose** in the grass that the ruminant eats. The ruminant can't digest grass itself because it hasn't got a cellulase enzyme to break down the cellulose found in grass.

The Tapeworm, Taenia solium, is a Parasite

Parasites live **on** or **in** their **larger host**. The parasite gets its **nutrition** from the host, and this **harms the host**. *Taenia solium* is an example — it's a type of tapeworm that can grow up to 3 metres long. It has a complex life cycle — it starts off its life living in a pig and end it living in the human gut. Nice.

The *Taenia* tapeworm's body is made up of lots of small sections. One of these sections is called a proglottis, several of them are called proglottides — another one of those funny plurals. The proglottides move further from the head as they mature, and eggs develop inside them.

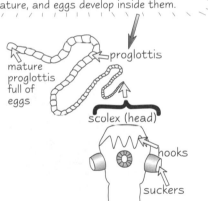

mature proglottis full of eggs

proglottis

scolex (head)

hooks

suckers

Taenia solium has lots of adaptations to make it an effective parasite:

1) It's **long and thin**, giving it a **large surface area** to absorb more nutrients from the human gut.

2) The long thin shape also prevents the gut getting blocked, because parasites obviously don't want to kill their hosts.

3) *Taenia* has **hooks** and **suckers** on its **scolex** (head part) so it can **grip** onto the intestine wall.

4) There's no digestive system in the tapeworm — the host does the digestion for it, and *Taenia* just absorbs the products of digestion from the gut. Cheeky.

5) The tapeworm's body is covered in a **cuticle**, which prevents its living cells being digested by the host.

6) *Taenia* produces **loads of eggs**, to increase the chances of infecting a new host. The eggs leave in the host's **faeces**.

Practice Questions

Q1 What mode of nutrition does *Rhizopus* use?

Q2 What is meant by mutualism?

Q3 Define a parasite.

Q4 Draw a diagram of *Taenia solium* and label it.

Exam Questions

Q1 Parasites often have adaptations to help them survive in or on their hosts. Give four examples of these adaptations, with reference to a named parasite. [4 marks]

Q2 Explain how the saprophyte, *Rhizopus*, is able to digest food outside of its body. [4 marks]

Fungus, tapeworms and faeces — do not attempt to snack while learning...

I know there's a lot of hard-to-remember names and easily-mixed-up terms on this page. But some people have worms inside them that are 3 m long and used to be inside a pig. So count yourself lucky, stop whining and start learning.

Human Influences on the Environment

Skip these pages if you're doing OCR, AQA A or AQA B.

Humans can really hurt the environment. Luckily, stuff can be done to limit our nastiness and — added bonus — if you know about it you'll do better in your exams.

Fossil Fuels are Non-Renewable, but there are Renewable Alternatives

Fossil fuels are **non-renewable** resources because they take **millions of years** to form. Supplies of fossil fuels will **run out** one day — they're being used up faster than they can be replaced. **Alternatives** to fossil fuels include:

1) **Renewable** energy resources like wind, wave and solar energy.
2) Renewable **biomass** energy resources, like wood, gasohol and biogas.

> • **Wood** is the main biomass energy resource. Fast-growing trees like **poplar** and **willow** can be **logged sustainably**. The wood can be burnt for heat energy directly, or it can be used to heat water. This creates **steam**, which can turn **turbines** to generate **electricity**.
>
> • **Gasohol** — can be used in **engines** instead of petrol and is a cleaner fuel. It's produced from **ethanol**, when sugar is **fermented** by yeast.
>
> • **Biogas** — is mostly **methane**, and is produced during **anaerobic fermentation** of organic waste by bacteria. The methane burns to produce carbon dioxide and water, without any other pollutants.

Deforestation Damages the Environment

Deforestation can lead to changes in the **climate**, **soil erosion**, and **reduction** in the number of **species** in an ecosystem.

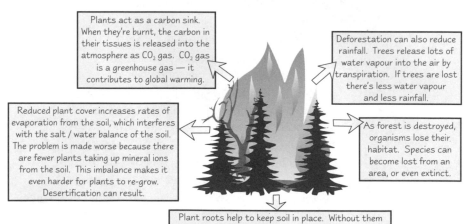

Plants act as a carbon sink. When they're burnt, the carbon in their tissues is released into the atmosphere as CO_2 gas. CO_2 gas is a greenhouse gas — it contributes to global warming.

Deforestation can also reduce rainfall. Trees release lots of water vapour into the air by transpiration. If trees are lost there's less water vapour and less rainfall.

Reduced plant cover increases rates of evaporation from the soil, which interferes with the salt / water balance of the soil. The problem is made worse because there are fewer plants taking up mineral ions from the soil. This imbalance makes it even harder for plants to re-grow. Desertification can result.

As forest is destroyed, organisms lose their habitat. Species can become lost from an area, or even extinct.

Plant roots help to keep soil in place. Without them there is more risk of soil erosion, which makes the land less fertile. Without trees and vegetation the soil can dry out and desertification can result.

Deforestation? What deforestation?

Burning Fossil Fuels Causes Global Warming and Acid Rain

1) CO_2 and other **greenhouse gases** form a **layer** around the Earth. The **Sun's radiation** has a **short wavelength**, and it passes easily through the layer. The radiation from the Sun warms the Earth. As the **Earth** warms up, it **radiates heat** (infrared radiation) from its surface. This radiation has a **longer wavelength**, and gets **trapped** by the greenhouse gases. Because the heat doesn't all escape into space, the Earth gets very slowly warmer and warmer.

2) **Sulphur dioxide** and **oxides of nitrogen** are also produced when fossil fuels are burnt. These gases dissolve in water vapour to make **acids**, which fall to Earth in acid rain or snow. Acid rain can harm plants and animals, mostly by interfering with their **metabolic reactions**.

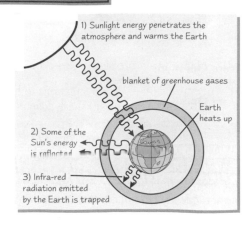

1) Sunlight energy penetrates the atmosphere and warms the Earth

blanket of greenhouse gases

Earth heats up

2) Some of the Sun's energy is reflected

3) Infra-red radiation emitted by the Earth is trapped

Human Influences on the Environment

Raw Sewage and Fertilisers Cause Eutrophication

If **raw sewage** or **fertilisers** get into rivers and lakes, they increase the levels of **nitrate** and **phosphate** in them. This leads to **eutrophication**.

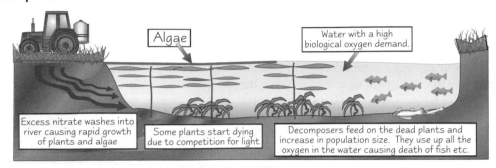

Algae

Water with a high biological oxygen demand.

Excess nitrate washes into river causing rapid growth of plants and algae

Some plants start dying due to competition for light

Decomposers feed on the dead plants and increase in population size. They use up all the oxygen in the water causing death of fish etc.

1) Growth of **algae** and other plants increases due to the higher levels of nitrates and phosphates. There become so many producers that they're **overcrowded**, and start to die faster than they're eaten.

2) The dead producers produce lots of food for **decomposers**, which flourish. They use up a lot of the oxygen in the water, increasing its **biological oxygen demand** (BOD). With raw sewage, which is full of bacteria anyway, the BOD of the water is even greater.

3) The lack of oxygen leads to the **death** of fish, plants and other aerobic organisms.

4) This whole process is called eutrophication. There's more about it on page 68.

Conservation Aims to Protect Natural Resources

1) An important aim of conservation is to maintain **species diversity**. If one organism becomes extinct it affects other organisms in the ecosystem — because a food supply or predator is removed.

2) **Sustainable agriculture** can help maintain species diversity by allowing the environment time to recover between crops. **Sustainable forestry** involves planting new trees to replace ones that are cut down.

3) Having a **variety** of **habitats** in an area encourages species diversity. This is hard if the area is being used to grow one particular crop or tree, but things like allowing old hedgerows to remain can really improve species diversity.

4) **EU legislation** has been drawn up to control air and water quality, protect the environment and avoid over-exploitation of natural resources.

Practice Questions

Q1 Name four types of renewable energy resources.

Q2 How is gasohol produced?

Q3 Name two pollution problems that can be caused by burning fossil fuels.

Q4 Name three problems caused by deforestation.

Exam Question

Q1 Fertilisers can be damaging to lakes and rivers. Explain why. [8 marks]

I was told gases are better out than in — obviously not for fossil fuels...

Not a very cheerful page, but pretty important, and therefore loved by examiners everywhere. And you know what that means... tear it out of the book and pretend it never happened. Just kidding — it's actually got to be learned, learned, and then learned some more. Well, at least I amuse myself.

Genetic Engineering

Skip these pages if you're doing Edexcel.
Genetic engineering is a dead popular exam topic because it shows how biology relates to real life — and examiners love all that stuff. These pages explain the process for manufacturing genes and, you've got to admit, it's kinda cool.

Recombinant DNA is like 'Home-Made' DNA

DNA has the **same** structure of **nucleotides** in **all organisms**. This means you can **join together** a piece of DNA from one organism and a piece of DNA from another organism.

DNA that has been **genetically engineered** to contain DNA from another organism, is called **recombinant DNA**. It has **useful applications**. In the example below, a **human gene** coding for a **useful protein** is inserted into a bacterium's DNA. When the **bacterium reproduces**, the **gene** is **reproduced** too. The gene is **expressed** in the bacterium, and so the bacterium **produces** the **protein** which is coded for by the gene.

1) First you **find** the gene you want in the donor cell. The **DNA** containing the gene is **removed** from the cell and any **proteins** surrounding the extracted DNA are removed using **peptidase enzymes**.

2) Next you **cut out** the **useful gene** from the DNA using **restriction endonuclease** enzymes. These leave a **sticky end** (tail of unpaired bases) at each end of the useful gene. This stage is called **restriction**.

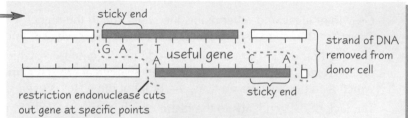

restriction endonuclease cuts out gene at specific points

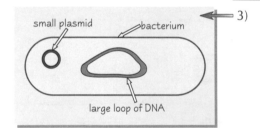

3) Then you need to **prepare** the other bit of DNA that you're **joining** the useful gene to (called a **vector**). The main vectors used are **plasmids** — these are small, **circular molecules** of DNA found in **bacteria**. They're useful as vectors because they can **replicate** without interfering with the bacterium's own DNA (see p.62 for more on vectors). The same **restriction enzyme** is used to **cut out** a section of the plasmid. The **sticky ends** that are left have bases that are **complementary** to the bases on the sticky ends of the **useful gene**.

4) Finally, you need to **join** the **useful gene** to the **plasmid vector DNA** — this process is called **ligation**. This is where the **sticky ends** come in — **hydrogen bonds** form between the **complementary bases** of the sticky ends. The DNA molecules are then 'tied' together with the enzyme, **ligase**. The new DNA is called **recombinant DNA**.

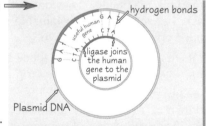

The useful gene is now in the recombinant DNA of a plasmid vector in a bacterium. So now the bacterium is made to reproduce loads, so you get loads of copies of the gene (see next page for how this happens). Clever, huh.

Reverse Transcriptase makes DNA from *mRNA*

Transcription is when mRNA is made from DNA (see p.34). **Reverse transcriptase** is a nifty enzyme that runs this process backwards and makes DNA from mRNA. It's useful in genetic engineering because **cells** that make **specific proteins** usually contain **more mRNA molecules than genes**. For example, **pancreatic cells** produce the protein **insulin**. They have loads of mRNA molecules on their way to ribosomes to make the insulin — but only two copies of the DNA gene for insulin, one on each pair of chromosomes.

1) mRNA is **extracted** from donor cells.

2) The mRNA is mixed with **free DNA nucleotides** and **reverse transcriptase**. The reverse transcriptase uses the mRNA as a **template** to synthesise a new strand of **complementary** DNA.

3) The complementary DNA can be made **double-stranded** by mixing it with DNA nucleotides and **polymerase enzymes**. Then the useful gene from the double-stranded DNA is inserted into a plasmid (see section above) so the bacteria can make lots of the product of the gene.

4) The diagram shows a monkey swinging from a strand of DNA. Try to ignore him — he's attention-seeking.

Genetic Engineering

Genetic Engineering has *Important Medical Uses*

Sometimes humans can't produce a certain **protein** because the **gene** that codes for it is **faulty**. By creating recombinant DNA, genes can be artificially **manufactured**, to replace the faulty genes. This has important **medical benefits**. For example:

1) **Diabetics** don't have the healthy gene needed to make the protein **insulin**, which controls blood sugar levels.
2) **Haemophiliacs** lack the healthy gene that codes for the protein, **factor VIII**, which allows blood to clot.
3) Genetic engineering allows these genes to be manufactured in bacterial cells and used to help sufferers.

Industrial Fermenters are Used for Large Scale *Protein Production*

Once a useful gene is in a bacterium, it has to start working to produce the **protein**. An **industrial fermenter** is used to culture the bacteria and produce a **large amount** of the gene product (the protein).

1) A **promoter** gene is often included along with the **donor** gene when the **recombinant DNA** is made. This 'switches on' the useful donor gene so it starts making the **protein**.
2) The **bacteria** containing the recombinant DNA are grown or cultured in a **fermenter**. Inside the fermenter, they're given the **ideal conditions** needed for rapid growth (see p.22 for more on industrial fermenters). They **reproduce quickly**, until there are millions of bacteria inside the fermenter.
3) The **plasmids**, including plasmids made of recombinant DNA, **replicate** at each cell division — so each new bacterium contains the useful gene.
4) As the bacteria grow, they start producing the **human protein** that the donor gene in the plasmid codes for, e.g. **human factor VIII** or **human insulin**.
5) The bacteria can't use human protein, so it **builds up** in the medium inside the fermenter. When enough has built up, it can be **extracted** and processed for use.

Practice Questions

Q1 What is recombinant DNA?

Q2 What do restriction endonuclease enzymes do?

Q3 How are useful genes joined to plasmids?

Q4 How does reverse transcriptase work?

Q5 What proteins do diabetics and haemophiliacs lack?

Exam Questions

Q1 Plant breeders have found a variety of cabbage that is resistant to a pest called root fly. This is because the cabbage produces a protein that inhibits one of the fly's digestive enzymes. Plant breeders want to manufacture this protein so they can insert it into carrots too. Describe how scientists could:

a) remove the gene that produces the inhibitor from the cabbage. [2 marks]

b) insert this gene into the DNA of a bacterium. [2 marks]

Q2 One technique used to produce human factor VIII by genetic engineering involves inserting a gene for human factor VIII into the DNA of a bacterium. Name the enzyme which would be used to:

a) cut the bacterial DNA; [1 mark]

b) insert the DNA for human insulin into the cut bacterial DNA. [1 mark]

Monkey vectors — Plasmid of the Apes...

You see, biology isn't just an evil conspiracy to keep students busy — it has loads of really important uses in real life. For example, sufferers of genetic diseases now have a far greater chance of having successful treatment, which is nice. Round of applause for biology, that's what I say.

Genetic Fingerprinting

Skip these pages if you're doing OCR or Edexcel.

*The tiniest bit of DNA is enough to identify you. You're shedding hairs and flakes of skin-scum all the time (nice) — it's like leaving a personal trail of, well, **you** wherever you go. Scary (and quite grim) thought.*

The **Polymerase Chain Reaction** (PCR) Creates Millions of **Copies** of DNA

Some samples of DNA are too small to analyse. The **Polymerase Chain Reaction** makes millions of copies of the smallest sample of DNA in a few hours. This **amplifies** DNA, so analysis can be done on it. PCR has **several stages**:

1) The DNA sample is **heated** at **95°C**. This breaks the hydrogen bonds between the bases on each strand. But it **doesn't** break the bonds between the ribose of one nucleotide and the phosphate on the next — so the DNA molecule is broken into **separate strands** but doesn't completely fall apart.

2) **Primers** (short pieces of DNA) are attached to both strands of the DNA — these will tell the **enzyme** where to **start copying** later in the process. They also stop the two DNA strands from joining together again.

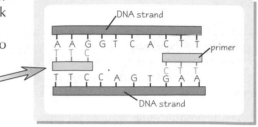

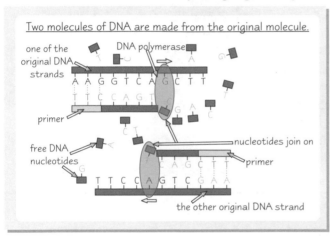

Two molecules of DNA are made from the original molecule.

3) The DNA and primer mixture are **cooled** to **40°C** so that the primers can **fully bind on** to the DNA.

4) Free **DNA nucleotides** and the enzyme **DNA polymerase** are added to the reaction mixture. The mixture is heated to **70°C**. Each of the original DNA strands is used as a **template**. Free DNA nucleotides pair with their complementary bases on the template strands. The DNA polymerase attaches the new nucleotides together into a strand, starting at the primers.

5) The cycle starts again, using **both** molecules of DNA. Each cycle **doubles** the amount of DNA.

You can **Identify People** from their **DNA** by **Cutting** it into **Fragments**

It's possible to **identify a person** from a sample of their DNA, if the sample is big enough. This is done by using **enzymes** to cut the DNA up into **fragments**, then looking at the **pattern** of fragments, which is **different** for everyone (except identical twins). This is called a person's **genetic fingerprint**.

1) To **cut up** the DNA into DNA fragments you add specific **restriction endonuclease** enzymes to the DNA sample — each one **cuts** the DNA every time a **specific base sequence** occurs. **Where** these base sequences occur on the DNA **varies** between everyone (except identical twins), so the number and length of DNA fragments will be different for everyone.

2) Next you use the process of **electrophoresis** to separate out the DNA fragments by size:

How Electrophoresis Works:

1) The DNA fragments are put into **wells** in a slab of **gel**. The gel is covered in a **buffer solution** that **conducts electricity**.

2) An **electrical current** is passed through the gel. DNA fragments are **negatively charged**, so they move towards the positive electrode. **Small** fragments move **faster** than large ones, so they **travel furthest** through the gel.

3) By the time the current is switched off, all the fragments of DNA are **well separated**.

Electrophoresis

DNA moves towards the anode, with smallest fragments moving furthest

−ve cathode
wells
DNA fragment (invisible)
gel, with buffer solution on top
+ve anode

In electrophoresis the DNA fragments **aren't visible** to the eye — you have to do something else to them before you can **see their pattern**. Coincidentally, that's what the next page is all about...

Genetic Fingerprinting

Gene Probes Make the Invisible 'Genetic Fingerprint' Visible

DNA fragments separated by electrophoresis are invisible.
A radioactive DNA probe (also called **gene probe**) is used to show them up:

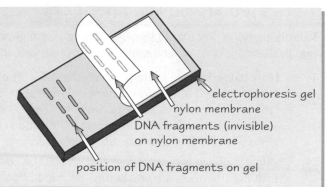

electrophoresis gel
nylon membrane
DNA fragments (invisible)
on nylon membrane
position of DNA fragments on gel

1) A **nylon membrane** is placed over the electrophoresis gel, and the DNA fragments **bind** to it.

2) The DNA fragments on the nylon membrane are **heated** to separate them into **single strands**.

3) **Radioactive gene probes** are then put onto the nylon membrane. (It's the **phosphorus** in the gene probes' sugar-phosphate backbones that's radioactive.) The probes are warmed and **incubated** for a while so that they'll attach to any bits of complementary DNA in the DNA fragments.

4) The nylon membrane is then put on top of unexposed **photographic film**. The film goes **dark** where the radioactive gene probes are **present**, which **reveals the position** of the **DNA fragments**. The pattern is different for every human — it's **unique** like a fingerprint.

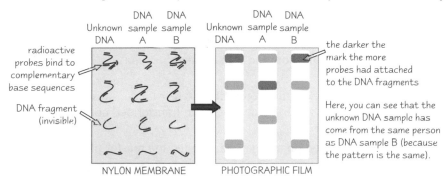

radioactive probes bind to complementary base sequences

DNA fragment (invisible)

NYLON MEMBRANE

PHOTOGRAPHIC FILM

the darker the mark the more probes had attached to the DNA fragments

Here, you can see that the unknown DNA sample has come from the same person as DNA sample B (because the pattern is the same).

Genetic fingerprinting is incredibly useful. **Forensic investigations** use it to confirm the identity of suspects from blood, hair, skin, sweat or semen samples left at a crime scene, or to establish the identity of victims. **Medical investigations** use the same technique for **tissue typing**, **paternity tests** and **infection diagnosis**.

Practice Questions

Q1 Give the full name of the technique used to increase the amount of DNA from a very small sample.

Q2 Name the enzyme added to DNA before gel electrophoresis.

Q3 Which part of a gene probe is radioactive?

Q4 State three uses of genetic fingerprinting in medical investigations.

Q5 Name the enzyme used in PCR.

Exam Question

Q1 Police have found incriminating DNA samples at the scene of a murder.
They have a suspect in mind, and want to prove that the suspect is guilty.

a) Name the technique that the police could use to confirm the guilt of the suspect. [1 mark]

b) Explain how this technique would be carried out. [5 marks]

You see that sweat stain there — that's you, that is...

Genetic fingerprinting has revolutionised medicine and forensic science. Remember that the PCR amplifies small DNA samples so genetic analysis can be done. You need to learn the PCR process, plus the process of electrophoresis and how it's involved in genetic fingerprinting. Also, learn what genetic fingerprinting is used for in the real world.

Vectors and Micro-organisms

Skip these pages if you're doing OCR or Edexcel.

Having a single copy of a useful gene is all very well, but thousands of copies are even better. Fortunately, we can use microbes as micro-factories. They can copy the gene and make the gene product, but only if you treat 'em right.

Genes are Moved into *Micro-organisms* using *Vectors*

Vectors carry recombinant DNA containing useful genes into microbes. They're usually plasmids (see p.58 for making recombinant DNA in plasmids) or viruses, like the λ (**Lambda**) **phage virus**.

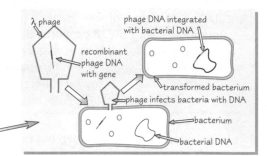

1) **Host bacteria** have to be **persuaded** to take up **plasmid** vectors. They're placed into cold **calcium chloride** solution to make their cell membranes more **permeable**. Then the plasmids are added and the mixture warmed up. The **sudden cold** causes some of the bacteria to take up the plasmids.

2) When a **phage** is used as a vector, the phage DNA is combined with the useful gene to make recombinant DNA. The phage then **infects** a bacterium by injecting its DNA strand into it. The phage DNA is then **integrated** into the bacterium's DNA.

3) Bacteria that have taken up vectors are said to be **transformed**.

Transformed Bacteria can be Identified Using Marker Genes

Not all the bacteria will take up vectors, so you need a way to **pick out** the **transformed** bacteria. The easiest way is to use **antibiotic marker genes**.

1) When recombinant DNA is produced in plasmids, a marker gene for **antibiotic resistance** is inserted into the plasmid as well as the donor gene. This means bacteria that have been transformed contain both the donor gene **and** the gene for antibiotic resistance.

2) After being mixed with plasmids, the bacteria are cultured on an agar plate called the **master plate**.

3) Once bacteria have grown on the master plate, **replica plating** is used to isolate **transformed bacteria**:

- A **sterile velvet pad** is pressed onto the master plate. This picks up some bacteria from each colony.

- The pad is pressed onto a fresh agar plate, **containing an antibiotic**. Some of the bacteria from each colony are transferred onto the agar surface.

- Only transformed bacteria can grow and reproduce on the replica plate — the others don't contain the antibiotic-resistant gene, so they stop growing.

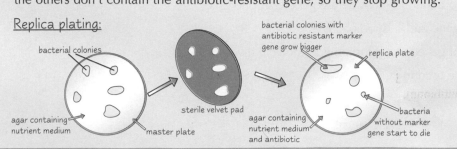

Genetically Engineered Microbes are *Micro-factories*

AQA B ONLY

Genetically engineered microbes can be used to produce large quantities of many **useful substances** like the ones below:

1) **Antibiotics** like penicillin.

2) **Hormones**, like insulin and human growth hormone.

3) **Enzymes** used in manufacturing processes, like those in biological washing powders.

Flick back to page 59 to see how large-scale production of microbes in industrial fermenters produces large quantities of useful products.

Vectors and Micro-organisms

Genetic Engineering Raises **Ethical** and **Moral** Issues

The **Human Genome Project** has mapped our DNA and we now have the technology to manipulate genes. But there are **ethical**, **moral**, **social** and **economic** issues to consider.

Potential Benefits of Genetic Engineering	Concerns over Genetic Engineering
Specific medicines could be developed to treat diseases. A current example of this is the production of genetically engineered human insulin to control diabetes.	Risk of foreign genes entering **non-target** organisms and disrupting functions.
Faulty genes could be identified and replaced, preventing genetically inherited diseases (see p.64).	Risk of **accidental transfer** of unwanted genes, which could damage the recipient.
Parents could make sure their babies didn't have faulty genes before they were born.	Doctors might be under pressure to implant embryos that could provide **transplant material for siblings**. Those who can afford it might decide which characteristics they wish their children to have (**designer babies**), creating a 'genetic underclass'. The **evolutionary consequences** of genetic engineering are unknown. **Religious concerns** about 'playing God'.
Crops could be engineered to give **increased yields** or exploit new habitats	**Health concerns** over human consumption of genetically modified foods.

Practice Questions

Q1 What is a vector? Give two examples.

Q2 What is a marker gene?

Q3 How can you use replica plating to isolate transformed bacteria?

Q4 Name three useful substances produced by genetically engineered microbes.

Q5 Give three ethical concerns about genetic engineering.

Q6 Give three potential benefits of genetic engineering.

Exam Questions

Q1 A human gene was combined with a plasmid which also contained a gene coding for resistance to ampicillin (an antibiotic).

The plasmid was added to a bacterial culture.

a) Which technique could be used to find out whether the bacteria had taken up the plasmid containing the gene? [1 mark]

b) Explain how this technique works. [5 marks]

Q2 Explain how a virus could be used as a vector. [3 marks]

Designer babies — mine's Gucci, daahling...

The antibiotic-resistance gene is the genetic marker that you need to know about — learn how it's used to identify transformed bacteria, including how replica plating isolates the transformed bacteria. Then ponder for a while, with an earnest, serious look, the ethical issues surrounding genetic engineering. Hmmmmmmmm.

Gene Therapy

Skip these pages if you're doing OCR, AQA A or Edexcel.

Gene therapy isn't about group hugs and biscuits — it's to do with replacing faulty genes with healthy ones.
Sounds great, but bear in mind the ethical concerns over genetic engineering (on p.63) when you're reading this stuff.

Gene Therapy Replaces Faulty Genes with Healthy Ones

Gene therapy replaces defective genes with healthy ones to treat **genetically inherited diseases**. The **cause** of the disease is tackled, not just the symptoms. The **healthy gene** is isolated and **cloned** and inserted into the cells where it's needed. The healthy gene **codes** for the **protein** that the **sufferer** of the disease **lacks**.
Cystic fibrosis is a genetic disease that can be treated by gene therapy.

Cystic Fibrosis is Caused by a Defect in the CFTR Gene

People who suffer from cystic fibrosis produce **thick, sticky mucus**. This stays in the lungs, causing them to become congested, which makes breathing difficult. The sticky mucus is caused by a **mutation** in the **CFTR gene**.

1) The **CFTR protein** is found in the cell membranes of **epithelial cells** lining the **airways** and the **gut**. It's a **channel protein**, which lets **chloride ions** out of the cells.

2) The **defective** CFTR protein is missing an **amino acid**. This affects the **3D shape** of the protein so that chloride ions can't move out of the cell.

3) The **ion concentration** in the cell increases, so more water's retained instead of moving out by osmosis. The **mucus lining** the airways becomes **thicker** and **stickier** as a result.

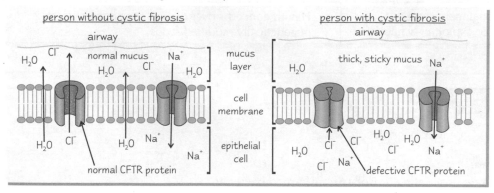

Vectors Transfer Healthy CFTR Genes in Epithelial Cells

Two main types of **vectors** are used to transfer healthy CFTR genes into body cells.

1) **Liposome vectors**. Recombinant DNA technology is used to put healthy CFTR genes into plasmids which are 'wrapped' in **liposomes**. Liposomes are minute lipid droplets that fuse with the cell membrane. The liposomes are sprayed into the lungs using **aerosols**. Liposomes can be produced on a large scale and patients don't develop an **immune reaction** to them.

2) **Adenovirus vectors**. Adenoviruses are the viruses that cause the **common cold**. First they're **inactivated**, by disabling the genes needed for them to replicate. Then the healthy CFTR gene is combined with the virus DNA. Then the viruses are **sprayed** into the lungs, where they **inject** the recombinant DNA into cells (see p.62).

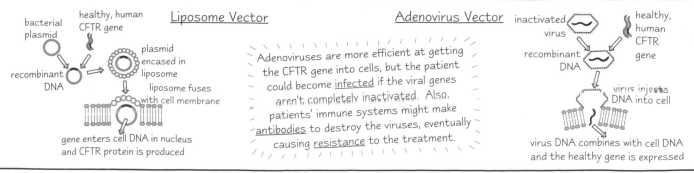

Gene Therapy

Important **Human Proteins** are Produced by **Genetically Engineered Animals**

People who can't produce the **glycoprotein alpha-1-antitrypsin (AAT)** suffer from **emphysema**.
Sheep can be genetically engineered to produce human **AAT**, which they secrete in their milk, bless 'em.

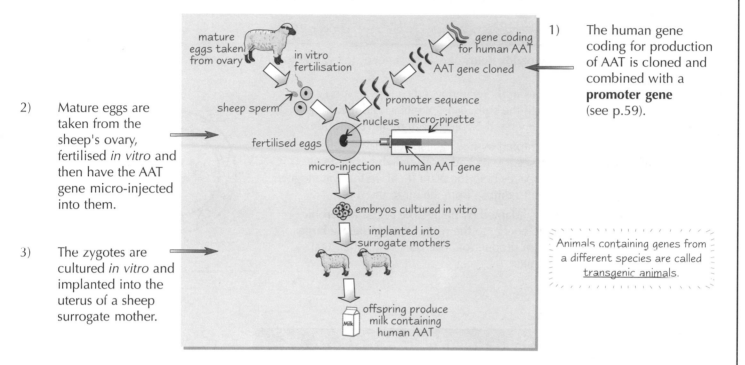

1) The human gene coding for production of AAT is cloned and combined with a **promoter gene** (see p.59).

2) Mature eggs are taken from the sheep's ovary, fertilised *in vitro* and then have the AAT gene micro-injected into them.

3) The zygotes are cultured *in vitro* and implanted into the uterus of a sheep surrogate mother.

Animals containing genes from a different species are called <u>transgenic animals</u>.

Practice Questions

Q1   What is gene therapy?

Q2   What are the symptoms of cystic fibrosis?

Q3   Give two examples of how humans can benefit from genetically modified organisms.

Q4   Which two vectors are used to transfer healthy CFTR genes into human cells?

Q5   Which gene determines whether someone suffers from emphysema or not?

Exam Questions

Q1   a) Explain why there is a decrease in the movement of chloride ions and water in the airway epithelial cells of someone with cystic fibrosis.   [4 marks]

b) Describe one way that the normal gene could be placed into the lung cells of someone suffering from cystic fibrosis.   [5 marks]

Q2   People who suffer from haemophilia lack a clotting agent, factor VIII, in their blood. They can be treated with factor VIII extracted from the milk of genetically engineered sheep.

a) Describe how sheep can be genetically engineered to produce human factor VIII in their milk.   [3 marks]

b) Give one advantage of using genetically engineered factor VIII instead of factor VIII that has been extracted from blood donations.   [1 mark]

<u>What do you get if you cross Aladdin with a cow? — a transgenie...</u>

Gene therapy is good news for cystic fibrosis sufferers — you need to learn what causes the disease and how it's treated by replacing the faulty gene. Make sure you know the difference between liposome and adenovirus vectors. Then learn about how we get important proteins from inserting the right genes into animals. Mmmm, milky.

Growing Crops

Skip these pages if you're doing OCR, AQA B or Edexcel.

*Cereal plants are really important in our diet. They provide **carbohydrate** for **energy**.*
So grab yourself a quick bowl of cornflakes, and get on with learning all these lovely facts.

Cereals have different **structural** and **physiological adaptations** so they can grow in **different environments**.

Rice is Adapted to Grow in Swampy Conditions

Rice is grown in the **swampy paddy fields** of Asia so it needs to be able to survive in **water**.

1) There are **no air spaces** in the waterlogged soil, so oxygen can't get to the roots through the soil. Most plants would **die** in these conditions because they need oxygen for **aerobic respiration**.

2) **Structurally**, rice is adapted by having a special tissue called **aerenchyma** in its leaves, stems and roots, which has large air spaces in it. The air spaces help the plant 'float' in the waterlogged soil and allow oxygen to diffuse from the air to the roots.

3) **Physiologically**, rice is adapted by being able to use **anaerobic respiration** to provide energy to the roots. It can **tolerate large quantities of ethanol**, a product of anaerobic respiration that's poisonous to most plants.

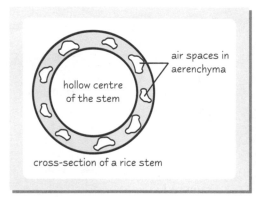

air spaces in aerenchyma

hollow centre of the stem

cross-section of a rice stem

Maize Uses a Special Method of Photosynthesis

Maize is a tropical plant that grows in **hot places** with **high light intensity**. These conditions affect **photosynthesis**:

1) **High temperatures** increase water loss by transpiration, which closes the stomata.

2) **Closed stomata** mean not much carbon dioxide can enter the plant, leading to low carbon dioxide levels in leaves.

Fortunately, you don't have to learn all the gritty biochemical details of photosynthesis. You see those examiners are human after all.

Physiologically, maize is adapted by having a **special method of photosynthesis** called **C4**. C4 works well at high temperatures and low carbon dioxide concentrations. The stomata don't need to be open for long in C4 plants, which helps to prevent water loss.

Structurally, it's adapted to the hot environment by being able to roll its leaves up to reduce the number of stomata exposed to the atmosphere. This reduces water loss.

I see the problem — you have a nasty case of sorghum.

Sorghum Grows Well in Hot, Dry Conditions

Sorghum has many **xerophytic** characteristics — it can live in hot, dry conditions that other plants can't survive in. Xerophytes have adaptations that allow them to conserve water. **Structurally**, sorghum is very well adapted:

1) **Long, extensive roots** reach **deep into soil** to find water.
2) **Thick waxy cuticles** reduce water loss.
3) There are **relatively few stomata**, which helps **reduce water loss** from leaves.
4) The **stomata are sunken**, which means water vapour builds up round the opening, reducing the diffusion gradient and slowing diffusion (see p.105).
5) Like maize, sorghum can roll its leaves.
6) Sorghum can also use **C4 photosynthesis**.

Physiologically, sorghum is adapted by containing enzymes that aren't denatured by extreme heat — so plants can survive in the heat, even when they are still developing structurally.

Growing Crops

Increasing the **Rate** of **Photosynthesis** Increases **Crop Yield**

Humans can control the **abiotic** (non-living) factors affecting photosynthesis — **light intensity**, **temperature**, **water**, CO_2, **soil fertility** and **pH**. They encourage growth by **maximising** the **rate of photosynthesis**:

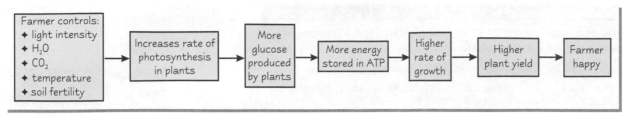

Farmers can Create Controlled, **Artificial Environments**

Farmers use large, commercial **greenhouses** to monitor and control the environment. They aim to maintain **optimum growing conditions**:

1) Increasing the light intensity raises the photosynthesis rate — so farmers supply **artificial light** for **longer hours** than natural sunlight. But too much light can damage chloroplasts, so they have to be careful.

2) 25°C is the optimum temperature for photosynthesis so farmers use **paraffin heaters** in winter and **shade** and **ventilation** in summer to maintain this temperature in greenhouses.

3) **Carbon dioxide** is needed for photosynthesis. Farmers give greenhouse plants a good supply of carbon dioxide, but don't usually add more than around **0.4%**, otherwise the stomata would close up.

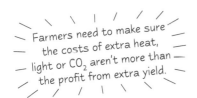

Farmers need to make sure the costs of extra heat, light or CO_2 aren't more than the profit from extra yield.

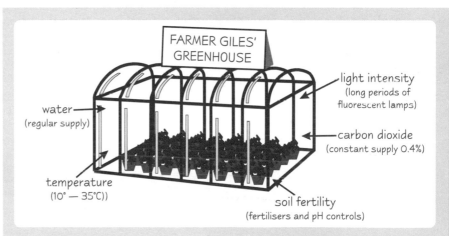

Practice Questions

Q1 Describe two ways rice adapts to growing in swampy conditions.

Q2 List four structural adaptations of sorghum.

Q3 How does maize reduce its water loss?

Q4 Which abiotic factors do farmers control in commercial greenhouses?

Exam Questions

Q1 Explain how a tolerance for ethanol has helped rice adapt to waterlogged soil. [4 marks]

Q2 Describe how farmers can use greenhouses to improve crop yields. [4 marks]

What an a-maize-ing topic...

Credit where credit's due — I'd like to see how well you'd survive standing in a puddle of water your entire life or living in the Sahara desert. But even with all the plants' clever adaptations, that doesn't stop humans stepping in to make them grow even better. But then, I can't quite imagine a life without bread, so I'm not complaining.

Fertilisers and Pesticides

Skip these pages if you're doing OCR, AQA B or Edexcel.

Soil, fertilisers and pesticides — sounds like a recipe for maximum crop yield if ever I heard one.
Learn what farmers do to make their crops grow well — and don't try this recipe at home, kids.

Fertilisers Replace Nutrients Lost from the Soil

Plants use **mineral ions** (nutrients) in soil for growth. The main ones
they use are **nitrate** (NO_3^-), **phosphate** (PO_4^{3-}) and **potassium** (K^+) ions.

1) Normally, mineral ions used in plants **re-enter the soil** when the plants die and decompose. But in agriculture, when crops are harvested, this doesn't happen.

2) When nutrient levels in soil become **too low**, crops won't grow as well, which means a lower yield and smaller profit for farmers.

3) So farmers use **fertilisers** to replace the lost nutrients.

Fertilisers can be Organic or Inorganic

There are two types of fertiliser — organic and inorganic. Both have advantages and disadvantages.

1) **Organic fertilisers** (e.g. manure) are **natural products** that are put onto the soil. They decompose, releasing minerals into the soil.

2) **Inorganic fertilisers** are commercially manufactured from **mineral ions** and sprayed onto crops.

TYPE OF FERTILISER	ADVANTAGES	DISADVANTAGES
Organic	• Cheap. • Adds humus to soil, which improves soil structure. • Helps soil's water retention, so there's less leaching. • Less eutrophication. • Recycles animal waste.	• Hard to obtain in large quantities. • Expensive to transport. • Has a haphazard mineral content. • Slow release of nutrients. • Difficult to spread accurately.
Inorganic	• Can be manufactured to match the needs of a specific soil or crop. • Can be sprayed easily and accurately. • Fast release of mineral ions.	• Expensive. • Doesn't have the organic matter to 'glue' soil particles together. Repeated use can damage the soil structure. • Soil is more prone to leaching. • Causes eutrophication.

Farmers have to work out how much fertiliser to use to get the **best yield possible** without spending too much **money**:

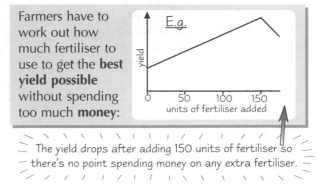

The yield drops after adding 150 units of fertiliser so there's no point spending money on any extra fertiliser.

Fertilisers can Lead to Leaching and Eutrophication

Over use of NPK (nitrate, phosphate and potassium) fertilisers can be bad news for nearby lakes, rivers and streams. Learn these flow charts to see how leaching and eutrophication happen.

1) **Leaching** is the 'washing out' of mineral ions from the soil:

See diagram of eutrophication on p.57.

Too many NPK mineral ions in soil → The rain washes mineral ions out through the soil → Mineral ions are washed into streams, rivers and lakes

2) **Eutrophication** is what happens when too many mineral ions are leached into streams, rivers and lakes:

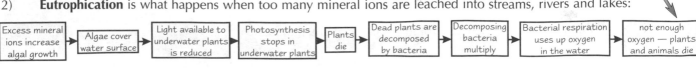

Excess mineral ions increase algal growth → Algae cover water surface → Light available to underwater plants is reduced → Photosynthesis stops in underwater plants → Plants die → Dead plants are decomposed by bacteria → Decomposing bacteria multiply → Bacterial respiration uses up oxygen in the water → not enough oxygen — plants and animals die

Crop Yield can be Reduced by Competition and Insects

Plants compete for light, space, nutrients, water, oxygen and carbon dioxide.

1) **Intraspecific competition** is competition between plants of the **same species**. Farmers reduce this by making sure there's enough of everything to go around. E.g. by irrigating crops and using fertilisers.

2) **Interspecific competition** is competition between **different species**, like weeds and crop plants. Farmers reduce this by using **herbicides** to **kill weeds**.

Insects can reduce crop yield by eating the parts of crops that humans use and by damaging photosynthetic tissue.

Fertilisers and Pesticides

Pesticides are Used to Kill Organisms That Reduce Crop Yield

Pesticides are **manufactured chemicals** that are used to kill pests.
They're split into different types, depending on what they're killing:

Pesticides are **easy** and **quick** to apply. But, **resistance** builds
up in the target pest, so they stop being effective after a while.
Also, pesticides can have damaging effects on the **environment**:

Type of Pesticide	Type of Organism Killed
Herbicide	Weeds
Insecticide	Insects
Fungicide	Fungi

1) Pesticides can be toxic to **non-pest organisms** as well.
2) Some pesticides (like the insecticide, **DDT**) aren't broken down by organisms — instead they build up in the organism's body. Anything that eats the organism eats the pesticide too — so toxins can therefore **enter food chains** and pass along them.
3) This leads to **bio-accumulation** — higher levels of toxin accumulate at each trophic level of a food chain.
4) **Predators** at the top of the food chain can be **killed** by the toxins from pesticides.

Biological Agents are More Environmentally Friendly

Biological agents are **organisms** used to control pests. E.g. farmers can release predators to **eat the pests** or release **bacteria** that cause **disease** in the pests. Biological control is **better for the environment** but it has some problems:

1) It's **slow**.
2) Biological agents don't eliminate all the pests, so you get **resurgence** — the pests that aren't killed reproduce and the pest population increases again.
3) Introducing new organisms into existing ecosystems can **disrupt food chains and webs**.

Integrated Systems are the Best of Both Worlds

More farmers are now using **integrated systems of pest management** — they control pests with a combination of:

1) **biological agents**;
2) **chemical pesticides**;
3) **good crop management** (e.g. timing crops so they miss seasons when pests are more common);
4) using genetically-modified **pest-resistant crops**.

Having **more than one** control method reduces the risk of pests becoming **resistant** to control. Also, it's **better for the environment** — fewer pesticide toxins and biological agents are used, so existing organism populations **aren't disrupted** as much.

Practice Questions

Q1 What does NPK stand for?

Q2 Draw up a table of advantages and disadvantages of using inorganic and organic fertilisers.

Q3 What is bio-accumulation?

Q4 What is integrated pest management?

Exam Questions

Q1 Why is a root crop yield reduced when insects eat the leaves of the crop? [4 marks]

Q2 Give two advantages and two disadvantages of using biological control instead of pesticides. [4 marks]

Farmers like to watch TOTC — Top of the Crops...

Make sure you get eutrophication sorted in your head — it's a bit tricky and can throw you if you're not careful. Remember that it's not the algae that use up all the oxygen — it's the decomposing bacteria. So next time you see someone being a bit over-keen with their fertilisers, tell them on behalf of all the little fishies that it's not big and it's not clever. Then run away.

Health and Disease

Skip these pages if you're doing AQA A, AQA B or Edexcel.

Health is more than just absence from disease. The World Health Organisation defines health as "a state of complete physical, mental and social well being". But you still need to learn about diseases, though — bummer.

There are **Different Categories** of **Disease**

You need to learn all these categories of disease, and an example for each one.

NB — a disease can fall into more than one of these categories. For example, you could have a self-inflicted physical disease or a non-infectious degenerative disease.

Type of Disease	Description	Example
Physical	Temporary or permanent damage to your body.	torn knee cartilage
Mental	Psychological disorder	depression
Social	Disease caused by social conditions or environment.	obesity or asbestos poisoning
Infectious	Body is entered by another organism.	influenza virus
Non-infectious	Can't be passed from one person to another.	cancer
Degenerative	Age-related wear and tear of tissues or organs.	osteo-arthritis
Inherited	Defective genes are passed on from parents.	cystic fibrosis
Self-inflicted	Damage you have done to yourself.	emphysema from smoking
Deficiency	A health problem caused by inadequate diet.	scurvy due to lack of vitamin C

Infectious Diseases are Caused by **Micro-Organisms**

There are many different **micro-organisms** that can cause infectious disease — they can be viruses, bacteria, fungi, algae or protozoa.

1) Organisms that cause infectious diseases are called **pathogens**.
2) **Animal diseases** are usually caused by bacteria or viruses.
3) **Plant diseases** are usually caused by fungi and viruses.

BUT, it's important to remember that not all micro-organisms are harmful.

Statistics can Reveal the **Health** of a **Population**

Epidemiology is the **study of patterns of disease** using statistics. Most epidemiological studies look at either **incidence** of disease (the **number of cases** over a period of time) or **mortality** (the **number of deaths** from a disease over time).

1) Epidemiology is often used to **identify links** between a disease and its **cause**. For example in the 1950s, epidemiological studies linked smoking to deaths from lung cancer. More recently, studies have linked sunbathing with skin cancer.

2) Epidemiology is also used to decide **suitable cures** and treatments for diseases:

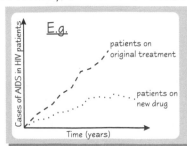

This graph shows that fewer HIV patients developed AIDS when given a new drug. This would go some way towards proving that the new drug is a suitable treatment for HIV patients.

Diseases can **Spread Across** the **World**

You need to know these terms about how diseases **spread**.

1) **Pandemic** — the spread of disease **internationally**, e.g. SARS or HIV.
2) **Epidemic** — the **rapid spread of disease** through a population, e.g. new strains of 'flu.
3) **Endemic** — a common disease, **always present** in a population, e.g. measles.

Health and Disease

Standards of Health Care Vary Between Countries

Wealth **varies** between countries — the world is often described as being made up of **More Economically Developed Countries (MEDCs)** and **Less Economically Developed Countries (LEDCs)**. Health care is generally worse in LEDCs — so their populations suffer more from diseases.

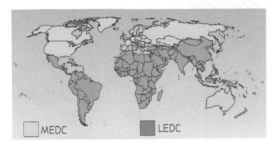

MEDC   LEDC

In **LEDCs**:

1) People suffer **more deaths from infectious diseases** (like malaria and TB).

2) People have a **lower life expectancy**.

3) There's poor medical care, housing and diet, which **increases the incidence of disease**.

4) There are **high infant mortality rates** from diseases like diarrhoea and measles.

In **MEDCs**:

1) People suffer **fewer deaths from infectious diseases**.

2) People have a **higher life expectancy**.

3) There are better medical services, housing and diet, which **lowers the incidence of disease**.

4) Children are immunised against infectious diseases early on, so there are **low infant mortality rates**.

5) People suffer **more deaths from degenerative diseases** due to unhealthy lifestyles — things like coronary heart disease, obesity and cirrhosis of the liver due to alcoholism.

Results from the Human Genome Project May Help Treat Disease

The **Human Genome Project** is an international project that has **identified** every human gene and now aims to work out what each one **codes for**. This has **potential advantages** for improving health:

1) We might be able to change our **genetic inheritance** by eliminating genes that code for inherited diseases.

2) Doctors can make more **accurate diagnoses** of diseases.

3) Better drugs can be made to **target** specific diseases.

4) Drugs with **fewer side-effects** can be made.

5) There'll be more information to base **medical research** on.

Many people have ethical arguments against changing our natural genetic make-up. Some scientists are attempting to clone humans and it could be possible in the future to choose a 'designer' baby, with the genetic make-up of your choice. Many people dislike the idea of this level of interference. (See p.63 for more on ethics.)

Practice Questions

Q1   Define health in relation to disease.

Q2   Give an example of a deficiency disease.

Q3   What can epidemiological studies tell us?

Q4   What's the difference between endemic and pandemic diseases?

Q5   What's the aim of the Human Genome Project?

Exam Questions

Q1   Discuss the advantages and disadvantages of manipulating genes for the treatment of diseases.   [4 marks]

Q2   Over 12 million children in Africa and Asia under the age of 5 years die from diseases every year. Give reasons for the spread of disease in these continents.   [4 marks]

The Human Gnome Project — it started in my garden...

Good mix of facts to learn and ethical issues to get your teeth into here. If the ethical side of manipulating genes to prevent disease crops up in the exam you need to be able to show that you're aware of both sides of the arguments. To clone or not to clone — that is the (essay) question.

A Balanced Diet and Essential Nutrients

Skip these pages if you're doing AQA A, AQA B or Edexcel.

A page all about diet — no glossy mag would be complete without one.
Now here comes the science part — concentrate. Why? Because you're worth it.

A **Balanced Diet** Supplies All the **Essential Nutrients**

A balanced diet gives you all the **essential nutrients** you need, plus fibre and water.
The 5 essential nutrients are **carbohydrates**, **proteins**, **lipids**, **vitamins** and **minerals**.

Large molecules are broken down into small molecules during digestion.
Nutrients are absorbed as small molecules through **microvilli** in the small intestine.

1) **Carbohydrates** are broken down and absorbed as **monosaccharides**.
2) **Lipids** are broken down and absorbed as **fatty acids** and **glycerol**.
3) **Proteins** are broken down and absorbed as **amino acids**.

Different nutrients are required for different functions in the body.

NUTRIENTS	FUNCTIONS
Carbohydrates	Provide energy.
Lipids	Store energy, provide insulation, constituent of cell membranes, physically protect organs.
Proteins	Growth and repair of tissue.
Vitamins	Various functions: e.g. vitamin B is needed for ATP production; vitamin K is needed for blood clotting.
Mineral ions	Various functions: e.g. iron is needed for healthy blood; calcium is needed for bone formation and strength.
Fibre	Keeps the gut in good working order.
Water	Used in hydrolytic reactions. We need a constant supply to replace water lost through urinating, breathing and sweating.

Essential Amino Acids and **Fatty Acids** have to be Obtained from **Food**

1) There are **10** amino acids that the body can't make. These are called **essential amino acids** because it's essential that they're in our food.
2) Some essential amino acids **make non-essential ones**. For example, the essential amino acid **phenylalanine** can be converted into the non-essential amino acid **tyrosine**.
3) Similarly, our body makes some fatty acids, but **essential fatty acids** can't be made by cells — they have to be provided by our diet.

> Essential amino acids and fatty acids have many uses —
> 1) Amino acids are used to **make proteins** required by the body.
> 2) Essential fatty acids **heal wounds** and prevent hair loss.
> 3) Fatty acids also ensure healthy growth in **babies**.
> 4) **Linolenic acid** is an essential fatty acid that makes the phospholipids found in cell membranes and lowers cholesterol levels in blood plasma. It can also be converted into lots of other fatty acids.

The Body Needs **Small Amounts** of Vitamins for Specific Functions

Vitamins are a group of chemicals needed to keep you healthy. They're only required in very **small amounts**.
You need to know the **functions** of **vitamins A** and **D**:

1) You get **vitamin A** from **meat** and especially from **vegetables**. It's essential for keeping **epithelial cells** in good condition and for **healthy eyesight**.

2) **Vitamin D** is found in oily fish and eggs. It **controls calcium absorption** to make strong bones and teeth. It also helps **absorb the phosphorous** needed for making **ATP** and **nucleic acids**.

A Balanced Diet and Essential Nutrients

Energy and Nutrient Needs Vary Between People

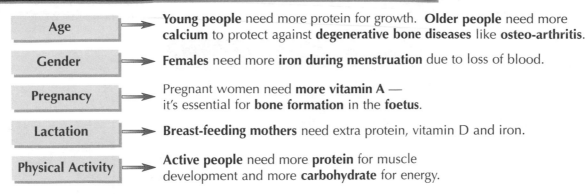

Age → **Young people** need more protein for growth. **Older people** need more **calcium** to protect against **degenerative bone diseases** like **osteo-arthritis**.

Gender → **Females** need more **iron during menstruation** due to loss of blood.

Pregnancy → Pregnant women need **more vitamin A** — it's essential for **bone formation** in the **foetus**.

Lactation → **Breast-feeding mothers** need extra protein, vitamin D and iron.

Physical Activity → **Active people** need more **protein** for muscle development and more **carbohydrate** for energy.

DRVs are Dietary Reference Values

DRVs are **recommendations** made by the Government on estimated **energy and nutritional requirements** for particular groups of the UK population. The recommendations are related to age, gender, level of fitness and body size.

> These are all the codes used in working out DRVs, so you need to learn 'em.
> **DRV**   **Dietary Reference Values** — Government recommendations based on scientific studies.
> **EAR**   **Estimated Average Requirement** — of energy or nutrients.
> **BMR**   **Basal Metabolic Rate** — the speed at which energy is used up in the body.
> **PAL**   **Physical Activity Levels** — varies with type and length of activity and your own body size.

DRVs should be used when assessing or planning the dietary intake of a group. People have **different energy needs** depending on the rate at which energy is used up in their bodies. If you burn energy quickly then you have a **high BMR**. Physical activity **increases BMR**. Calculations on energy needs can be made using DRVs.

> The equation used is **EAR = BMR x PAL**

Practice Questions

Q1 Name the uses of carbohydrate and protein in the body.

Q2 Why would someone with a sedentary lifestyle need to eat less food than a professional athlete?

Q3 Which vitamin:
a) is needed for strong teeth?
b) improves vision?

Q4 What use does water have in the body?

Q5 What does BMR stand for?

Exam Questions

Q1 What is the estimated average requirement of energy for a 16 year old female with a low physical activity level of 1.4 and a basal metabolic rate of 7.2 MJ per day? [3 marks]

Q2 Describe why humans need essential amino acids. [4 marks]

I have a balanced diet — one doughnut for every kebab...

Everyone needs the same essential nutrients, but how much we need of each depends on things like age, job and gender — champion cheese-hurlers will need more carbohydrates than champion chess players. As you're learning all the posh names (like phenylalanine), learn the spelling too. It'll save time thinking about it in the exam and will help you remember them.

Malnutrition

Skip these pages if you're doing AQA A, AQA B or Edexcel.

Two rather sobering pages for you. We need food to survive — simple as that. The sad thing is, loads of people in the world don't have enough to eat, whilst other people suffer from problems due to over-eating. It's not a fair world.

Malnutrition is When You Don't Get the Proper Nutrients

Malnutrition is basically having too little or too much of some nutrient. There are four causes:

1) Not having **enough food**. This can lead to **starvation**.

2) Having an **unbalanced diet** — so you aren't getting all the essential nutrients you need from your diet. This leads to all kinds of **deficiency illnesses**.

3) **Defective assimilation** of nutrients — this means your body isn't absorbing the nutrients from digestion into your bloodstream properly. This also causes **deficiency illnesses**.

4) Having **too much** food. This can lead to **obesity**.

Protein-energy Malnutrition (PEM) — not getting enough Protein and Energy

Inadequate **protein** intake means **growth** and **development** slow down. Inadequate **energy** causes the **basal metabolic rate** to slow down (see p.73) so that physical activity becomes difficult.

1) **Children** are particularly vulnerable to PEM because they need extra protein and energy to help them grow. Children suffering from PEM have **muscle wasting**, **skin rashes** and **swollen abdomens**.

2) PEM can cause **failure of the pancreas** and **intestines**.

3) Extreme forms of PEM lead to the deficiency diseases **marasmus** and **kwashiorkor**. These are more common in **LEDCs**.

4) If it carries on long enough, a child's growth and development stops completely, causing permanent damage.

Vitamin D Deficiency Affects Healthy Bone Development

Vitamin D is involved in **bone formation**. It stimulates **gut cells** to absorb calcium, and stimulates **bone cells** to use the stored calcium to form bones. So if you don't get enough vitamin D in your diet, your bones don't form properly and you can get one of two deficiency diseases:

1) **Rickets** — bone softening in children, which causes legs to become bowed. It also causes enlargement of the liver and the spleen.

2) **Osteomalacia** — the same bone softening symptoms, but in adults.

Vitamin A Deficiency Affects your Eyes and Immune System

You get vitamin A from meat and vegetables. It's used for two main things in the body:

1) **Epithelial cells** (in the digestive tract, skin and lungs) convert it to **rhetonoic acid** — used to **fight pathogens**.

2) **Rod cells** in the eye convert it into **rhodopsin**, which is used to help us **see in dim light**.

Deficiency in Vitamin A can cause three health problems:
- **poor defence** against pathogens,
- **poor night vision** or
- **xerophthalmia**, where the skin of the cornea is scarred, causing blindness.

Malnutrition

Over-Nutrition and Lack of Exercise can Lead to Obesity

Some people, especially in **MEDCs**, have **dietary diseases** caused by **too much food**.

1) **Obesity** is a common dietary disease — it's defined as being **20% (or more) over recommended body weight**.

2) **Too much sugary or fatty food** and **too little exercise** are the main causes of obesity.

3) People can also be obese due to an **underactive thyroid gland**, but this problem isn't common.

4) Obesity can increase the risk of **diabetes**, **arthritis**, **high blood pressure, coronary heart disease** (CHD) and even some forms of **cancer**.

I'm just big boned.

Anorexia Nervosa is a Particular Form of Starvation

Anorexia nervosa is a **mental disease** with **physical effects**. It's caused by an **emotional refusal to eat**.

1) Anorexia is usually caused by **low self esteem** and **anxiety about body fat**. Sufferers have a **poor self-image**. Even though they lose loads of weight, they still see themselves as fat and **continue starving themselves**.

2) Symptoms of anorexia are muscle wasting, depression, delayed sexual development, retarded growth and decreases in BMR and heart function. Severe anorexia can lead to **death by starvation**.

Practice Questions

Q1 What causes marasmus?

Q2 Name four symptoms of anorexia nervosa.

Q3 Name a deficiency disease caused by lack of vitamin D.

Q4 What percentage over recommended body weight is classified as obese?

Q5 Explain what PEM is.

Exam Questions

Q1 Describe the dietary causes of a named disease found mainly in:

a) LEDCs; [2 marks]

b) MEDCs. [2 marks]

Q2 Explain why we need vitamin A in our diet. [4 marks]

Supercalorificdiet-totallyatrocious... (*in a Mary Poppins style)

Remember that people in both developed and developing countries suffer from dietary illnesses through malnutrition — but the diseases are different. In LEDCs, they're usually deficiency diseases or starvation, and in MEDCs they're more to do with over-eating and having high-fat diets.

Prevention and Cure

Skip these pages if you're doing AQA A, AQA B or Edexcel.

Most diseases can either be prevented, or cured.
Prevention is better than cure as my old mum used to say — but what did she mean...

CHD is an example of a Disease with Prevention and Cure

Coronary Heart Disease (**CHD**) is when not enough oxygen gets to the heart so it can't function efficiently. If the blood supply to an area of the heart is cut off then the heart muscle can't respire and fails. This causes a **heart attack**.

There are many factors which affect your chances of getting CHD:

1) Some people are **naturally more prone** to heart disease, for example if they've inherited high blood pressure or high cholesterol levels in their blood.

2) The **width of arteries** carrying blood to the heart affects how much oxygen is provided to the heart muscle. **Cholesterol** clogs up arteries, making them **narrower**, so less blood can get to the heart.

3) **Smoking** is another **risk factor** that increases the chance of suffering from coronary heart disease.

4) People with **diabetes mellitus** or high **blood pressure** are also more likely to develop heart disease. Excess alcohol intake increases blood pressure, so that increases the risk too.

5) One important inherited factor is a person's **sex** — men are three times as likely as women to suffer from coronary heart disease.

Some risk factors are preventable:

1) Over-nutrition and high-fat diets lead to **excess weight**. This should be avoided, because otherwise the heart muscle is **put under strain** pumping blood to the extra body cells.

2) **Diets** with too much cholesterol should be avoided to prevent narrowing of arteries.

3) Regular exercise is also needed to keep the heart muscle strong.

4) Cutting out the '**self-inflicted**' risk factors like smoking and alcohol abuse. There are many ways to help people give up smoking, from nicotine replacement patches to hypnosis.

Death Rate from Coronary Heart Disease Varies Around the World

Death rates aren't the same in every country. For example, the number of deaths from coronary heart disease is higher in Finland and Scotland than in France or China. This difference in the death rate is mainly due to the factors below:

1) Differences in the **inheritance** of disease — Inherited factors aren't preventable, but an awareness of family health history does help people make better decisions about their lifestyle.

2) **Diet** varies between countries. Some countries (like Scotland and Finland) have, overall, more fatty diets than other countries.

3) **Attitudes** towards drinking and smoking vary between these countries.

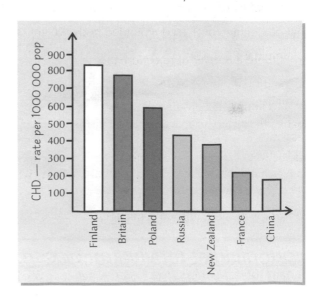

Prevention and Cure

By-pass Operations Improve Heart Function

A **coronary artery bypass** operation only relieves the **symptoms** of coronary heart disease — the causes can't be treated by surgical methods. By-pass surgery is used when coronary arteries can't be unblocked. Sections of **veins** taken from a leg are attached to the heart. These are used to **link blood vessels**, by-passing the blockage.

Blood flow is increased, improving the supply of oxygen and nutrients to **heart muscle**.

Transplanted Hearts can be Rejected

If a person's heart is severely damaged, a **transplant** can be their only chance of survival. Hearts become available for transplant usually after accidents like **road accidents**, which kill someone but leave their heart undamaged. But hearts for transplants aren't plentiful, and even if one were available, it might be **rejected**:

1) The function of white blood cells in the immune system is to destroy 'foreign' tissue like bacteria and viruses.
2) Unfortunately, heart tissue from another person is identified as foreign by the immune system.
3) Heart transplant patients are treated with drugs to **prevent rejection** of new heart tissue.
4) If these fail the heart tissue is **rejected** — it's attacked by the immune system.
5) If another transplant isn't available at once, the patient will die.

Antibiotics are used to Treat Infectious Bacterial Diseases

Antibiotics are chemicals produced by some **micro-organisms**. They can be used to inhibit or destroy **harmful bacteria**, because they interfere with the bacteria's metabolism without interfering with ours.

1) The first antibiotic to be discovered was **penicillin**. Most antibiotics were originally produced from the **actinomycete** fungus that occurs naturally in soil.
2) Antibiotics can be used to treat most bacterial diseases in humans, from **typhoid** to sore throats. But some bacteria have developed a **resistance** to antibiotics due to **misuse** or **overuse** of the drugs. For example, if a person doesn't finish their full course of antibiotics, the most resistant bacteria will be left to reproduce. Bacteria reproduce **asexually**, so their offspring will be clones and will therefore also be resistant to the antibiotic. This may result in a resistant strain. Uh-oh.
3) Antibiotics are made in large quantities in **fermentation reactions** (see p.59). The biochemical industry constantly researches and develops new strains.

Practice Questions

Q1 List four risk factors which lead to coronary heart disease.

Q2 Why is there a danger of rejection after a heart transplant?

Q3 Why might the death rate from heart disease be lower in China than Scotland?

Q4 How are antibiotics produced?

Exam Questions

Q1 Describe what happens in a coronary artery by-pass operation and explain how this can help a patient suffering from coronary heart disease. Why are such patients not simply given a new heart in a transplant operation? [8 marks]

Q2 Explain how bacterial resistance to antibiotics can occur. [4 marks]

Take your pick — prevention or cure...

This isn't a hard topic, but don't just rush through it or you'll forget little details. Like why heart transplants aren't always straightforward, and how antibiotics are made in large quantities. So, same old, same old — keep going over the page and scribbling down all the details until you know them all, without having to look.

Effects of Smoking

Skip these pages if you're doing AQA A, AQA B or Edexcel.

Don't worry, I'm not about to launch into a lecture. Everyone has a choice to make about whether or not they're going to start smoking. All these pages do is tell you the scientific stuff about it that you need to know to pass your exam.

Smoking Damages the Body

Some of the health problems caused by smoking include:

1) Toxic chemicals in the tar can cause cancer

Scientific evidence was first used to show the link between smoking and **lung cancer** in the **1950s**. **Tar** from cigarette smoke collects in the lungs. It's full of toxic chemicals, some of which are **carcinogens** (cause cancer). Carcinogens make mutations in the DNA of the **alveoli** more likely. If this happens, cell division goes out of control and **malignant tumours** form. Lung cancer's one of the main causes of early deaths in the UK.

2) Inhaling smoke can cause chronic bronchitis

The smoke destroys the **cilia** on the epithelial tissue lining the trachea. It also irritates the **bronchi and bronchioles**, which encourages mucus to be produced. Excess mucus can't be cleared properly because the cilia are damaged. It sticks to air passages causing smoker's cough and **chronic bronchitis**. Micro-organisms multiply in the extra mucus. (Not a happy thought if you're snogging a smoker.)

3) Emphysema is a breathing disorder caused by reduced gas exchange

People suffering from emphysema have a reduced surface area for gas exchange, and a loss of **elasticity** in their lungs. A lot of smokers develop it eventually, because chemicals in tobacco smoke destroy **fibrous elastin** tissue in alveoli. This means the alveoli can't expand as air enters the lungs. The smoke also increases the number of protein-eating **phagocyte cells**, which digest the alveoli tissue (see p.82 and p.94). This reduces the surface area for gas exchange. Sufferers gasp for breath because their lungs can't absorb enough oxygen, and they might need an oxygen cylinder to help them live longer.

Smoking can cause Artery and Heart Disease

Smoking is a risk factor in **atherosclerosis** (a disease caused by narrowing of the arteries), coronary heart disease and strokes.

This is because tobacco smoke —

1) Destroys **elastin**, so blood vessel elasticity is reduced. This leads to narrowing of the arteries.
2) Encourages **blood clots** to form more easily.
3) Contains nicotine, which activates **adrenalin**. (It's also the substance that smokers become addicted to). This raises blood pressure and puts more strain on heart muscle.
4) Contains **carbon monoxide**, which combines irreversibly with haemoglobin — so there's less haemoglobin available for oxygen transport.

A **stroke** can be caused when an artery narrows or become blocked by a clot. This reduces oxygen supply to the brain and causes loss of certain functions, like memory, and can be fatal.

Coronary heart disease is caused by increased heart rate and slower delivery of oxygen to the heart due to blocked arteries. This means the heart can't keep functioning properly.

Thromboses (blood clots) happen in narrowed arteries. They can block the arteries, which means oxygen fails to reach heart muscles.

Effects of Smoking

Statistics show Smokers are more likely to Die Early

Epidemiological (see p.70) and **experimental** evidence link cigarette smoking with disease and early death:

1) **Richard Doll's** statistical study in the 1950s first showed the link between smoking and lung cancer.

2) **Animal experiments** conducted in the 1960s showed that tumours developed when tobacco smoke was present in the lungs.

3) **Chemical analysis** of the chemicals in tobacco smoke has proved the presence of **carcinogenic substances**.

4) **Epidemiological** studies have shown that **passive smoking** (breathing in other people's smoke) increases the chances of developing lung cancer. They have also shown that the risk is reduced if a smoker stops smoking.

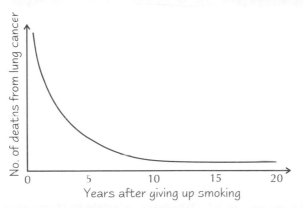

The **graph** shows the results from epidemiological studies. It shows that smokers are less likely to die from lung cancer once they've given up smoking.

Jeff — living proof that smoking isn't necessarily cool.

Practice Questions

Q1 What is a carcinogenic substance?

Q2 List three effects of tobacco smoke on the body.

Q3 List three diseases that smokers are more likely to suffer from.

Q4 Why does smoking increase the likelihood of blood clots?

Q5 Give three types of study that have shown smoking causes cancer.

Exam Questions

Q1 Give four health reasons why it is sensible to ban smoking in restaurants, theatres and other public places.   [4 marks]

Q2 'Emphysema is damage to the exchange surface of the lungs'. Explain how smoking causes this damage.   [4 marks]

Disease, death, mucus — such a delightful subject...

It might not be pleasant, but I'm afraid it's all true and you're going to have to learn it. This is another thing that often comes up. Maybe the examiners are trying to catch out the people who quickly turned the page so they weren't reminded about what they're doing to their lungs. Don't be shy, smokers — these pages are all about you and your body. Fame at last.

AIDS, Malaria, Cholera and TB

Skip these pages if you're doing AQA A, AQA B or Edexcel.

Another joyful page. Lots more lovely bacteria, viruses and disease for you to get your teeth into. Yummy.

AIDS stands for Acquired Immune Deficiency Syndrome

AIDS is caused by the **Human Immunodeficiency Virus** (HIV). So far over **30 million** people have been infected with HIV, and there's no vaccine available to stop it spreading more. There's no known cure for AIDS either.

1) HIV's a **retrovirus** — it injects its own RNA into the **nuclei** of host cells.

2) HIV can remain **dormant** for many years, then it replicates and kills the host cells.

3) The host cells targeted by the virus are the cells responsible for fighting pathogens (**T-cells**), so the infected person ends up with a **weakened immune system**.

4) This weakened immunity is called **AIDS**. It means the body can't defend itself against diseases like **pneumonia**, which it would usually recover from.

HIV is transmitted in **body fluids**

Body fluids include semen during unprotected sex, and **blood** — so drug users who share needles are at risk. Babies can be born with the disease after infection through the **placenta** if their mother has HIV. It can also be transmitted through **breast milk**.

Attempts are being made to **stop the spread of HIV**

Donated blood is **screened** for HIV to reduce transmission through **blood transfusions**. Using condoms during sex helps to stop you catching HIV (and other unpleasant diseases). Free **needle exchange centres** have been set up to provide drug addicts with clean needles, and there are drugs available to reduce the risk of a pregnant woman infecting her unborn child.

The main preventative measure for HIV and AIDS is education — leaflets were delivered throughout the UK in the 1990s with the message "Don't Die of Ignorance."

Malaria is Caused by Plasmodium

Plasmodium is a **protozoan** — a eukaryotic, single-celled organism (see p.2). It's carried by **mosquitoes**, which feed on blood from animals like humans. The mosquitoes are **vectors**, meaning they carry the disease without getting it themselves. They transfer the malarial parasite (*Plasmodium*) from one animal to another by inserting it into animals' blood vessels when they feed on them. Mosquitoes infect up to **500 million** people a year. Malaria kills **3000 children a day**, and a total of **1 million people** a year.

The main prevention measures are —

1) Drain the areas of water where mosquitoes lay their eggs.

2) Spray these areas with insecticides.

3) Introduce fish into the water to eat mosquito larvae.

4) Protect people from mosquitoes using insecticides and using mosquito nets.

Biological control can be used to reduce infection rates

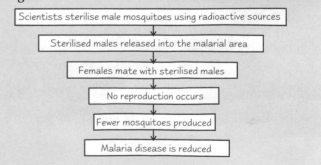

Scientists sterilise male mosquitoes using radioactive sources
↓
Sterilised males released into the malarial area
↓
Females mate with sterilised males
↓
No reproduction occurs
↓
Fewer mosquitoes produced
↓
Malaria disease is reduced

Cholera is Caused by Vibrio cholerae, a Waterborne Bacterium

Cholera is an infectious disease which causes severe diarrhoea. It is initially transmitted by **drinking contaminated water**. An infected person can then pass it on by handling food with unclean hands.

Some areas of the world regularly suffer from **epidemics** due to poor housing and sanitation. Investment in sewage treatment works and **chlorination** of drinking water would help eradicate the disease.

AIDS, Malaria, Cholera and TB

Tuberculosis (TB) Kills over 2 Million People a Year

Tuberculosis is caused by the bacterium *Mycobacterium tuberculosis*, and spreads rapidly by **droplet infection** (where bacteria are inhaled from the air).

The bacteria can live for years in the lungs before they become active. This **dormant** period prevents **contact tracing** (i.e. you don't know **when** you caught the disease so you don't know **who** you caught it from or who might have caught it from you) — so it's very difficult to eradicate the disease completely.

TB can be prevented with the **BCG vaccine** and controlled using the antibiotic **Streptomycin**, but **resurgence** often happens because of **resistance** to the drug.

> The number of reported cases of TB has been rising steadily in the UK — from **5010** in 1990, to **6379** in 2000. A major group affected by the disease is homeless people. Improved housing conditions with less overcrowding would reduce the spread of the infection.

Poorer Countries Need Help to Control these Diseases

LEDCs often lack the resources needed to treat and prevent the spread of these diseases. Money is needed for things like:

> 1) improved water treatment (to prevent **cholera**);
> 2) elimination of mosquito breeding areas (to prevent **malaria**);
> 3) improved housing conditions, vaccinations and antibiotics (to prevent **TB**);
> 4) education (to prevent **AIDS**).

The **World Health Organisation** helps eliminate diseases around the world. One of the biggest problems is the spread of **HIV in Africa**. Africa has the highest incidence of HIV per head of its population in the world.

Practice Questions

Q1 How is TB spread?

Q2 Which of these diseases is caused by water contamination: Malaria, Cholera, TB?

Q3 How does increasing fish stocks in lakes reduce malaria?

Q4 List four ways money could be spent to eradicate TB, cholera and AIDS in LEDCs.

Q5 Blood transfusions are used regularly in hospitals. How are patients protected from HIV?

Exam Questions

Q1 Explain why contact tracing is important in treatment of infectious disease.   [3 marks]

Q2 Give three ways that HIV is transmitted.   [4 marks]

TB or not TB? That is the question…

…and 'hopefully not,' is the answer. I don't know — first cancer and emphysema, then heart disease, and now TB and AIDS. Don't they realise AS levels are depressing enough without all this? Don't bother learning these pages because we're all going to die anyway. Dooooom. Glooooom.

The Immune System

Skip these pages if you're doing AQA B or Edexcel.

The immune system protects the body from pathogens (organisms that cause disease). It helps the body recognise them as foreign, and destroys them with a mixture of funny-sounding cells, like phagocytes and lymphocytes. Hurrah.

Antigens and Antibodies know What Should and Shouldn't be in our Body

Antigens and **antibodies** work together to let our cells distinguish 'self' from 'non-self' — they know when something is in our body that shouldn't be.

1) **Antigens** are large, organic molecules found on the surface of **cell membranes**. Every individual has their own **unique** cell surface molecules, which the immune system recognises. So when a **pathogen** like a bacterium invades the body, the antigens on its cell surface are identified as **foreign** by the immune system.

2) When the body detects foreign antigens, it makes **antibodies** — **protein molecules** that bind to specific antigens, giving an **antigen-antibody complex**.

3) Antibodies have **two binding sites**, so they can attach to two antigen molecules. They deal with pathogens by **clumping** or **linking** them together to make it easier for them to be engulfed by **phagocytes**. They can also **rupture** foreign cells, (which kills them) and inactivate any **toxins** they produce.

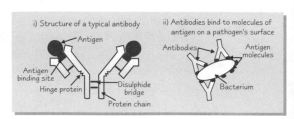

i) Structure of a typical antibody

Antigen
Antigen binding site
Hinge protein
Disulphide bridge
Protein chain

ii) Antibodies bind to molecules of antigen on a pathogen's surface

Antibodies
Antigen molecules
Bacterium

Phagocytes Get Rid of Cell Debris and Bacteria

1) **Phagocytes** are large white blood cells that encircle and **engulf** pathogens — a process called **phagocytosis**. Phagocytes use phagocytosis to clear away the antigen-antibody complexes formed in an **immune response**.

2) **Macrophages** and **neutrophils** are types of phagocytes (see p.94). They're both made in the **bone marrow**. Neutrophils are found in the **blood** and macrophages in **tissues**.

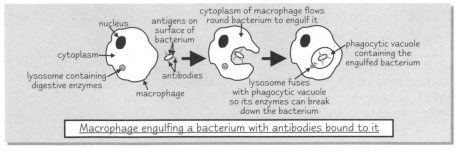

nucleus
cytoplasm
lysosome containing digestive enzymes
antigens on surface of bacterium
antibodies
macrophage
cytoplasm of macrophage flows round bacterium to engulf it
lysosome fuses with phagocytic vacuole so its enzymes can break down the bacterium
phagocytic vacuole containing the engulfed bacterium

Macrophage engulfing a bacterium with antibodies bound to it

Lymphocytes Control our Immune Response

Lymphocytes are white blood cells with **glycoproteins** on their surface to **recognise foreign antigens**. The two main types are: **B-lymphocytes** (**B-cells**) that mature in the **b**one marrow; and **T-lymphocytes** (**T-cells**) that mature in the **t**hymus gland.

Our bodies carry out **two types** of immune response:

1) **The CELLULAR RESPONSE** — This uses **T-cells**, either to attach to foreign antigens and attack pathogens directly, or to trigger the **humoral response** (see below). There are **four types of T-cell**.

- **Killer or cytotoxic T-cells** — stick to a pathogen's antigens and secrete substances that kill pathogen directly.
- **Helper T-cells** — help the **plasma cells** produced by **B-lymphocytes** to secrete antibodies, and secrete substances that attract **macrophages**.
- **Memory T-cells** — Keep the ability to recognise a particular antigen in the future. Allows the immune system to respond very quickly to a future attack by **the same pathogen**.
- **Suppressor T-cells** — suppress activity of killer T-cells and B-cells when antigens have been destroyed.

2) **The HUMORAL RESPONSE** — This uses **B-cells** to release antibodies. Each **B-cell** has a **specific antibody** on its membrane. When they meet a complementary foreign **antigen**, the antigen binds to the antibody's **receptor site**. This stimulates the B-cell to release the antibody into the blood. The B-cell then divides by mitosis, producing many clones, called **plasma cells**. These cells release large quantities of the same antibody, hopefully killing the pathogen. Some of the clones become **memory B-cells**, which provide us with immunity against a pathogen if it enters the body again. The next page has more on memory cells.

The Immune System

The **Immune Response** for Antigens can be **Memorised**

The first time a particular antigen enters the body the **immune response** is slow, because there aren't many B-cells that can make the antibody needed to bind to it. This is the **primary response**. Eventually the body will probably produce enough of the right antibody to overcome the infection, but while it's doing this the infected person will show **symptoms** of the disease. After being exposed to an antigen, both T- and B-cells produce **memory cells**. Memory T cells record the **invading antigen**, and memory B- cells record the '**recipe' for antibodies** to fight them.

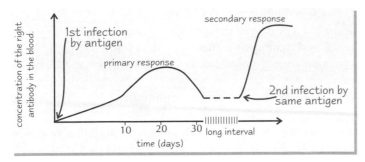

If the same pathogen enters the body again, these memory cells can produce the right cells and antibodies for fighting the pathogen very quickly.
This is known as the **secondary response**. It often gets rid of the pathogen before you begin to show any symptoms.

The **Two Immune Responses** can be Summarised as Shown

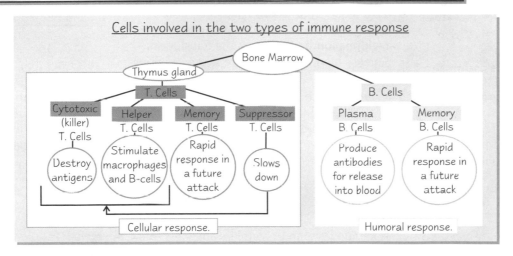

Practice Questions

Q1 What are antigens?

Q2 What is an antibody?

Q3 Where do B-lymphocytes come from, and what is their function?

Q4 Name the four types of T-lymphocyte.

Q5 What is phagocytosis?

Exam Questions

Q1 How does the cellular response protect the body from disease? [8 marks]

Q2 Explain how antibodies are produced, and describe their function. [6 marks]

This is getting scary — there's a battle being fought in my own nose...

And the names of some of the soldiers are even scarier. I'm sure we're all very grateful to these macrophages, neutrophils and cytotoxic T-lymphocytes for doing their bit to defend us from the attacking hordes. But why couldn't they have names like Bill, Jim and Dave?

Immunity and Vaccinations

Skip this page if you're doing AQA B or Edexcel.

This page is pretty darn interesting. It's nice to know there's a reason for hay fever making your life hell all summer, and to understand why people sticking needles in you is a good thing.

AQA A ONLY

There are **Four Blood Groups** — **A, B, AB** and **O**

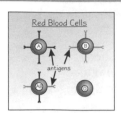

Red Blood Cells

antigens

1) **Red blood cells** carry special **antigens** (called **agglutinogens**) on their surface. There are two types of red blood cell antigen — **A** and **B**.

2) These determine **blood groups** — a person with type A antigens will be blood group A, a person with type A **and** B antigens = blood group AB and so on... If you don't have any antigens on your red blood cells you're blood group O.

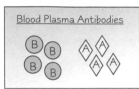

Blood Plasma Antibodies

1) **Blood plasma** carries special **antibodies** (called **agglutinins**). Again there are two types — A and B.

2) If blood antigens and antibodies of the **same type** mix, **agglutination** occurs — the agglutinins bind to the agglutinogens on the blood cells, forming a **clump**. This can be **fatal** because the clumps can **block arteries**.

3) So we **don't** have agglutinogens and agglutinins of the **same type** in our bodies. If we have type A agglutinogens, we'll have type B agglutinins and so on...

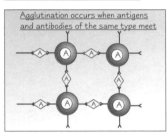

Agglutination occurs when antigens and antibodies of the same type meet

Most **blood transfusions** have to be from someone of the same blood group to prevent **agglutination** happening in the transfusion patient's blood. But there are two exceptions.

Blood groups	Red Blood Cell Antigens	Blood Plasma Antibodies
A	A	B
B	B	A
AB	A+B	none
O	none	A+B

People with **blood group O** (with **no agglutinogens** on their red blood cells) can **donate** blood to anyone. Also, people with **blood group AB** (with **no agglutinins** in their blood plasma) can **receive** blood from anyone. The reason for this is that it doesn't usually matter if donated blood contains the wrong **agglutinins**, because there won't be a high enough concentration of them to cause serious agglutination. BUT, donated blood can't contain the wrong **agglutinogens**, because the high concentration of **agglutinins** in the patient's blood will attack them, causing fatal agglutination.

OCR ONLY

An **Allergy** is a Reaction to a 'Harmless' Substance

Allergies are over-reactions by the immune system to harmless antigens, called **allergens**. People with **hay fever** are sensitive to pollen. When they breathe it in the body over-reacts and increases production of chemicals like **histamine**. This causes **inflammation** of the affected area, excessive mucus secretion and constriction of the **bronchi** (so you're swollen, snotty and can't breathe). **Anti-histamine** is used to treat hay fever, insect bites and skin allergies.

Asthma can be caused by an allergic reaction too. The allergen is the **house dust mite** and its faeces. Asthma causes inflammation in the **bronchioles**. This obstructs the airways, making it hard to breathe.

OCR ONLY

Immunity can be Active or Passive

1) **Active immunity** — the immune system makes antibodies of its own after being stimulated by an **antigen**. This can happen **naturally**, when you catch a disease and it promotes an immune response. Or it can happen **artificially**, when you get a vaccination containing a harmless dose of the **antigen**. Your body makes antibodies against it, but you don't get the disease. Active immunity involves producing **memory cells** to enable a rapid **secondary response** to pathogens.

2) **Passive immunity** — uses antibodies made by **another** organism. This can be **natural**, e.g. when antibodies pass from mum to baby through the placenta and breast milk. Or it can be **artificial**, when someone's injected with **antibodies** from someone else rather than antigens — e.g. a **tetanus jab** contains antibodies against tetanus toxin, collected from blood donations. **Memory** cells aren't produced in passive immunity, so it's only **short-term** protection. But it's **immediate** — with active immunity the primary immune response takes a while.

Immunity and Vaccinations

Skip this section if you're doing AQA A, AQA B or Edexcel.

Vaccines are Made From Harmless Antigens

Vaccines contain harmless **antigens** that are injected or swallowed. The dose is very small, and a killed or weakened form of the pathogen is used. The body then starts making **antibodies** against the antigens in the vaccine. T-lymphocyte and B-lymphocyte **memory cells** store the information about the antigen and its required antibody. If the real pathogen then enters the body, the immune system can work fast enough so that you don't get ill.

The **World Health Organisation** (WHO) uses vaccination as a major weapon in the fight against disease. A vaccination programme, coordinated by the WHO, **eradicated smallpox** from the world. Yay!

This was possible because —

1) Only one vaccine and no **boosters** (extra doses of the vaccine needed after the first one) were needed, so it was cheap to make.

2) There was only **one strain** of the pathogen, and it couldn't infect animals as well as people.

3) The disease was easily **diagnosed**, and everyone who got infected showed the symptoms.

4) So when the disease started dying out, there was no pathogen still hidden in the population or in animals to infect people again in the future.

Measles, **TB**, **malaria** and **cholera** can all be vaccinated against but haven't been eradicated yet.

Some of the reasons are —

1) The pathogens exist in many strains, which keep changing by **mutation**, e.g. influenza virus.

2) Some live in animals too, e.g. **malaria** lives in mosquitoes.

3) Some invade the **gut** where the immune system doesn't work as well, like **cholera**.

4) It can be hard to organise vaccination programmes — e.g. for **measles** in Less Economically Developed Countries, vaccinations aren't always readily available, so babies often can't be vaccinated soon enough after birth to give them protection when they're most vulnerable.

Practice Questions

Q1   How is asthma caused?

Q2   What does anti-histamine do?

Q3   What is the difference between passive and active immunity?

Q4   What is the difference between an agglutinogen and an agglutinin?

Q5   Which type of immunity is passed from mother to unborn baby — passive or active?

Exam Questions

Q1   Explain what would happen if a person of Blood Group A received a transfusion of Blood Group B.
Why could this be life-threatening?   [7 marks]

Q2   Whooping cough is a bacterial disease which kills one million infants a year throughout the world.
What are the benefits of producing vaccines for this disease by genetic engineering
rather than traditional techniques of injecting weakened forms of the pathogen antigens?   [6 marks]

So asthma's an allergy to mite poo — you learn something every day...

Or in your case you learn 492 new things. So perhaps you're not as excited about mite poo as I am. Make sure you learn all the facts on these pages. Spot check — how is passive immunity different from active immunity? What's an allergy? If you can't answer these questions then back you go to the start of page 84. Wachoo.*

*The sound of a whip cracking, in case you were wondering.

Nutrient and Gaseous Exchange

These pages are about surface area. Basically, things get into and out of organisms across exchange surfaces, which are usually cell membranes. There needs to be a big enough area of surface (see what I did there?) for this to happen.

Smaller Animals have Higher Surface Area : Volume Ratios

A mouse has a bigger surface area **relative to its volume** than a hippo. This can be hard to imagine, but you can prove it mathematically. Imagine these animals as cubes:

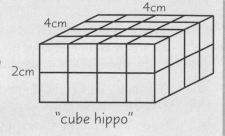

The hippo could be represented by a block with an area of 2 cm × 4 cm × 4 cm.

Its **volume** is 2 × 4 × 4 = **32 cm³**

Its **surface area** is 2 × 4 × 4 = 32 cm² (top and bottom surfaces of cube)
+ 4 × 2 × 4 = 32 cm² (four sides of the cube)

Total surface area = **64 cm²**

So the hippo has a **surface area : volume ratio** of 64 : 32 or **2 : 1**.

"cube hippo"

"cube mouse"

Compare this to a mouse cube measuring 1 cm × 1 cm × 1 cm
Its **volume** is 1 × 1 × 1 = **1 cm³**
Its **surface area** is 1 × 1 × 6 = **6 cm²**
So the mouse has a **surface area : volume ratio** of 6 : 1

The cube mouse's surface area is six times its volume. The cube hippo's surface area is only twice its volume. Smaller animals have a bigger surface area compared to their volume.

Organisms Need to Exchange Materials with the Environment

Cells need oxygen (for aerobic respiration) and nutrients. They need to excrete waste products like CO_2.

1) Microscopic one-celled organisms have very **high** surface area : volume ratios, so they can exchange materials with the environment over their whole surface by diffusion.

2) Larger multicellular organisms have **lower** surface area : volume ratios. They need **organs** with **big surface areas** and **specialised cells** for exchange (e.g. lungs — see below). Many have also developed specialised **transport systems** like blood, to carry gases, nutrients and wastes to and from inner cells.

Surface area is also important for **body temperature**. Animals release heat energy when their **cells respire** and lose it to the **environment**. So **small animals** with high S.A. : volume ratios, like mice, have to use lots of energy just **keeping warm**, while **big animals** with low S.A. : volume ratios, like elephants, are more likely to **overheat**.

Elephants have a low S.A. : volume ratio, but their big, flat ears have a very small volume and a big surface area. Elephants use their ears for heat exchange, to help heat escape from the body quickly.

Lungs are Specialised Organs for Breathing

Mammals like humans exchange oxygen and carbon dioxide through their **lungs**. The lungs have special **features** that make them well-adapted to **breathing**:

Cartilage — rings of strong but bendy cartilage keep the **trachea** open.
Goblet cells — produce **mucus** to trap inhaled dust and other particles.
Cilia — **hairs** on the cells that line the trachea, bronchi and bronchioles. They **move** to push the mucus with trapped particles **upwards**, away from the lungs.
Smooth muscle — round the bronchi and bronchioles. **Involuntary** muscle contractions narrow the airways.
Elastic fibres — between the alveoli. Stretch the lungs when we breathe in and recoil when we breathe out to help push air out.
Pleural membrane — protective lining on the lungs.

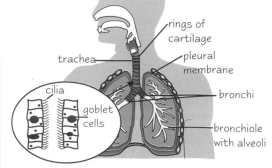

rings of cartilage
pleural membrane
trachea
cilia
goblet cells
bronchi
bronchiole with alveoli

Nutrient and Gaseous Exchange

In Humans Gaseous Exchange Happens in the Alveoli

Lungs contain millions of microscopic air sacs called **alveoli**, which are responsible for gas exchange. They're so tiny, but so important — size ain't everything.

1) The huge number of alveoli means a **big surface area** for exchanging oxygen and carbon dioxide.

2) **O_2** diffuses **out of** alveoli, across the **alveolar epithelium** (the single layer of cells lining the alveoli) and the **capillary endothelium** (the single layer of cells of the capillary wall), and into **haemoglobin** in the **blood**.

3) **CO_2** diffuses **into** the alveoli from the blood, and is breathed out through the lungs, up the trachea, and out of the mouth and nose.

4) The alveoli secrete liquid called **surfactant**. This stops the alveoli collapsing by lowering the surface tension of the water layer lining the alveoli.

alveoli ('air sacs') covered in a network of capillaries
bronchiole
one alveolus

Alveoli have **adaptations** that make them a really good surface for gas exchange. They have the following features, which all **speed up** the **rate of diffusion**:

- **thin exchange surfaces** (the alveolar epithelium cells are very thin);
- **short diffusion pathways** (the alveolar epithelium layer is only one cell thick);
- **a large surface area to volume ratio**;
- **a steep concentration gradient** between the alveoli and the capillaries surrounding them.

Fish Use a Counter-Current System for Gaseous Exchange

There's a **lower concentration** of oxygen in water than in air. So **fish** have special **adaptations** to get **enough oxygen**.

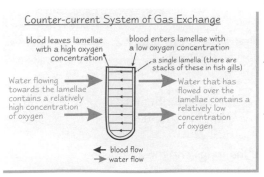

Counter-current System of Gas Exchange

blood leaves lamellae with a high oxygen concentration
blood enters lamellae with a low oxygen concentration
a single lamella (there are stacks of these in fish gills)
Water flowing towards the lamellae contains a relatively high concentration of oxygen
Water that has flowed over the lamellae contains a relatively low concentration of oxygen
blood flow
water flow

1) Water containing oxygen enters the fish through its **gills**. In the gills there's a **one-way current** of water that's continually kept flowing by a **pumping mechanism**.

2) Each gill contains very many **thin plates** called **lamellae**, which give a **big surface area** for **exchange** of **gases**. The lamellae have lots of blood capillaries and a thin surface layer of cells to speed up diffusion.

3) In the gills, the **blood** flows over the lamellae in one direction and **water** flows over the lamellae in the opposite direction. This is called a **counter-current system**. It means that a **concentration gradient** is maintained between the water and the blood — so as much oxygen diffuses from the water into the blood as possible.

Practice Questions

Q1 Draw a flow diagram of gas exchange in the alveoli.

Q2 Why is surfactant important?

Q3 Name three ways the lungs are adapted for gas exchange.

Exam Questions

Q1 Describe how gaseous exchange in fish is adapted to cope with the relatively low oxygen levels in water. [4 marks]

Q2 Explain why a specialised gas exchange system is required in humans. [4 marks]

Alveoli — useful things...always make me think of pasta...

I know you've just got to the end of a page — but it would be a pretty smart idea to have another look at Diffusion and Osmosis (page 26). It's all the stuff about Fick's Law, and transport across membranes. Not the most thrilling prospect I realise, but it'll help these pages make more sense.

Ventilation and Cardiac Output

A person's breathing rate and heart rate change when they exercise. For some reason, biologists see this as an excuse to start using technical terms and sticking them in equations. Don't let that bother you — it's all pretty straightforward.

PV is the **Volume of Air** Taken into the **Lungs** in **One Minute**

PV stands for **Pulmonary Ventilation** and is measured in dm³ min⁻¹ (cubic decimetres per minute — a decimetre is 10 centimetres). Biologists put it into an equation , to show that they're just as good as other scientists:

$$PV = TV \times BR$$

Tidal Volume (TV) is the volume of air in each breath — usually about **0.4 dm³** per breath.

Breathing Rate (BR) is the number of breaths per minute. For a person at rest it's about **15 breaths**.

So a normal person at rest would have a PV of about 15 x 0.4 dm³ min⁻¹ = **6 dm³ min⁻¹**.

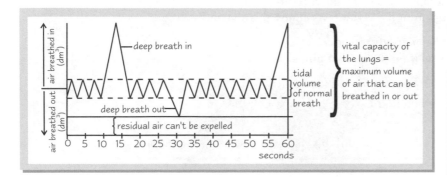

The table below shows the difference in composition between the air you breathe in and the air you breathe out again a moment later — the main difference is you've used up some oxygen and added a bit of CO_2.

Gas	% Inhaled	% Exhaled
Oxygen	20.96	16.50
Carbon Dioxide	0.04	4.00
Nitrogen	79.00	79.00
Water Vapour	Variable	Saturated

The **Medulla Oblongata** in the Brain Controls **Rate of Breathing**

Your **breathing rate** changes according to how much **physical activity** you're doing. When you're exercising you use more **energy**. Your body needs to do more **aerobic respiration** to release this energy, so it needs more **oxygen**.

The **ventilation cycle** is the cycle of breathing in and out. It involves **inspiratory** and **expiratory** centres in the **medulla oblongata** (an area of the brain) and **stretch receptors** in the lungs.

> The Ventilation Cycle:
>
> 1) The medulla's **inspiratory centre** sends nerve impulses to the **intercostal** (rib) and **diaphragm** muscles to make them **contract**. It also sends nerve impulses to the medulla to **inhibit** the **expiratory centre**.
>
> 2) Air enters the lungs due to the **pressure difference** between the lungs and the air outside.
>
> 3) The **lungs inflate**. This stimulates **stretch receptors**, which send nerve impulses back to the **medulla** to **inhibit** the **inspiratory centre**.
>
> 4) Now the expiratory centre (no longer inhibited) sends nerve impulses to the muscles to relax and the **lungs deflate**, expelling air. This causes the **stretch receptors** to become **inactive**, so the inspiratory centre is no longer inhibited and the cycle starts again.
>
> 5) This ventilation cycle happens **automatically** without you having to think about it.

Chemoreceptors Detect **Chemical Changes** in the **Blood**

1) During exercise, CO_2 levels rise and this decreases the **pH** of the blood.

2) **Chemoreceptors** are sensitive to these chemical changes in the blood. They're found in the **medulla oblongata**, in **aortic bodies** (in the aorta), and in **carotid bodies** (in the carotid arteries carrying blood to the head).

3) If the chemoreceptors **detect** a **decrease** in the **pH** of the blood, they send a **signal** to the **medulla** to send more frequent nerve impulses to the intercostal muscles and diaphragm. This **increases** the **rate** of **breathing** and the **depth** of breathing.

4) This allows **gaseous exchange** to **speed up**. CO_2 levels drop and the demand for extra O_2 by the muscles is met.

Ventilation and Cardiac Output

Skip this page if you're doing AQA B.

There are **Four Terms** You Should Know About the **Heart**

1) **Pulse Rate / Heart Rate** — Pulse rate is a measure of the heart rate. Blood is forced through the arteries by the heart contracting. You can feel your pulse where arteries are near the skin's surface, like in your wrist. During exercise the pulse (heart rate) speeds up. Afterwards it returns to resting rate.

2) **Fitness** is measured by how quickly the pulse returns to **resting rate**. The quicker it returns, and the lower the resting pulse, the fitter you are.

3) **Stroke volume** — the volume of blood pumped during each heart beat.

4) **Cardiac Output** — the amount of blood pumped by the heart per minute.

   cardiac output = stroke volume × heart rate

Matilda had a very low stroke volume compared to other cats.

During exercise:

1) the blood flow to the skeletal muscles and heart **increases**;
2) the blood flow to the digestive system **decreases**;
3) the blood flow to the brain and kidneys **stays the same**.

AQA A ONLY

There are **Three Terms** You Should Know About **Blood Pressure**

You need to learn these terms about blood pressure too. The fun never ends...

1) **Systolic Pressure** — the pressure in the ventricles (heart chambers — see p.98) when heart muscle **contracts**.
2) **Diastolic Pressure** — the pressure when the ventricular muscle **relaxes**.
3) **Hypertension** — When **blood pressure** is too **high**. This puts extra strain on the heart muscle and on the blood vessels, which causes heart problems.

Practice Questions

Q1 Explain the role of stretch receptors in the ventilation cycle.

Q2 What structures detect changes in pH in the blood?

Q3 Where is the rate of breathing controlled?

Q4 What is stroke volume?

Q5 How would you calculate cardiac output?

Exam Questions

Q1 Explain how and why distribution of blood flow changes during exercise. [4 marks]

Q2 Explain why hypertension is a danger to health. [3 marks]

Q3 How would you expect pulmonary ventilation to change when an athlete starts to run a race? Explain your answer. [5 marks]

You need to learn about TV — watching Eastenders doesn't count...

I may have been a bit optimistic when I said this was straightforward. OK, I was lying. There are loads of terms to learn, and it's tempting just to read them and hope for the best. But the safest way is to close the book and try to write them out, along with their meanings. Keep doing this until the cows come home and the fat lady sings — or, until you know them all.

Energy Sources and Exercise

Skip this page if you're doing AQA A or Edexcel.

*Respiration is the release of energy from food. **Glucose** is the main substrate for respiration, but if it's not available the body can use **glycogen** (stored energy) or a **triglyceride**. The energy is stored in **ATP**, a **short-term** energy store.*

Anaerobic Respiration Doesn't Use Oxygen

Anaerobic respiration releases a different amount of energy from aerobic respiration, and gives different end products.

Aerobic Respiration —

1) Uses oxygen and produces waste CO_2 that's excreted through the lungs.

2) Releases more energy from each glucose molecule than anaerobic respiration.

$$C_6H_{12}O_6 + 6O_2 \longrightarrow 6CO_2 + 6H_2O + 38\ ATP$$
glucose + oxygen $\longrightarrow$ carbon dioxide + water + ATP (contains energy)

Anaerobic Respiration —

1) In humans it's called **lactate fermentation**.

2) It's less efficient at releasing energy.

3) It doesn't need oxygen to release energy.

$$C_6H_{12}O_6 \longrightarrow 2CH_3CHOHCOOH + 2ATP$$
glucose $\longrightarrow$ lactic acid + ATP (contains energy)

4) It produces **lactic acid**, which builds up in the blood. This lowers the pH in muscle cells that are respiring anaerobically, which causes the pain known as **muscle fatigue**.

During Exercise an Oxygen Debt May Build Up

During **vigorous exercise** the body demands more oxygen than is available:

1) In skeletal muscles, **aerobic** respiration changes to **anaerobic** respiration.

2) **Lactic acid** is produced, which builds up in the blood. Lactic acid is **toxic** and the body can only deal with **small amounts**. Too much lactic acid in the blood means exercise has to stop.

3) **Oxygen** is needed to get rid of the lactic acid. When exercise stops, more oxygen can be used for this job.

4) The oxygen needed to convert lactic acid to the chemical **pyruvate** is called the **oxygen debt**. This is why you keep **panting** after hard exercise — you're still **repaying** the oxygen debt.

Aerobic exercise is exercise using oxygen. If you pace yourself well you can have a good work-out without going into anaerobic respiration. Athletes train regularly to train their muscles to work harder whilst staying in aerobic respiration (which provides more energy). Aerobic exercise improves **ventilation** and makes the **circulatory system** more efficient.

The Effects of Exercise can be Investigated

Long term research has been conducted into the benefits of exercise — one way of doing this is by comparing people with different fitness levels:

1) Expose people with **different fitness levels** (e.g. an athlete compared to a person who does little exercise) to a measured exercise regime.

2) Make sure that the fitness level is the only variable and keep everything else **constant,** — like age, sex, duration of activity, etc.

3) **Take measurements** such as:

- **tidal volume** and **vital capacity** of lungs;
- heart rate, **stroke volume** and blood pressure;
- body temperature;
- blood concentration of CO_2 and lactic acid.

This type of experiment has shown that people who exercise regularly have improved heart and lung function.

4) Do this before, during and after exercise, using appropriate equipment — like a **spirometer** to measure the volume of air moving in and out of lungs.

5) **Analyse** results to work out things like **recovery rates**, total oxygen consumed during exercise, etc.

Energy Sources and Exercise

Skip this page if you're doing AQA A, AQA B or Edexcel.

You Need to do **Exercise** to **Stay Healthy**

Recent studies have found that **two thirds** of adults in the UK don't do enough exercise to stay healthy. Frequent, moderate exercise keeps the body working at its maximum efficiency, and increases the amount of the chemicals in the brain which make you feel good.

Look how happy you could be.

Exercise makes you happy:

The **pituitary gland** releases an increased level of **ß-endorphin** into the blood during exercise. Endorphins belong to a family of chemicals that includes **morphine** — used to relieve pain. It's thought that ß-endorphin is responsible for the "jogger's high" — a feeling of well-being after exercise.

There are **Three Types** of **Exercise**

1) **Aerobic Exercise** — activities that increase **heart rate** and **lung efficiency**, e.g. walking, running, swimming or cycling.

Benefits
- Keeps heart muscle healthy.
- Increases **oxygen delivery** to body cells.
- Improves lung efficiency.
- Decreases **cholesterol**.
- Improves resistance to disease.
- Reduces excess weight.

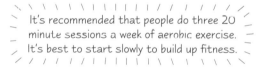
It's recommended that people do three 20 minute sessions a week of aerobic exercise. It's best to start slowly to build up fitness.

2) **Muscle Strengthening Exercise** — works the muscles against resistance.

Benefits
- Improves muscle control of skeleton and body shape.
- Improves strength.

3) **Flexibility Exercises** — stretching exercises like **yoga** and **pilates**.

Benefits
- Improves posture, muscle tone and body shape.
- Also said to improve mental fitness such as the ability to concentrate or relax.

Practice Questions

Q1 What is the main respiratory substrate used by animals?

Q2 Write out both the word and formula equations for aerobic and anaerobic respiration.

Q3 What causes muscle fatigue?

Q4 Would you expect a trained athlete to consume more or less energy than other people during exercise? Why?

Q5 Name three types of exercise and give the benefits of each.

Exam Questions

Q1 Explain what happens during vigorous exercise in terms of respiration. [4 marks]

Q2 Explain why regular exercise can prolong an active life. [5 marks]

First revision, now you're nagging about exercise — leave me alone...

Actually, exercise can help you revise — put down your Revision Guide for a bit (the first and last time I'll ever say that) and do some gentle exercise. When you come back to it, you'll find it easier to concentrate and you'll remember things more quickly. And now you know what causes those vicious pains if you exercise a bit too much. Marvellous.

Transport Systems

The idea behind this page is simple. You take stuff in through specially adapted organs. You move it around to where its needed in specially adapted transport systems. Then you move waste to where it can be got rid of.

Multicellular Organisms need Transport Systems

All cells need energy — most cells get energy via **aerobic respiration**. The raw materials for this are **glucose** and **oxygen**, so the body has to make sure it can deliver enough of these to all its cells. In single-celled creatures, these materials can **diffuse directly** into the cell across the cell surface membrane. The diffusion rate is quick because of the small distances the substances have to travel (see p.26).

In **multicellular** animals, diffusion across the outer membrane is too slow for their needs. This is because:

1) some cells are **deep within the body**;
2) they have a **low surface area to volume ratio**;
3) they have a **high metabolic rate**, which means they respire quickly, so they need a **constant supply** of glucose and oxygen.
4) they have a **tough outer surface**.

So multicellular animals need **transport systems** to carry raw materials from specialised **exchange organs** to their body cells. In mammals this is the **circulatory system**, which uses **blood** to carry glucose and oxygen around the body. It also carries hormones, antibodies (to fight disease) and waste like CO_2. The bulk movement of blood is called **mass flow** (see p.98)

Exchange Organs are Specialised for their Function

For **exchange surfaces** to be efficient, they need to have:

1) thin membranes to provide a **short diffusion path**;
2) a **big surface area** for exchanging sufficient gases or nutrients.

In mammals gas exchange happens in the **alveoli** of the lungs. **Nutrients** are absorbed in the **villi** of the small intestine. Both alveoli and villi:

1) transfer substances into **blood capillaries**;
2) have blood capillaries very close to the surface;
3) are extremely small and numerous to give a big **surface area to volume ratio**;
4) have thin walls to speed up **diffusion rates**.

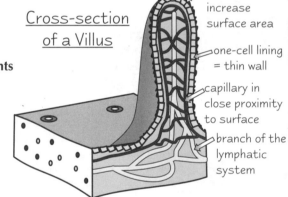

Cross-section of a Villus

- microvilli to increase surface area
- one-cell lining = thin wall
- capillary in close proximity to surface
- branch of the lymphatic system

Large Organisms Maintain Concentration Gradients at Exchange Surfaces

If there's a big difference in the concentration of a substance between two areas (a steep **concentration gradient**), the rate of diffusion is faster. Substances diffuse from an area of **higher** concentration to an area of **lower** concentration. One function of the **specialised exchange organs** of larger organisms is to maintain concentration gradients so things diffuse quickly. A good example of this is the **alveoli** in human lungs:

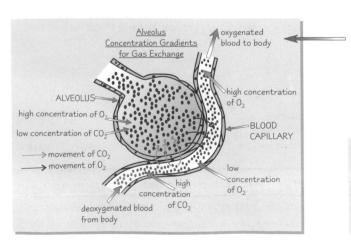

Alveolus Concentration Gradients for Gas Exchange

- oxygenated blood to body
- high concentration of O_2
- ALVEOLUS
- high concentration of O_2
- low concentration of CO_2
- movement of CO_2
- movement of O_2
- BLOOD CAPILLARY
- low concentration of O_2
- high concentration of CO_2
- deoxygenated blood from body

After exchanging gases with cells, **deoxygenated blood** full of CO_2 returns to blood capillaries in the lungs. There's a higher level of O_2 in the **alveoli** compared to the capillaries. This gives a good concentration gradient for **diffusion of oxygen** into the **blood**. The low level of CO_2 in the **alveolar space** helps to remove the CO_2 from the blood. CO_2 **diffuses** down the concentration gradient and **into the lungs**, where it's breathed out.

Other exchange surfaces have similar features. E.g. blood delivers glucose to cells for respiration. When blood returns "empty" to the microvilli in the gut, more glucose diffuses down the concentration gradient into the capillaries. Most larger organisms have special ways of maintaining concentration gradients, like the counter-current exchange system in the gill lamellae of fish (see p.87).

Transport Systems

There are **Five** Main Types of **Blood Vessel**

The five main types of blood vessels are **arteries**, **arterioles**, **capillaries**, **venules** and **veins**.

1) **Arteries** carry blood **from** the heart **to** the rest of the body. They're thick-walled, muscular and have elastic tissue in the walls to cope with the **high pressure** caused by the heartbeat. All arteries carry **oxygenated** blood except the **pulmonary arteries**, which take deoxygenated blood to the lungs.

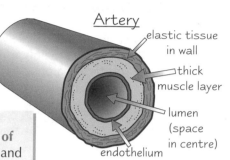

Artery
elastic tissue in wall
thick muscle layer
lumen (space in centre)
endothelium

2) Arteries divide into smaller **arterioles** which form a network of vessels throughout the body. Blood is directed to different **areas of demand** in the body by muscles inside the arterioles contracting and restricting the blood flow or relaxing and allowing full blood flow.

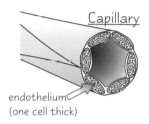

Capillary
endothelium (one cell thick)

3) Arterioles branch into **capillaries**, which are the **smallest** of the blood vessels. Substances are exchanged between cells and capillaries. Their walls are only **one cell thick** to allow efficient **diffusion** of substances (e.g. glucose and oxygen) to occur near cells. At their other end, capillaries merge into venules (see below). Networks of capillaries in tissue are called **capillary beds**.

4) **Venules** are a bit bigger than capillaries and form a network of vessels which spread away from capillary beds towards veins.

Vein
large lumen
endothelium
thin muscle wall

5) **Veins** take blood back **to the heart**. They're **wider** than equivalent arteries, with very little elastic or muscle tissue. Veins contain **valves** to stop the blood flowing backwards. Blood flow through the veins is helped by contraction of the **body muscles** surrounding them. All veins carry **deoxygenated** blood (because oxygen has been used up by body cells), except for the **pulmonary veins**, which carry oxygenated blood to the heart from the lungs.

Practice Questions

Q1 Why don't single-celled organisms need transport systems?

Q2 How does a concentration gradient influence speed of diffusion?

Q3 What are the 5 main types of blood vessel?

Q4 Do arteries mainly carry oxygenated or deoxygenated blood?

Q5 What is the smallest type of blood vessel?

Exam Questions

Q1 "Structures involved in exchange are specialised for their function." Give two examples of exchange structures in the human body and describe the relationship between their structure and their function. [4 marks]

Q2 Why do multicellular organisms need extra features to aid diffusion of substances into and out of their cells? [6 marks]

If blood can handle transport this efficiently, the trains have no excuse...

Four hours I was waiting at Preston this weekend. Four hours! You may have noticed that biologists are obsessed with the relationship between structure and function, so whenever you're learning the structure of something, make sure you know how this relates to its function. Like the veins, arteries and capillaries on this page, for example.

Blood, Tissue Fluid and Lymph

For some people the word 'blood' is enough to make them cringe. Strange really, seeing as it's the substance that keeps us all alive. So sorry to all you blood-phobics out there, because these pages are all about the stuff.

Blood Contains **Blood Cells**, **Platelets** *and* **Plasma**

Blood is a **specialised tissue** that's composed of 45% **blood cells** and **platelets** suspended in a liquid called **plasma** (55%). Plasma's mainly **water**, with various nutrients and gases dissolved in it. The main role of blood is **transporting substances** around the body **dissolved** in the **plasma**. Substances move into and out of the plasma through **blood capillaries** at exchange surfaces.

Substance	Exchange surface where substance enters blood through capillaries	Exchange surface where substance leaves blood through capillaries
nutrients from digestion (glucose, amino acids, fatty acids, mineral ions)	epithelium of the villi in the small intestine	body tissues
hormones	glands	target organs
oxygen	alveoli in the lungs	body tissues
carbon dioxide	body tissues	alveoli in the lungs
urea	liver cells	kidney cells

Also, antibodies are secreted directly into plasma by white blood cells

Blood Cells *are* Adapted *to* Specific Jobs

1) **Red blood cells** (**erythrocytes**) are responsible for absorbing **oxygen** and transporting it round the body. They're made in the **bone marrow** and are very small.

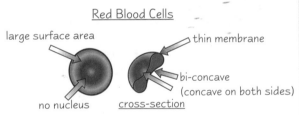

Red Blood Cells

large surface area — thin membrane — bi-concave (concave on both sides) — no nucleus — cross-section

1) They have **no organelles** (including no nucleus) to leave more room for **haemoglobin**, which carries the oxygen.

2) They have a large surface area due to their **bi-concave disc** shape. This allows O_2 to diffuse quickly into and out of the cell.

3) They have an **elastic membrane**, which allows them to change shape to squeeze through the small blood capillaries, then spring back into normal shape when they re-enter veins.

2) **White blood cells** (**leucocytes**) are larger than red blood cells but there are fewer of them in blood. They are responsible for fighting disease (see p.82).

There are two main types of white blood cell:

White Blood Cell	Diagram	Function and Structure
phagocytes (neutrophils and macrophages)		• engulf pathogens and micro-organisms and digest them (phagocytosis) • contain many lysosomes to aid digestion • elongated nucleus and flowing cytoplasm enables them to squeeze through gaps between cells to move to the site of infection in body tissues
lymphocytes		• produce antibodies to prevent disease • large nucleus

In addition, white blood cells can be divided into two general types — those with a **granular cytoplasm** and those without.

Granular cytoplasm, e.g.

neutrophils (phagocyte)   eosinophils (antihistamine)

Non-granular cytoplasm, e.g.

monocytes (phagocyte)   lymphocytes (produce antibodies)

3) **Platelets** are tiny bits of **cytoplasm** held within a cell membrane. They have no nucleus. They release an enzyme that produces **fibrin fibres** to form a **blood clot** when blood vessels are cut open — this is what forms **scabs**.

Blood, Tissue Fluid and Lymph

Tissue Fluid is Formed from Blood Plasma

Tissue fluid surrounds the cells in tissues — providing them with the conditions they need to function. Tissue fluid is made from substances which leave the plasma from the blood capillaries. Substances move out of blood capillaries by **pressure filtration**:

1) At the **arteriole end** of the capillary bed, pressure inside the capillaries is **greater** than pressure in the tissue fluid. This difference in pressure forces fluid to **leave** the **capillaries** and enter tissue space.

2) As fluid leaves, pressure reduces in the capillaries — so the pressure's much lower at the **venule end** of the capillary bed.

3) Due to the fluid loss, the **water potential** at the **venule end** of the capillaries is **lower** than the water potential in the **tissue fluid** — so some **water re-enters** the capillaries from the tissue fluid at the venule end, by **osmosis**.

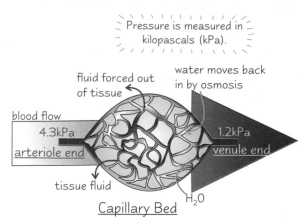

Capillary Bed

Unlike blood, tissue fluid **doesn't** contain **red blood cells** or **big proteins**, because they are **too large** to be pushed out through the capillary walls. It does contain smaller molecules, e.g. oxygen, glucose and mineral ions. Tissue fluid helps cells to get the oxygen and glucose they need, and to get rid of the CO_2 and waste they don't need.

Lymph is Formed from Excess Tissue Fluid

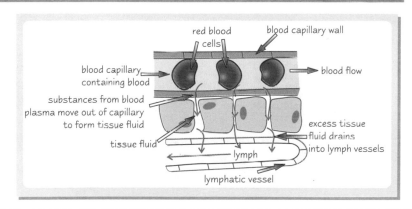

Lymph is a fluid that forms when excess tissue fluid drains into the lymphatic vessels, which lie close to blood capillaries. Lymph takes away waste products from the cells. It then travels through the **lymphatic system** and eventually enters blood plasma.

It's similar to tissue fluid, except it contains more fats, proteins and white blood cells, which it picks up at **lymph nodes** as it travels through the lymphatic system.

Practice Questions

Q1 What does blood contain?

Q2 What do white blood cells do?

Q3 What are all cells surrounded by?

Q4 Explain pressure filtration.

Q5 What makes lymph different from tissue fluid?

Exam Questions

Q1 How does tissue fluid move into and out of blood capillaries? [5 marks]

Q2 Explain how the structure of phagocytes helps them to fight disease in the body. [3 marks]

That's the end of this bloody topic — and you can't get me for swearing...

It's time to conquer any fears of blood and start appreciating it for the amazing tissue it is. Learn its functions, and which bits do each function — plasma does transport, red blood cells do oxygen and white blood cells do disease-fighting. If I were a blood cell I'd be a great leucocyte warrior, instilling fear into the nuclei of pathogens everywhere. Aaanyway.

Haemoglobin and Oxygen Transport

Skip these pages if you're doing AQA A.

Aaagh, complicated topic alert. Don't worry though, because your poor, over-worked brain cells will recover from the brain-strain of these pages thanks to oxyhaemoglobin. So the least you can do is learn how it works.

Oxygen is Carried Round the Body as Oxyhaemoglobin

Oxygen is carried round the body by **haemoglobin** (Hb), in red blood cells. When oxygen joins to it, it becomes **oxyhaemoglobin**. This is a **reversible reaction** — when oxygen leaves oxyhaemoglobin (**dissociates** from it), it turns back to haemoglobin.

$$Hb + 4O_2 \rightleftharpoons HbO_8$$
Haemoglobin + oxygen $\rightleftharpoons$ oxyhaemoglobin

1) **Haemoglobin** is a large, **globular protein** molecule made up of four polypeptide chains (see p.14).

2) Each chain has a **haem group** which contains **iron** and gives haemoglobin its **red** colour.

3) Haemoglobin has a **high affinity for oxygen** — each molecule carries **four oxygen molecules**.

'Affinity' for oxygen means willingness to combine with oxygen.

Partial Pressure Measures Concentration of Gases

The **partial pressure of oxygen** (pO_2) is a measure of **oxygen concentration**. The **greater** the concentration of dissolved oxygen in cells, the **higher** the partial pressure. Similarly, the **partial pressure of carbon dioxide** (pCO_2) is a measure of the concentration of carbon dioxide in a cell.

Oxygen **loads onto** haemoglobin to form oxyhaemoglobin where there's a **high pO_2**. Oxyhaemoglobin **unloads** its oxygen where there has been a **decrease in pO_2**.

1) Oxygen enters blood capillaries at the **alveoli** in the **lungs**. Alveoli cells have a **high pO_2** so oxygen **loads onto** haemoglobin to form oxyhaemoglobin.

2) When our **cells respire**, they use up oxygen. This **lowers pO_2**, so red blood cells deliver oxyhaemoglobin to respiring tissues, where it unloads its oxygen.

3) The haemoglobin then returns to the lungs to pick up more oxygen.

Athletes train at **high altitude** because there's **low pO_2** in the air, which makes the body start producing **more red blood cells**. This means extra oxygen can be carried, so muscles respire more efficiently.

The extra red blood cells stay in the blood for a couple of weeks after returning to normal altitudes, giving the athlete an advantage. Sneaky.

Dissociation Curves Show How Affinity for Oxygen Varies

Dissociation curves show how the willingness of haemoglobin to combine with oxygen varies, depending on partial pressure of oxygen (pO_2).

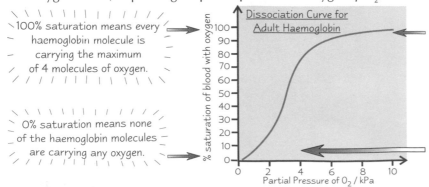

100% saturation means every haemoglobin molecule is carrying the maximum of 4 molecules of oxygen.

0% saturation means none of the haemoglobin molecules are carrying any oxygen.

Where pO_2 **is high** (e.g. in the lungs), haemoglobin has a **high affinity** for oxygen (i.e. it will **readily combine** with oxygen), so it has a **high saturation** of oxygen.

Where pO_2 **is low** (e.g. in respiring tissues), haemoglobin has a **low affinity** for oxygen, which means it **releases oxygen** rather than combines with it. That's why it has a **low saturation** of oxygen.

The graph is 'S-shaped' because when haemoglobin (Hb) combines with the **first O_2 molecule**, it **alters the shape** of the Hb molecule in a way that makes it **easier** for other molecules to join too. But as the haemoglobin starts to become fully saturated, it becomes harder for more oxygen to join. As a result, the curve has a **steep** bit in the middle where it's really easy for oxygen molecules to join, and **shallow** bits at each end where it's harder for oxygen molecules to join. When the curve is steep, a small change in pO_2 causes a big change in the amount of oxygen carried by the haemoglobin.

Haemoglobin and Oxygen Transport

Different Blood Pigments have Different Affinities for Oxygen

1) **Foetal haemoglobin:**

In the **womb**, the foetus gets oxygen from its **mother's blood** across the placenta. This can only happen if its blood is **more likely** to absorb oxygen than its mother's blood. Because of this, **foetal haemoglobin** has a **higher affinity for oxygen** than adult haemoglobin. This means that foetal haemoglobin **always** has a slightly **higher saturation of oxygen** than adult haemoglobin, as you can see on the **graph**.

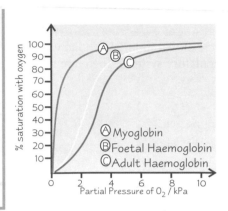

Ⓐ Myoglobin
Ⓑ Foetal Haemoglobin
Ⓒ Adult Haemoglobin

2) **Myoglobin:**

Myoglobin is a **blood pigment** that stores emergency supplies of oxygen in **muscle tissue**. It only releases this oxygen when pO_2 drops to **very low levels**, for example when muscles are using up oxygen faster than haemoglobin can replace it. You can see on the **graph** that its saturation of oxygen remains high, except when pO_2 is very low.

Carbon Dioxide Levels Affect Oxygen Unloading

To complicate matters, haemoglobin gives up its oxygen **more readily** at **higher partial pressures of carbon dioxide** (pCO_2). It's a cunning way of getting more oxygen to cells during activity. When cells respire they produce carbon dioxide, which raises pCO_2, increasing the rate of oxygen unloading. The reason for this is linked to how CO_2 affects blood pH.

1) CO_2 from respiring tissues diffuses into red blood cells and is converted to **carbonic acid**.

2) The carbonic acid **dissociates** to give **hydrogen ions** and **hydrogencarbonate ions**.

3) If left alone, the hydrogen ions would increase the cell's acidity. To prevent this, oxyhaemoglobin **unloads** its oxygen so that haemoglobin can take up the hydrogen ions.

4) The **hydrogencarbonate ions** diffuse out of the red blood cells and are **transported in the plasma**.

5) When the blood reaches the **lungs** the low concentration of CO_2 causes the hydrogencarbonate and hydrogen ions to **recombine into CO_2**.

6) The CO_2 then diffuses into the **alveoli** and is breathed out.

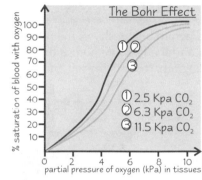

The Bohr Effect

① 2.5 Kpa CO_2
② 6.3 Kpa CO_2
③ 11.5 Kpa CO_2

When carbon dioxide levels increase, the dissociation curve 'shifts' down, showing that more oxygen is released from the blood (because the lower the saturation of O_2 in blood, the more O_2 is being released). This is called the Bohr effect.

Practice Questions

Q1 How is HbO_8 formed?

Q2 What is pO_2?

Q3 What are the differences between myoglobin and haemoglobin?

Q4 What is carbon dioxide converted to in red blood cells?

Exam Questions

Q1 Explain why foetal haemoglobin is different from adult haemoglobin. [3 marks]

Q2 Explain the importance of the Bohr effect during a marathon race. [4 marks]

The Bore effect — it's happening right now...

Dissociation graphs can be a bit confusing — but basically, when tissues contain lots of oxygen (i.e. pO_2 is high), haemoglobin readily combines with the oxygen, so blood has a high saturation of oxygen (and vice versa when pO_2 is low). Simple. Also, make sure you get the lingo right, like 'partial pressure' and 'affinity' — hey, I'm hip, I'm groovy.

Circulation, the Heart and the Cardiac Cycle

*Blood pumps **continually** round your body. It's happening right now as you read this rather long and dull sentence that I'm writing to keep you reading without stopping to try and highlight the **unceasingness** of blood flow. And relax.*

Mammals Have a Closed Double Circulation

Blood transports respiratory gases, products of digestion, metabolic wastes and hormones round the body in a **closed circulatory system**. There are two routes:

1) **Systemic circulation**

(heart ⟹ body ⟹ heart)

Oxygenated blood travels to the body cells and **deoxygenated** blood returns to the heart.

2) **Pulmonary circulation**

(heart ⟹ lungs ⟹ heart)

Deoxygenated blood travels to the lungs and **oxygenated** blood returns to the heart.

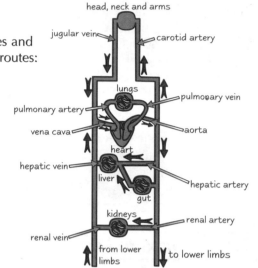

Mass Flow of Blood — Human Closed Circulatory System

The Heart Consists of Two Muscular Pumps

The diagram below shows the **internal structure** of the heart. The **right side** pumps **deoxygenated blood** to the **lungs** and the **left side** pumps **oxygenated blood** to the **whole body**. NB — the **left and right side** are **reversed** on the diagram, 'cos it's the left and right of the person that the heart belongs to.

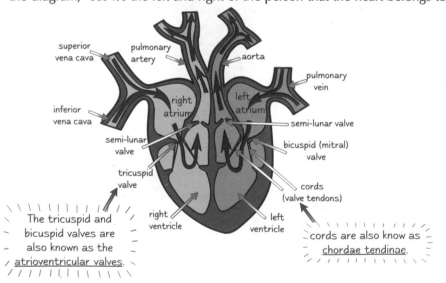

The tricuspid and bicuspid valves are also known as the *atrioventricular valves*.

cords are also know as *chordae tendinae*.

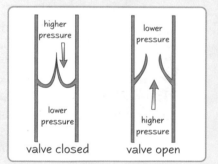

valve closed   valve open

The **valves** only open one way — whether they open or close depends on the relative pressure of the heart chambers. If there's higher pressure behind a valve, it's forced open, but if pressure is higher above the valve it's forced shut.

Each bit of the heart is adapted to do its job effectively.

1) The **left ventricle** of the heart has thicker, more muscular walls than the **right ventricle**, because it needs to contract powerfully to pump blood all the way round the body. The right side only needs to get blood to the lungs, which are nearby.

2) The **ventricles** have thicker walls than the **atria**, because they have to push blood out of the heart whereas the atria just need to push blood a short distance into the ventricles.

3) The **tricuspid** and **bicuspid** valves link the atria to the ventricles and stop blood getting back into the atria when the ventricles contract.

4) The **semilunar valves** stop blood flowing back into the heart after the ventricles contract.

5) The **cords** attach the atrioventricular valves to the ventricles to stop them being forced up into the atria when the ventricles contract.

Circulation, the Heart and the Cardiac Cycle

The Cardiac Cycle Pumps Blood Round the Body

The cardiac cycle is an on-going sequence of **systole** (contraction) and **diastole** (relaxation) of the atria and ventricles that keeps blood continuously circulating round the body. The systole and diastole alter the **volume** of the different heart chambers, which alters **pressure** inside the chambers. This causes **valves** to open and close, which directs the **blood flow** through the system. There are 3 stages:

① **Ventricular diastole, atrial systole**

The **ventricles both relax**. The atria then contract, which decreases their volume. The resultant higher pressure in the atria causes the atrioventricular valves to open. This forces blood through the valves into the ventricles.

② **Ventricular systole, atrial diastole**

The **atria relax** and the **ventricles then contract**. This means pressure is higher in the ventricles than the atria, which shuts off the atrioventricular valves to prevent backflow. Meanwhile, the high pressure opens the semilunar valves and blood is forced out into the pulmonary artery and aorta.

③ **Ventricular diastole, atrial diastole**

The **ventricles and the atria both relax**, which increases volume and lowers pressure in the heart chambers. The higher pressure in the pulmonary artery and aorta closes the semilunar valves to prevent backflow. Then the atria fill with blood again due to higher pressure in the vena cava and pulmonary vein and the cycle starts over again.

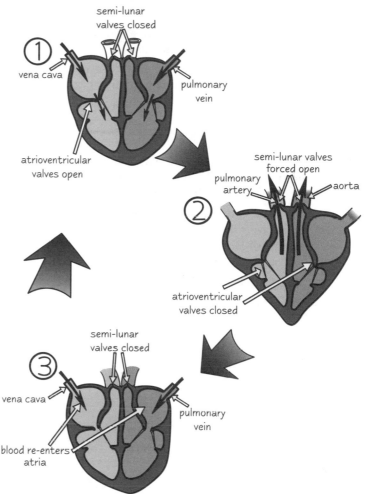

Practice Questions

Q1   What is the difference between the systemic and pulmonary circulatory systems?

Q2   Which side of the heart carries oxygenated blood?

Q3   Why is the left ventricle more muscular than the right ventricle?

Q4   What is the purpose of heart valves?

Exam Questions

Q1   Describe the pressure changes which occur in the heart during systole and diastole.   [3 marks]

Q2   Explain how valves stop blood going back the wrong way.   [6 marks]

Learn these pages off by heart...

Some of this will be familiar to you from GCSEs — so there's no excuse for not learning it really well. The diagram of the heart can be confusing — it's like looking at a mirror image, so right is left and left is right. (So in fact, when you look in the mirror you don't see what you actually look like — you see a reverse image — weird.)

Control of Heartbeat

You don't have to think consciously about making your heart beat — your body does it for you.
So you couldn't stop it beating even if for some strange reason you wanted to. Which is nice to know.

Cardiac Muscle Controls the Regular Beating of the Heart

Cardiac muscle is '**myogenic**' — this means that, rather than receiving signals from **nerves**, it contracts and relaxes on its own. This pattern of contractions controls the **regular heartbeat**.

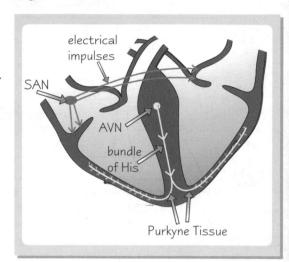

electrical impulses

SAN

AVN

bundle of His

Purkyne Tissue

1) The process starts in the **sino-atrial node (SAN)** in the wall of the **right atrium**.

2) The SAN is like a pacemaker — it sets the rhythm of the heart beat by sending out regular **electrical impulses** to the atrial walls.

3) This causes the right and left atria to contract **at the same time**.

4) A band of non-conducting **collagen tissue** prevents the electrical impulses from passing directly from the atria to the ventricles.

5) Instead, the **atrio-ventricular node (AVN)** picks up the impulses from the SAN. There is a **slight delay** before it reacts, so that the ventricles contract **after** the atria.

6) The AVN generates its own **electrical impulse**. This travels through a group of fibres called the **bundle of His** and then into the finer fibrous tissue in the right and left ventricle walls called **Purkyne tissue**.

7) The impulses mean both ventricles **contract simultaneously**, from the bottom up.

> Sometimes the heart rhythm gets <u>out of control</u>. The wave of stimulation to heart muscle becomes chaotic. Different parts of the heart contract and relax at the same time. This is called <u>fibrillation</u> and can be fatal. Luckily, doctors can stop it using <u>defibrillating equipment</u>, which sends an electric shock to the heart, returning it to its proper rhythm.

Skip this section if you're doing OCR or Edexcel.

The Brain Controls Changes in the Heart Rate

Nerve impulses from the brain **modify the heart rate** — making the heart beat faster or slower.

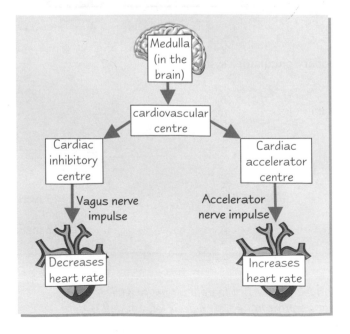

Medulla (in the brain)

cardiovascular centre

Cardiac inhibitory centre

Cardiac accelerator centre

Vagus nerve impulse

Accelerator nerve impulse

Decreases heart rate

Increases heart rate

1) **Heart rate** is controlled in the **cardiovascular centre** in the **medulla oblongata** area of the **brain**.

2) **Nerve impulses** from the **cardiovascular centre** reach the SAN.

3) An **accelerator nerve impulse** from the cardiac accelerator centre stimulates the SAN to **increase the heartbeat**.

4) A **vagus nerve impulse** from the cardiac inhibitory centre stimulates the SAN to **slow the heart rate down**.

Doug's medulla oblongata was having trouble steadying his heart rate.

Control of Heartbeat

Skip this section if you're doing OCR or Edexcel.

Receptors *Inform the Brain About* Changing Blood Pressure *and* Blood pH

Pressure receptors inform the brain about changes in **blood pressure** so it can alter heart rate accordingly:

1) It's important that **blood pressure** is maintained at a constant level. **Pressure receptors** are found in the **aorta wall** and in **carotid arteries**. They detect changes in arterial blood pressure and inform the brain.

2) If the pressure is **too high**, they send impulses to the cardiovascular centre. In turn, this sends impulses to the SAN via the parasympathetic nervous system, to **slow down heart rate**.

3) If **pressure is too low**, pressure receptors send impulses to the cardiovascular centre, which sends its own impulses to, yep you guessed it, the SAN via the sympathetic nervous system, to **speed up heart rate**.

Chemoreceptors inform the brain about changes in **blood pH** so it can alter heart rate accordingly:

1) An **increase in respiration**, for example due to physical activity, increases the **level of CO_2** in the blood. Increased CO_2 levels **lower the pH of blood**, which is detected by **chemoreceptors** in the **carotid artery walls**.

2) In the same way as pressure receptors, these send impulses to the brain, which sends its own impulses to the SAN to **increase the heart rate**.

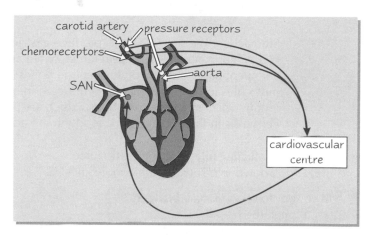

Practice Questions

Q1 What does myogenic mean?

Q2 What is the difference between SAN and AVN?

Q3 What two types of tissue do electrical impulses from the AVN travel through?

Q4 Which part of the brain modifies heart rate?

Q5 How do pressure receptors control blood pressure?

Q6 How do chemoreceptors control high CO_2 levels?

Exam Questions

Q1 Describe what would happen to the heart rate if the heart suffered a sudden loss of blood pressure. [4 marks]

Q2 Describe how the heart beat is stimulated. [6 marks]

What happened to the Bundle of Hers? — she lost her nerve & had to go...

*Did you know that your heart beat can continue beating for a while after you're 'clinically dead' — spooky stuff. The reason is that it doesn't need any input from the brain and nervous system to operate. But, although the brain doesn't control heartbeat it does control the **rate** of the heartbeat. That's where receptors and the cardiovascular centre come in.*

Digestion and Absorption

Skip these pages if you're doing OCR or AQA A.

Time for a bit of blood and guts — well, actually, mainly just the guts. The human digestive system demands respect — it's an amazing bit of kit that has to deal with whatever you trough. It's no coincidence that 'gutsy' means well 'ard.

The **Human Gut** is **Adapted** to its **Function**

There are two stages in human digestion:

1) **Mechanical breakdown** of large pieces of food into small pieces.
2) **Chemical breakdown** of large molecules into small molecules.

The human gut (**alimentary canal**) is composed of different parts, each with a specific job to do:

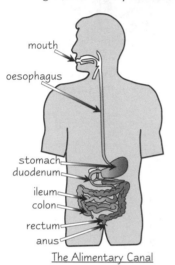

mouth
oesophagus
stomach
duodenum
ileum
colon
rectum
anus

The Alimentary Canal

1) **Mouth** — **Mastication** (chewing) of food by teeth **mechanically** breaks up food so there's a **larger surface** area for enzymes to work on. Mixing food with saliva (water, **amylase** and mucus) partly digests food so it can be swallowed easily. The amylase **hydrolyses** starch into maltose.

2) **Oesophagus** — A tube that takes food from the mouth to the stomach using waves of muscle contractions called **peristalsis**. Mucus is secreted from glandular tissue in the walls, to lubricate the food's passage downwards.

3) **Stomach** — The stomach walls produce **gastric juice**, which consists of hydrochloric acid (HCl), **pepsin** (an enzyme) and mucus. Pepsin is an **endopeptidase** — it hydrolyses peptide bonds in the **middle** of polypeptide molecules (proteins), breaking them down into smaller polypeptide chains. It only works in **acidic conditions**, which are provided by the HCl. Peristalsis in the stomach turns food into an acidic fluid, called **chyme**.

4) **Duodenum** (small intestine) — Contains **alkaline bile** and **pancreatic juice**, which neutralise chyme and break food down into small, soluble molecules:

- Bile is produced in the **liver** and stored in the **gall bladder**, then enters the duodenum through the bile duct. It **emulsifies** lipids into small droplets, which speeds up hydrolysis of lipids by **pancreatic lipase**.
- Pancreatic juice contains **digestive enzymes**:

  Lipase — Hydrolyses **lipids** into fatty acids and glycerol.
  Amylase — Hydrolyses **starch** into maltose.
  Trypsin — An **endopeptidase** that hydrolyses polypeptides into smaller polypeptides.
  Exopeptidases — Hydrolyse peptide bonds found at the **end** of polypeptide chains, giving **free amino acids**.

- **Intestinal juice** is produced by the gut wall. It contains more digestive enzymes — more lipases, **maltase** (hydrolyses maltose into glucose), more exopeptidases and also **dipeptidases** that hydrolyse dipeptides into amino acids.

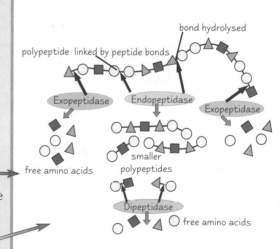

polypeptide linked by peptide bonds
bond hydrolysed
Exopeptidase   Endopeptidase   Exopeptidase
free amino acids
smaller polypeptides
Dipeptidase
free amino acids

5) **Ileum** (small intestine) — The small, soluble molecules of digested food (glucose, amino acids, fatty acids and glycerol) are absorbed through the **microvilli** lining the gut wall. Absorption is through diffusion, facilitated diffusion and active transport (see p.26 - 29):

Method of Absorption	Affected Molecules
Diffusion	Fatty acids, glycerol, water
Facilitated Diffusion	Some glucose, some amino acids
Active Transport	Mineral ions, some glucose, some amino acids

6) **Colon** (large intestine) — **Water** is **absorbed** by the body and waste is pushed along towards the rectum.

7) **Rectum** — Stores **faeces** until they're expelled through the **anus**.

Digestion and Absorption

The **Gut Wall** Consists of **Four Layers** of Tissue

The gut wall has the same **general structure** all the way through the human gut:

1) The **mucosa** (inner lining) lubricates the passage of food with **mucus**. This prevents **autodigestion** (enzymes attacking the gut wall). It's lined with **surface epithelium** cells.

2) The **submucosa** contains capillary beds and nerve fibres.

3) The **circular and longitudinal muscles** control the shape and movement of the gut.

4) The **serosa** contains tough tissue, which provides protection from friction against other organs.

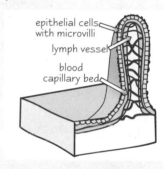

The gut wall in different regions of the alimentary canal has **special features** so it can carry out specific functions:

The mucosa in the **stomach** contains **gastric pits**, which secrete gastric juice.

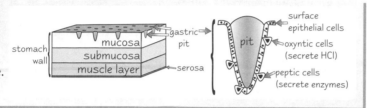

The gut wall in the **oesophagus** uses its circular and longitudinal muscles to perform **peristalsis**. These muscles work as an **antagonistic pair** — as one contracts, the other relaxes. Food is pushed along in front of the contractions.

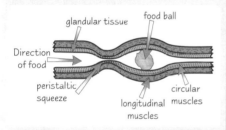

Epithelial cells in the mucosa of the **duodenum** release **digestive enzymes**.

The mucosa in the **ileum** has **villi** and **microvilli** to **increase the surface area** for absorbing the products of digestion. It also has other adaptations for effective absorption:

- It consists of a **single layer** of epithelial cells, so there's a **short diffusion pathway**.
- A **moist lining** helps substances **dissolve** so they can pass through cell membranes.
- The **capillary bed** takes away **absorbed molecules** so the diffusion gradient is maintained.
- **Lymph vessels** take away absorbed **glycerol** and **fatty acids** to join the lymphatic system (see p.95). This maintains the diffusion gradient.
- **Carrier proteins** in epithelial cell membranes allow **facilitated diffusion**.
- The epithelial cells contain lots of **mitochondria** to make ATP, needed for **active transport**.

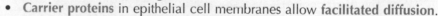

Practice Questions

Q1 What is saliva made of?

Q2 What is peristalsis?

Q3 What is an exopeptidase?

Q4 What is the difference in function between the duodenum and the ileum?

Q5 Draw the layers of the gut wall, label them and describe the functions.

Exam Questions

Q1 Explain how protein is broken down in the digestive system. [4 marks]

Q2 Describe what role the ileum plays in the human digestive system. [3 marks]

My mum told me mastication would make me go blind...

Quite a bit to learn here — it's understandable, 'cos digestion is a complicated process with many stages. The key thing is to learn what each bit of the gut does and how it's adapted to do this function. Make sure you know the difference between endo- and exopeptidases. Then eat some food, and revise its process down the body, not lingering on the last stage though.

SECTION TEN — EXCHANGE AND TRANSPORT IN ANIMALS

Exchange and Transport in Plants

Skip these pages if you are doing AQA A.

Plants can't sing, juggle or tap-dance (as you will hopefully be aware). But they can exchange gases — how exciting. What makes it all the more thrilling is that they lose water vapour as they do it. Gripping stuff.

Plants **Exchange Gases** at the **Surface** of the **Mesophyll Cells**

Two processes in plants involve gas exchange:

1) **Respiration takes in oxygen** and **releases carbon dioxide** — just like in animals.

2) **Photosynthesis** involves **taking in carbon dioxide** and **releasing oxygen**.

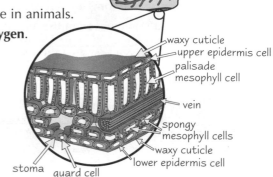

The main gas exchange surface is the **surface of the mesophyll cells** in the leaf. This is well adapted for its function — it's **moist**, and there's a **large surface area**.

The mesophyll cells are inside the leaf. Gases pass back and forth from the outside through special pores in the **epidermis** called **stomata** (singular = stoma). The stomata can open to allow exchange of gases, and close if the plant is losing too much water.

waxy cuticle
upper epidermis cell
palisade mesophyll cell
vein
spongy mesophyll cells
waxy cuticle
lower epidermis cell
stoma   guard cell

Guard Cells Help Control when Stomata Open and Close

1) Each stoma is surrounded by **guard cells**.

2) The stoma opens when the guard cells **increase in turgidity**.

3) They become turgid by absorbing water by **osmosis**. When this happens, each guard cell changes shape because its **inner cell wall** is **thicker** than its outer one. This opens the pore, as the diagram shows. ⇒

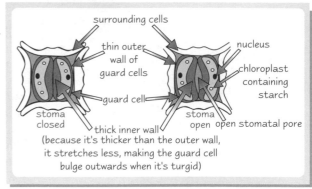

surrounding cells
thin outer wall of guard cells
nucleus
chloroplast containing starch
guard cell
stoma closed
thick inner wall
stoma open open stomatal pore
(because it's thicker than the outer wall, it stretches less, making the guard cell bulge outwards when it's turgid)

Stomata are generally **open** during the **day** so that CO_2 can enter the plant for **photosynthesis** (which needs **light**). They are usually **closed at night** to **save water**, because CO_2 is no longer needed (photosynthesis can't happen in the dark). The **plant controls** when stomata open and close:

When **light shines** on the guard cells, or when there are **low CO_2 concentrations** in the leaf, **two things happen**:

1) A **potassium pump** is triggered, which actively pumps **K^+ ions** into the guard cells from **surrounding cells**.

2) Starch, stored in the **chloroplasts** of guard cells is converted to **malate ions**. **Starch** is insoluble and **doesn't** affect osmosis. **Malate** is soluble and **does affect osmosis**.

This **increases the concentrations** of potassium and malate ions in the guard cells, which **reduces the water potential** of the guard cells (see p.27). This means water is drawn in by osmosis, which **opens the stomata**.

The <u>opposite</u> happens in the <u>dark</u> — the potassium pump stops and malate is converted back to starch. This reduces the concentration of ions in guard cells, so water potential increases. Water leaves the guard cells by osmosis and the <u>stomata close</u> for the night. Sweet dreams.

Transpiration is Loss of Water from a Plant's Surface

Transpiration is a side effect of photosynthesis. **Photosynthesis** uses up **carbon dioxide** and **water** and produces **oxygen** and **glucose**. Water **evaporates** from the moist cell walls and accumulates in the spaces between cells in the leaf. Then it diffuses out of the **stomata** when they open. This happens because there is a **diffusion gradient** — there's more water inside the leaf than in the air outside.

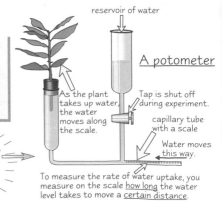

reservoir of water

A potometer

As the plant takes up water, the water moves along the scale.

Tap is shut off during experiment.

capillary tube with a scale

Water moves this way.

A <u>potometer</u> is a special piece of apparatus used to <u>measure transpiration</u>. It actually measures <u>water uptake</u> by a plant, but it's assumed that uptake by the roots is <u>directly related</u> to water loss by the leaves. This lets you see how different factors affect the transpiration rate.

To measure the rate of water uptake, you measure on the scale <u>how long</u> the water level takes to move a <u>certain distance</u>.

NOT OCR

NOT OCR

OCR ONLY

Exchange and Transport in Plants

Four Main Factors Affect Transpiration Rate

The factors below affect transpiration rate. Temperature, humidity and wind alter the **diffusion gradient**, but **light** is a bit different:

1) **Light** — Transpiration happens mainly when the stomata are open. In the dark the stomata usually close, so there's little transpiration.

2) **Temperature** — Diffusion involves the movement of molecules. Increasing the temperature speeds this movement up. So as temperature rises, so does transpiration rate.

3) **Humidity** — If the air around the plant is humid, the **diffusion gradient** between the leaf and the air is reduced. This slows transpiration down.

4) **Wind** — Lots of air movement blows away water molecules from around the stomata. This **increases** the diffusion gradient, which increases the rate of transpiration.

So the rate of transpiration is fastest when it's light, warm, dry and windy.

Xerophytes are Plants that Live in Dry Climates

Xerophytes have adaptations which prevent them losing too much water. Examples of xerophytic adaptations include:

1) Stomata are sunk in **pits**, where water vapour is sheltered from wind.
2) Leaves are **curled** with the stomata inside, again protecting them from wind.
3) Layer of **'hairs'** on the epidermis traps moist air round the stomata, to reduce the diffusion gradient.
4) **Reduced number of stomata**, so there are fewer places where water can escape.
5) Thick, waxy, water-resistant **cuticle** on the epidermis to reduce water loss.
6) **Swollen stem** to store water.
7) **Roots** spread over a **wide area** just below the soil surface, to make the most of any rain.
8) Whole leaf reduced to a **spike** (e.g. cactus). This reduces the surface area for water loss.
9) **Take in CO_2 at night** so they can close their stomata in the day to reduce water loss, and use stored CO_2 for photosynthesis instead.

Practice Questions

Q1 What is the main gas exchange surface in plants?

Q2 What ions are important in the opening and closing mechanism of stomata?

Q3 Define the term 'transpiration'.

Q4 What piece of apparatus is used to measure transpiration?

Exam Questions

Q1 Stomata open and close due to internal changes in the guard cells.
Explain the mechanism that causes these changes. [6 marks]

Q2 Describe factors that can alter the rate of transpiration in a plant, and explain the effect of each. [8 marks]

Q3  The illustration shows a transverse section of a leaf of *Ammophila*, a xerophytic plant. State 4 ways, visible in the picture, that this leaf is adapted to dry conditions. [4 marks]

I don't get it — what's stomata with me?

Actually, that was just a bad joke. Most of it makes sense. The only tricky bit is this diffusion gradient business. All it means is that there's a difference between how many water molecules there are inside the leaf, compared to how many outside. If there aren't many outside but loads inside, they start rushing out to make up for it. The little devils.

Xylem and Phloem

Skip these pages if you are doing AQA A.

*There are two types of tissues in plants that are involved in transport. The **xylem** transports water and mineral salts, while the **phloem** transports dissolved substances, like sugars. The xylem falls in love with the phloem and they get married.*

The **Xylem** Helps **Support** Roots and Stems

Xylem and **phloem** are found throughout the plant — they **transport materials** to all parts of the plant. Where they're found in each structure is connected to the **xylem**'s other function — **support**:

1) In a **root**, which has to resist crushing as it pushes though the soil, the xylem is in the **centre**.

2) In **stems**, which need to resist bending, the xylem is **near the outside** to provide a sort of 'scaffolding'.

3) In a **leaf**, xylem and phloem make up a **network of veins**, which is needed for support because leaves are thin.

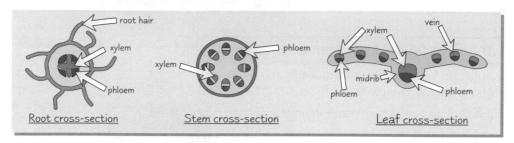

Root cross-section   Stem cross-section   Leaf cross-section

There are **Four Types** of Cell in the **Xylem**

The **xylem tissue** transports **water** and **mineral ions** up through plants. It consists of **vessel elements** and **tracheids**, that do the actual **transporting**, surrounded by extra cells for **packing** (**parenchyma** cells) and **support** (**fibre** cells).

Vessels — These are very long, **tube-like** structures formed from cells (**vessel elements**) joined end to end. There are **no end walls** on these cells, making an **uninterrupted tube** that allows water to pass through easily. The vessels are **dead**, containing **no cytoplasm**. Their walls are thickened with a woody substance called **lignin**, which helps with **support**. The amount of lignin increases as the cell gets older. Substances get into and out of the vessels through small **pits** in the walls, where there is **no lignin**.

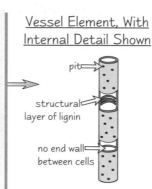

Vessel Element, With Internal Detail Shown

pit

structural layer of lignin

no end wall between cells

Tracheids — Like vessels, these are long, **lignified** cells with no cytoplasm. They don't form continuous tubes like vessels do — instead they **overlap** so that water can pass through. Where cells overlap the wall contains extra pits, so substances can pass easily between cells. These cells are a **more primitive** form of xylem — plants usually have more vessels than tracheids.

Parenchyma Cell

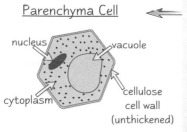

nucleus

vacuole

cytoplasm

cellulose cell wall (unthickened)

Parenchyma Cells — These are the only **living cells** in the xylem. Their cell walls aren't lignified or thickened. They surround the vessels and tracheids. Their functions include food storage and **radial transport** of food and water. **Radial transport** is movement **across** the stem from the outside to the middle, rather than up and down it.

Tracheid Cells

structural layer of lignin

pit

perforated end wall with lots of pits, where cells overlap

cells overlap like this

Cross-section of a Fibre Cell

Fibre Cells — These are small, dead cells with very **thick, lignified** cell walls. Their walls are so thick because the fibres are only used for **support and strength**. They **don't** carry water, so they don't need a wide lumen (the space in the middle).

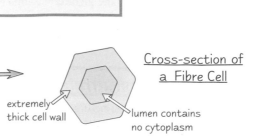

extremely thick cell wall

lumen contains no cytoplasm

Xylem and Phloem

There are Two Main Cell Types in Phloem

Phloem tissue transports **solutes** (dissolved substances — mainly sucrose) round plants.
Like xylem, **phloem** is formed from cells arranged in **tubes**, and these cells are modified for
transport. But, unlike xylem, it's purely a **transport tissue** — it isn't used for support as well.

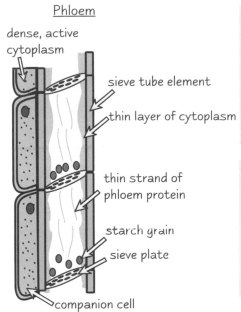

Phloem

dense, active
cytoplasm

sieve tube element

thin layer of cytoplasm

thin strand of
phloem protein

starch grain

sieve plate

companion cell

1) **Sieve tube elements** — These are **living cells** that **transport solutes** through the plant. They are joined end-to-end to form **sieve tubes**. The 'sieve' parts are the end walls, which have lots of holes in them. Unusually for living cells, sieve tube elements have **no nucleus** and only a **very thin layer of cytoplasm** without many organelles. The cytoplasm of adjacent cells is connected through the holes in the sieve plates.

2) **Companion cells** — The lack of a nucleus and other organelles in sieve tube elements means that they would have difficulty surviving on their own. So there is a companion cell for every sieve tube element. The companion cell has a very **dense and active cytoplasm**, and it seems to carry out the living functions for both itself and its sieve cell. Both are formed from a single cell during the development of the phloem.

Phloem tissue also contains **phloem fibres** and **phloem parenchyma**, but sieve tube
elements and companion cells are the most important cell types for transport.

Practice Questions

Q1   State two functions of xylem cells in plants.

Q2   Name four cell types that can be found in the xylem tissue.

Q3   What is the name of the substance that thickens the walls of xylem vessels?

Q4   What is the main solute transported by the phloem?

Q5   What are the two main types of cells found in phloem tissue?

Exam Questions

Q1   Describe the distribution of the xylem and phloem in stems, roots and leaves.
       Explain how this distribution is linked to the function of the xylem.   [10 marks]

Q2   The xylem tissue contains several different types of cell.
       Describe the structure and function of each type.   [12 marks]

Do you, xylem, take phloem, to be your lawful wedded tissue type...

Please don't write the part about them getting married in the exam. I just put that in to make sure you were paying atten
It's vital your mind doesn't wander on this page, because the structure and functions of some of these cell types are qu
It can be easy to get mixed up if you haven't learnt it properly, so take the time now to sort out which cell type does

Water Transport

Skip these pages if you are doing AQA A.

Water enters a plant through its roots and eventually, if it's not used, exits via the leaves. "Ah-ha," I hear you say, "— but how does it flow upwards, against gravity?" Well that, my friends, is a mystery that's about to be revealed.

Water Enters a Plant through its Root Hair Cells

Water has to get from the **soil**, across the **root** and into the **xylem**, which takes it up the plant. The bit of the root that absorbs water is covered in **root hairs**. This increases its surface area and speeds up water uptake. Once it's absorbed, the water has to get through two root tissues, the **cortex** and the **endodermis**, to reach the xylem.

> Water always moves from areas of **higher water potential** to areas of **lower water potential** — it goes down a **water potential gradient**. The **soil** around roots has a **high water potential** (i.e. there's lots of water there) and **leaves** have a **low water potential** (because water constantly **evaporates** from them). This creates a water potential gradient that keeps water moving through the plant in the right direction, **from roots to leaves**.

There are Three Routes Water can Take through the Root

Water can travel through the roots into the xylem by three different paths:

1) The **apoplast pathway** — goes through the **non-living** parts of the root — the **cell walls**. The walls are very absorbent and water can simply diffuse through them, as well as passing through the spaces between them.

2) The **symplast pathway** — goes through the **living** cytoplasm of the cells. The **cytoplasm** of neighbouring cells connects through **plasmodesmata** (small gaps in the cell walls).

3) The **vacuolar pathway** — water travels from the vacuole of one cell into the vacuole of the next by **osmosis**.

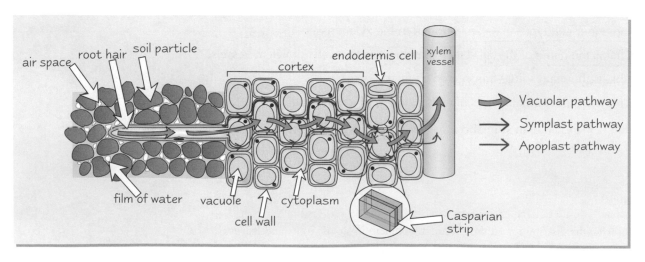

All three pathways are used, but the main one is the **apoplast pathway** because it provides the **least resistance**. When the water gets to the **endodermis** cells, though, the apoplast pathway is blocked by a **waxy strip** in the cell walls, called the **Casparian strip**, which the water can't penetrate. Now the water has to take one of the other pathways. This is useful, because it means the water has to go through a **cell membrane**. Cell membranes are able to control whether or not substances in the water get through (see p.24). Once past this barrier, the water moves into the **xylem**.

Water Transport

Water Moves *Up* a Plant *Against* the Force of *Gravity*

The **cohesion-tension theory** explains how water moves up plants from roots to leaves, against the force of gravity.

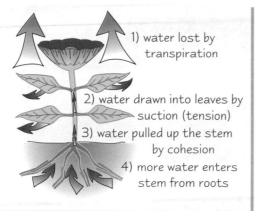

1) water lost by transpiration

2) water drawn into leaves by suction (tension)

3) water pulled up the stem by cohesion

4) more water enters stem from roots

1) Water evaporates from the leaves at the 'top' of the xylem (through transpiration).

2) This creates a **suction** ('tension'), which pulls more water into the leaf.

3) Water molecules **stick together** ('cohesion' — see p.16), so when some are pulled into the leaf others follow.

4) This means the whole **column** of water in the xylem, from the leaves down to the roots, moves upwards.

It's like what happens when you suck at the top of a drinking straw and the liquid moves up it.

Root pressure also helps move the water upwards. Water is transported into the xylem in the roots, which creates a pressure and tends to shove water already in the xylem further upwards. This pressure is weak, and couldn't move water to the top of bigger plants by itself. It helps though, especially in young, small plants where the leaves are still developing.

Plants Need to Absorb *Mineral Ions* as well as *Water*

Plants absorb **dissolved mineral ions** from the soil. This can happen by **diffusion**, but diffusion **isn't** a selective process — and plants often **only** need **certain ions** and not others. So instead, ions needed by a plant are absorbed by **active transport** (see p.28). This means a plant can absorb more of a certain ion, even if it already has a **high concentration** of them **inside** its cells — so it doesn't have to rely on there being a **diffusion gradient** into the plant. It also means that the plant can **pump out** any ions it **doesn't need**.

> Mineral ions travel up the plant with the water, in the **xylem**.
> Scientists know this because of experiments using **radioactive tracers**.
> This uses radioactive forms of ions, so that the radioactivity can be detected and the scientist will know where the ion has gone.

Practice Questions

Q1 In what way are roots adapted to absorb water?

Q2 Name the three pathways by which water travels across the root.

Q3 What is the Casparian strip and in which root tissue would you find it?

Q4 Explain why active transport is necessary for the absorption of mineral ions by the roots of a plant.

Exam Questions

Q1 Explain the role of each of the following in the transport of ions in the root.
a) cell walls
b) the endodermis
c) plasmodesmata
[6 marks]

Q2 Explain why movement of water in the xylem stops if the leaves of a plant are removed.
[4 marks]

So many routes through the roots...

Lots of impressive biological words on this page, to amaze your friends and confound your enemies. Go through the page again, and whenever you see a word like plasmodesmata, just stop and check you know exactly what it means. (Personally I think they should just call them cell wall gaps, but nobody ever listens to me.)

Translocation

Skip these pages if you are doing AQA A.

Translocation is the movement of organic solutes through a plant. It happens in the phloem.
Annoyingly, translocation sounds a lot like transpiration. Or is that just me? Don't confuse them anyway.

The Main Things **Translocated** are **Amino Acids** and **Sugars**

1) Sugars (mostly sucrose) are transported from the leaves (where they're made during photosynthesis) to **actively growing regions**, or to **storage sites**.

2) Amino acids are made in the **root tips** (where nitrogen is absorbed), and are carried to **growing areas** in the plant to **make proteins**.

The way that they're transported in the phloem isn't known exactly, but it is known that it's an active process, needing energy from respiration.

Translocation is the **movement of dissolved organic substances** (mainly sucrose) to **where they're needed** in the plant. Experiments show that it happens in the **phloem** (see section below).

Translocation moves substances from '**sources**' to '**sinks**'. The **source** of a substance is **where it's made** (so it's in **high concentration** there). The **sink** is the area where it's **used up** (so it's in **low concentration** there). For example, the source for sugars is the **leaves**, and the sinks are the other parts of the plant, especially the **food storage organs** and **growing points** in roots, stems and leaves.

Enzymes maintain a **concentration gradient** from the phloem to the sink by **modifying** the organic substances at the sink. For example, in **potatoes**, sucrose is converted to **starch** in the sink areas, so there's always a lower concentration of sucrose at the sink than inside the phloem. This makes sure a **constant supply** of new sucrose reaches the sink from the phloem.

Experiments Show **Where** Substances Move to by **Translocation**

Experiments done with **radioactive tracer substances** show how organic **solutes** (**dissolved** organic substances) **move around** in plants. **Radioactive sucrose** is put on a leaf and moves through the plant. This is detected by putting the plant in contact with **photographic film**. Wherever the radioactive sucrose goes, it can be 'seen', because it **fogs** the film. The experiment below shows that, unlike water and mineral ions, which **only move upwards** in the xylem, sucrose moves both **up and down** from the leaf it was added to. This movement can be stopped by **removing a ring of phloem** from the stem. The xylem is still there, so the experiment shows that translocation occurs in the phloem and not in the xylem.

Experiment Showing:

A) that sucrose moves up and down the plant,

B) that translocation occurs in the phloem, not the xylem.

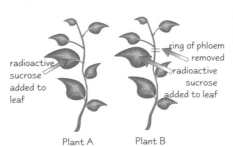

radioactive sucrose added to leaf

ring of phloem removed

radioactive sucrose added to leaf

Plant A   Plant B

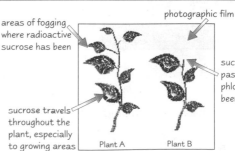

areas of fogging where radioactive sucrose has been

photographic film

sucrose can't pass point where phloem has been removed

sucrose travels throughout the plant, especially to growing areas

Plant A   Plant B

The **Mass Flow Hypothesis** Best Explains **Phloem Transport**

It's still not certain exactly how the solutes are transported from source to sink by translocation. The best supported theory is the **mass flow hypothesis**.

The mass flow hypothesis:

1) Dissolved sugars from photosynthesis (e.g. sucrose) are **actively transported** into the **sieve tubes** of the phloem at the **leaves** (the **source**). This **lowers the water potential** inside the sieve tubes, so water enters the tubes by **osmosis**. This creates a **high pressure** inside the sieve tubes at the source end of the phloem.

2) At the **sink** end, **sugars leave** the phloem to be used up, which **increases the water potential** inside the sieve tubes, so water also leaves the tubes by **osmosis**. This **lowers the pressure** inside the sieve tubes.

3) The result is a **pressure gradient** from source end to sink end, which pushes sugars along the sieve tubes to where they're needed.

Translocation

Mass Flow Hypothesis Can be Demonstrated in an Experiment

The idea behind the hypothesis can be shown in the experiment below.
In this model, **A** and **B** are two containers, each lined with a **selectively permeable membrane**.

1) **A** represents the **source** end and contains a **concentrated sugar solution**.

2) **B** represents the **sink** end, where **use** of the sugar **lowers** its concentration.

3) Water enters **A** by **osmosis**, causing the sugar solution to flow along the **top tube** — which represents the **phloem**.

4) **Hydrostatic pressure** increases in **B**, forcing water out and back through the **connecting tube** — which represents the **xylem**, because it just transports water.

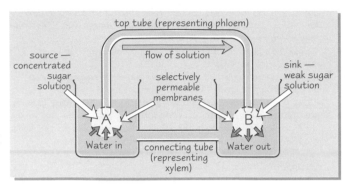

In the model, the **flow stops** when the sugar concentrations in the two containers **equal out**.
But in a plant this **wouldn't happen**, as sugar would constantly be produced by the source and used up by the sink.

Supporting evidence for this theory includes —
1) There is a suitable **water potential gradient** between the leaves and the other parts of the plant.
2) If the phloem is cut sap oozes out, showing that a **pressure gradient** does exist.

Objections to the theory are —
1) Sugar travels to many different sinks, not just to the one with the **highest water potential**, as the model would suggest.
2) The sieve plates would create a barrier to mass flow. A lot of pressure would be needed for the sugar solution to get through.
3) Mass flow doesn't require living cells, yet the **phloem cells** are alive and very active.

This book ain't over 'til the fat pig sings.

Practice Questions

Q1 Explain the terms 'source' and 'sink' in connection with translocation.
Q2 How can you detect the location of radioactive tracers in a plant?
Q3 State two pieces of evidence that support the mass flow hypothesis for translocation.

Exam Questions

Q1 Radioactive glucose is placed on the leaf of a plant, which is then left for 24 hrs. The radioactivity is then detected by placing the plant in contact with photographic film. In which areas of the plant would you expect to see most radioactivity? Give reasons for your answer. [2 marks]

Q2 The mass flow hypothesis depends on there being a difference in pressure in the phloem sieve tubes between the source and the sink. Explain how sugars cause the pressure to increase at the source end, according to the mass flow hypothesis. [4 marks]

Who cares whether the hypothesis is right — it's the last page...

Blimey it's the end of the book. A sad, sad moment for biology students everywhere. But hey, at least the pig's happy. He's still alive at the end of it all — he's survived cloning, coronary heart disease and the nitrogen cycle, amongst everything else. So I think we should all join in for a grand finale sing-song. OK, maybe not — I think I need to go now.

Answers

Section 1 — Cell Structure
Page 3 — Cell Organisation

1   Maximum of 9 marks available.
     1 mark for each example — e.g. ciliated epithelium, alveolar/
     squamous epithelium, intestinal epithelium [maximum of 3 marks].
     Up to 6 marks for explaining how their structure is linked to their
     function. E.g. Ciliated epithelium has cilia [1 mark] which allow the
     epithelium to move things [1 mark].
     It would be a good idea to give an example of what might be being
     moved (e.g. mucus, ova).
     Alveolar epidermis is thin [1 mark] so that respiratory gases can
     diffuse through it easily [1 mark].
     Intestinal epithelium has microvilli [1 mark] which increase its surface
     area [1 mark] for absorption of food.
     The examples above are from the syllabus. You could also get the marks if
     you know of any other examples from your reading / lessons.

2   Maximum of 12 marks available.
     Up to 6 marks for correctly naming each leaf tissue.
     Up to 6 marks for explaining each tissue's adaptation:
     Lower epidermis [1 mark] — has stomata which allow carbon dioxide
     and oxygen in and out [1 mark].
     Spongy mesophyll [1 mark] — has air spaces which allow gases to
     circulate [1 mark].
     Palisade mesophyll [1 mark] — has many chloroplasts to absorb
     sunlight [1 mark].
     Upper epidermis [1 mark] — waterproof to keep water in [1 mark].
     Xylem [1 mark] — delivers water to the leaf [1 mark].
     Phloem [1 mark] — transports sugars away from the leaf [1 mark].

Page 5 — Electron and Light Microscopy

1   Maximum of 6 marks available.
     Advantages: Greater resolution [1 mark].
     More detail / internal structure of organelles can be seen [1 mark].
     Disadvantages: Electron microscopes can't be used to study living
     tissues [1 mark].
     Natural colours can't be seen [1 mark]. They aren't portable
     [1 mark]. They are expensive [1 mark].

2   Maximum of 5 marks available.
     The cells are homogenised [1 mark] in ice cold isotonic
     buffer solution [1 mark]. The cold makes sure that any protein
     digesting enzymes that are released don't digest the organelles
     [1 mark]. The buffer keeps the pH constant [1 mark] and the isotonic
     solution ensures that osmosis does not occur as this could harm the
     organelles [1 mark].

Page 7 — Functions of Organelles

1   Maximum of 9 marks available.
     You could have written about any three of the four organelles given
     below.
     Mitochondria [1 mark] — Large numbers of mitochondria would
     indicate that the cell used a lot of energy [1 mark], because
     mitochondria are the site of (aerobic) respiration, which releases
     energy [1 mark].
     Chloroplasts [1 mark] — Large numbers of chloroplasts would be seen
     in cells that are involved in photosynthesis [1 mark] because the
     chloroplasts contain chlorophyll, which absorbs light for photosynthesis
     [1 mark].
     Rough endoplasmic reticulum [1 mark] —
     You find a lot of RER in cells that produce a lot of protein [1 mark]
     because the RER transports protein made in the attached ribosomes
     [1 mark]
     Lysosomes [1 mark] — Found in cells that are old / destroy other cells
     [1 mark] because lysosomes contain digestive enzymes that can
     break down cells [1 mark].
     There are 9 marks for this question and 3 organelles have to be
     mentioned — so it's logical that each organelle provides 3 marks. You
     get a mark for mentioning the correct organelles, so you need to give 2
     pieces of relevant information for each one.

2 a)   Maximum of 2 marks available.
       i)   mitochondrion [1 mark]
       ii)   Golgi apparatus [1 mark]
   b)   Maximum of 2 marks available:
       The function of the mitochondrion is to be the site of (aerobic)
       respiration / provide energy [1 mark].
       The function of the Golgi apparatus is to package materials made in
       the cell / to make lysosomes [1 mark].
       The question doesn't ask you to give the reasons why you identified the
       organelles as you did, so don't waste time writing your reasons down.

Section 2 — Biological Molecules
Page 9 — Biochemical Tests for Molecules

1   Maximum of 14 marks available.
     Test for starch [1 mark] by adding iodine in potassium iodide
     [1 mark]. A positive reaction would have a blue-black colour
     [1 mark].
     Test for reducing sugar [1 mark] by heating with Benedict's reagent
     [1 mark]. The formation of a brick red precipitate would indicate the
     presence of reducing sugar [1 mark].
     Instead of mentioning red precipitate, you could just describe a colour
     change from blue to brick red.
     Test for non-reducing sugars [1 mark] by boiling with hydrochloric
     acid and then neutralising before doing the Benedict's test [1 mark].
     Test for proteins [1 mark] by adding sodium hydroxide solution, then
     copper (II) sulphate solution [1 mark]. Protein is indicated by a
     purple colour [1 mark].
     Test for lipids [1 mark] by adding ethanol then mixing with water
     [1 mark]. Lipid is indicated by a milky colour [1 mark].
     For full marks, make sure you've mentioned what each biochemical group
     is, how you test for it and what results you might get.

2   Maximum of 7 marks available.
     Grind up the leaves in a solvent [1 mark].
     Add a drop of the extract to strip of chromatography paper [1 mark].
     Place the end of the paper into a solvent so that the solvent rises up
     the paper [1 mark].
     Measure the distance that the solvent has travelled [1 mark] and the
     distance that each spot of pigment has travelled [1 mark].
     To identify the pigments calculate their Rf values [1 mark] by using
     the formula Rf = distance travelled by pigment/distance travelled by
     solvent [1 mark].
     Sometimes it is easier or quicker to describe something in a diagram
     rather than in words (e.g. calculating Rf values). You can get full marks
     this way as long as the diagram shows what the examiner wants to know.

Page 11 — Carbohydrates

1   Maximum of 7 marks available.
     Glycosidic bonds are formed by condensation reactions [1 mark] and
     broken by hydrolysis reactions [1 mark].
     When a glycosidic bond is formed in a condensation reaction,
     a hydrogen [1 mark] from one monosaccharide combines with
     a hydroxyl / OH group [1 mark] from the other to form a molecule
     of water [1 mark].
     A hydrolysis reaction is the reverse of this [1 mark], with a molecule
     of water being used up to split the monosaccharide molecules apart
     [1 mark].
     The last 5 marks for this question could be obtained by a diagram
     showing the reaction, using structural formulae.

2   Maximum of 10 marks available.
     Glycogen is a chain of alpha glucose molecules [1 mark] whereas
     cellulose is a chain of beta glucose molecules [1 mark].
     Glycogen's chain is compact and very branched [1 mark] whereas
     cellulose's chain is long, straight and unbranched [1 mark] and these
     chains are bonded together to form strong fibres [1 mark].
     Glycogen's structure makes it a good food store in animals [1 mark].
     The branches allow enzymes to access the glycosidic bonds to break
     the food store down quickly [1 mark].
     Cellulose's structure makes it a good supporting structure in cell walls
     [1 mark]. The fibres provide strength [1 mark].

Answers

The function is helped by the fact that the cell doesn't have any enzymes that can break down beta bonds **[1 mark]**.

In questions worth lots of marks make sure you include enough details. This question is worth 10 marks so you should include at least 10 relevant points to score full marks. Also, the question asks you to compare and contrast, so make sure you don't just describe glycogen and cellulose totally separately from each other. You need to highlight how they differ from each other, and what this means for their functions.

Page 13 — Lipids

1 Maximum of 10 marks available.
Up to 5 marks for correctly naming the 5 functions.
Up to 5 marks for explaining the relevant features.
Energy store **[1 mark]** — lipids contain a lot of energy per gram **[1 mark]**.
Insulation **[1 mark]** — the lipid layer under the skin doesn't have an extensive blood supply so heat isn't lost from it **[1 mark]**.
Buoyancy **[1 mark]** — the lipid layer is less dense than muscle and bone **[1 mark]**.
Protection **[1 mark]** — the fat layer under the skin and around internal organs acts like a cushion to prevent damage from any blows **[1 mark]**.
Waterproofing **[1 mark]** — lipids don't mix / dissolve in water, so water can't penetrate a lipid layer **[1 mark]**.

2 Maximum of 8 marks available.
Triglycerides are made from a glycerol molecule **[1 mark]** and three molecules of fatty acids **[1 mark]**. They are formed by condensation reactions **[1 mark]**. These reactions result in the formation of ester bonds **[1 mark]** between the fatty acid and glycerol molecules, with the production of a molecule of water for each fatty acid added **[1 mark]**. Triglycerides are broken up by hydrolysis reactions **[1 mark]**, which are the reverse of condensation reactions **[1 mark]**, with one molecule of water being added for each fatty acid that's released **[1 mark]**.
It would be possible to get all the marks in this question by using labelled diagrams, as long as all the points listed have been illustrated.

3 Maximum of 8 marks available.
A triglyceride consists of glycerol **[1 mark]** and three fatty acid molecules **[1 mark]**. A phospholipid has the same basic structure, but one of the fatty acids is replaced by a phosphate group **[1 mark]**.
Triglycerides are hydrophobic / repel water **[1 mark]**. This is a property of the hydrocarbon chains that are part of the fatty acid molecules **[1 mark]**. The phosphate group in a phospholipid is hydrophilic / attracts water **[1 mark]**, because it's ionised **[1 mark]**. This means that the phospholipid has a hydrophilic 'head' and a hydrophobic 'tail' **[1 mark]**.
The words 'head' and 'tail' are not essential, as long as you have got across the idea that the molecule is partly hydrophobic and partly hydrophilic.

Page 15 — Proteins

Maximum of 10 marks available.
Proteins are made from amino acids **[1 mark]**.
The amino acids are joined together in a long (polypeptide) chain **[1 mark]**.
The sequence of amino acids is the protein's primary structure **[1 mark]**.
The amino acid chain / polypeptide coils in a certain way **[1 mark]**.
The way it's coiled is the protein's secondary structure **[1 mark]**.
The coiled chain is itself folded into a specific shape **[1 mark]**.
This is the protein's tertiary structure **[1 mark]**.
Different polypeptide chains can be joined together in the protein molecule **[1 mark]**.
This is the quaternary structure of the protein **[1 mark]**.
The question specifically states that you don't need to describe the chemical nature of the bonds in a protein. So, even if you name them, don't go into chemical details of how they're formed — no credit will be given.

2 Maximum of 6 marks available.
Collagen is a fibrous protein **[1 mark]**.
For this mark, mentioning that the molecule is fibrous is essential.
It forms supportive tissues in the body **[1 mark]**.
Collagen consists of three polypeptide chains **[1 mark]**.
These chains form a triple helix **[1 mark]**.
The chains are tightly coiled together **[1 mark]**.
The tightly coiled chains provide strength to the structure **[1 mark]**.
Minerals can bind to the collagen chain **[1 mark]**.
This makes it more rigid **[1 mark]**.
8 marks are listed, but the mark is given out of 6. This is common in longer exam questions. You would have to be a bit of a mind-reader to hit every mark the examiner thinks of, so to make it fair, there are more mark points than marks. You can only count a maximum of 6, though.

Page 17 — Water and Inorganic Ions

1 Maximum of 12 marks available, from any of the 15 mark points listed.
Water molecules have two hydrogen atoms and one oxygen atom **[1 mark]**.
The hydrogen and oxygen are joined by covalent bonds / sharing electrons **[1 mark]**.
Water molecules are polar **[1 mark]**.
Polarity leads to the formation of hydrogen bonds between water molecules **[1 mark]**.
Water is a solvent **[1 mark]**.
Water's polar nature allows water to dissolve polar solutes **[1 mark]**.
Water transports substances **[1 mark]**.
Substances are transported more easily when dissolved **[1 mark]**.
Water has a high specific heat capacity **[1 mark]**.
This is due to hydrogen bonds restricting movement **[1 mark]**.
This means it's difficult to change the temperature of water **[1 mark]**.
This allows cells to avoid sudden changes in temperature **[1 mark]**.
Water has a high latent heat of evaporation **[1 mark]**.
This is due to hydrogen bonding **[1 mark — but only awarded if hydrogen bonding hasn't already been mentioned]**.
It means the evaporation of water has a considerable cooling effect **[1 mark]**.
Be careful to stick to what the question asks for. The fact that ice floats on water and aquatic habitats have stable temperatures aren't things that happen "in living organisms".

2 Maximum of 7 marks available.
Magnesium is a constituent of chlorophyll **[1 mark]**.
If there's a lack of magnesium then chlorophyll can't be made, and the leaves will be pale or yellow **[1 mark]**.
If there is less chlorophyll, there will be less photosynthesis **[1 mark]**.
Low rates of photosynthesis will result in the plant growing less **[1 mark]**.
Nitrogen is needed for the manufacture of proteins **[1 mark]**.
Proteins are need for growth **[1 mark]**.
A nitrogen shortage will lead to a shortage of protein, and the plant's growth will be stunted **[1 mark]**.

Section 3 — Enzymes
Page 19 — Action of Enzymes

1 Maximum of 8 marks available.
'Lock and key' model —
The enzyme and the substrate have to fit together at the active site of the enzyme **[1 mark]**.
This creates an enzyme-substrate complex **[1 mark]**.
The active site then causes changes in the substrate **[1 mark]**.
This mark could also be gained by explaining the change (e.g. bringing molecules closer together, or putting a strain on bonds).
The change results in the substrate being assembled / broken down **[1 mark]**.
'Induced fit' model — has the same basic mechanism as the lock and key model **[1 mark]**.
The difference is that the substrate is thought to cause a change in the enzyme's active site **[1 mark]**, which enables a better fit **[1 mark]**.

Answers

2 Maximum of 4 marks available.
*Put the potato and hydrogen peroxide solution in a test tube joined by a delivery tube to an upturned measuring cylinder in a bowl of water [**2 marks available for correctly naming all the apparatus; 1 mark if most of the apparatus is named**].*
*You then use the measuring cylinder to measure the amount of oxygen produced by the reaction [**1 mark**] over a specified time (e.g. one minute) [**1 mark**].*
You could also draw an annotated diagram of the experiment to get all the marks. Other experiments are possible — for example, using a gas syringe.

Page 21 — Factors that Affect Enzyme Activity

1 Maximum of 8 marks available, from any of the 9 points below.
*If the solution is too cold, the enzyme will work very slowly [**1 mark**].*
*This is because, at low temperatures, the molecules move slowly and collisions are less likely between enzyme and substrate molecules [**1 mark**].*
The marks above could also be obtained by giving the reverse argument — a higher temperature is best to use because the molecules will move fast enough to give a reasonable chance of collisions.
*If the temperature gets too high, the reaction will stop [**1 mark**].*
*This is because the enzyme is denatured [**1 mark**] — the active site changes and will no longer fit the substrate [**1 mark**].*
*Denaturation is caused by increased vibration breaking bonds in the enzyme [**1 mark**].*
*Enzymes have an optimum pH [**1 mark**].*
*pH values too far from the optimum cause denaturation [**1 mark**].*
Explanation of denaturation here will get a mark only if it hasn't been explained earlier.
*Denaturation by pH is caused by disruption of ionic bonds, which destabilises the enzyme's tertiary structure [**1 mark**].*

2 Maximum of 4 marks available.
*Chemical X is an enzyme inhibitor [**1 mark**]*
*Reason — it reduces an enzyme controlled reaction [**1 mark**]*
*The inhibitor is probably competitive [**1 mark**]*
*Reason — increasing the concentration of the inhibitor makes it more effective, because if there are a lot of inhibitor molecules they're more likely to reach active sites before the substrate molecules and will block them [**1 mark**].*

Page 23 — Industrial Production of Useful Enzymes

1 a) Maximum of 3 marks available.
Any 3 of these:
*They're easier to isolate than intracellular enzymes [**1 mark**].*
*You don't need to break open cells to get to them [**1 mark**].*
*You don't need to separate them from all the other stuff inside a cell — they're usually secreted from the cell on their own [**1 mark**].*
*They're more stable than intracellular enzymes, which are often only stable within the cell environment [**1 mark**].*
 b) Maximum of 2 marks available.
Any 2 of these:
*May compete for nutrients [**1 mark**].*
*May produce toxic substances [**1 mark**].*
*Production time, and therefore money, wasted cleaning the equipment [**1 mark**].*
This question is basically just common sense. Sometimes you'll be asked questions that require you to think around a topic for yourself a bit. They'll always be very straightforward questions like this, though.

2 a) Maximum of 2 marks available.
*Immobilised enzymes aren't free in solution [**1 mark**].*
*Instead they're absorbed on / trapped in / encapsulated in an inert (non-reactive) material [**1 mark**].*
It might seem like these two points are saying the same thing but they are actually different, so you have to make sure you mention both of them.
 b) Maximum of 2 marks available. Any 2 of these:
*Does not contaminate the product [**1 mark**].*
*Can be easily recovered and used again [**1 mark**].*
*More stable [**1 mark**].*

Section 4 — Cell Membranes
Page 25 — The Cell Membrane Structure

1 a) Maximum of 1 mark available.
*In a triglyceride there are three fatty acids attached to a molecule of glycerol but in a phospholipid one of the fatty acids is replaced by a phosphate group [**1 mark**].*
 b) Maximum of 2 marks available.
*Phospholipids are arranged in a double layer / bilayer with fatty acid tails on the inside [**1 mark**].*
*Fatty acid tails are hydrophobic / non-polar so they prevent the passage of water soluble molecules through the cell membrane [**1 mark**].*
Occasionally a question may ask you to show how a single layer of phospholipid molecules would arrange themselves on the surface of a container of water. You should draw the molecules with their hydrophilic phosphate heads in the water and their hydrophobic fatty acid tails sticking up into the air.

2 a) Maximum of 2 marks available.
*A is an extrinsic protein / receptor protein [**1 mark**].*
*B is an intrinsic protein / carrier protein [**1 mark**].*
 b) Maximum of 2 marks available.
*Tertiary structure gives the receptor protein a particular shape [**1 mark**]*
*Only molecules with a specific shape will fit into (or bind with) the protein [**1 mark**]*

Page 29 — Transport Across the Cell Membrane

1 Maximum of 2 marks available.
*The ions are moving faster / have more kinetic energy [**1 mark**], so more ions will diffuse through the membrane in a given time [**1 mark**].*

2 a) Maximum of 3 marks available.
*Root hair cell has a more negative / lower water potential than the soil water [**1 mark**] because it has a greater concentration of dissolved solutes [**1 mark**].*
*So water moves into the cell by osmosis from a higher water potential to a lower water potential [**1 mark**].*
 b) Maximum of 3 marks available.
*Shape increases the outer surface area of the cell membrane in contact with the soil [**1 mark**].*
*There are many carrier proteins in the membrane for active transport [**1 mark**]. There are many mitochondria in the cytoplasm for the production of the ATP needed for active transport [**1 mark**].*
When answering questions on adaptations, always link the physical feature to its function.

Section 5 — DNA and RNA
Page 31— Structure of DNA and The Genetic Code

1 Maximum of 2 marks available.
*The long length and coiled nature of DNA molecules allows the storage of vast quantities of information [**1 mark**].*
You only get the mark here if you've mentioned the length <u>and</u> the coiled nature.
*Good at replicating itself because of the two strands being paired [**1 mark**].*
The question is worth two marks so you need to mention at least two things.

2 Maximum of 5 marks available.
*Nucleotides are joined by condensation reactions [**1 mark**].*
*This happens between the phosphate group and the sugar of the next nucleotide [**1 mark**].*
*The DNA strands join through hydrogen bonds [**1 mark**] between the base pairs [**1 mark**].*
*The final mark is given for at least one accurate diagram showing at least one of the above processes [**1 mark**].*
As the question asks for a diagram make sure you do at least one.

Answers

Page 33 — DNA Self-Replication and RNA

1   Maximum of 6 marks available.
DNA strands uncoil and separate *[1 mark]*.
Individual free DNA nucleotides pair up with their complementary bases on the template strand *[1 mark]*.
DNA polymerase joins the individual nucleotides together *[1 mark]*.
Students often forget to mention this enzyme in their answers.
Hydrogen bonds then form between the bases on each strand *[1 mark]*.
Two identical DNA molecules are produced *[1 mark]*.
Each of the new molecules contains a single strand from the original DNA molecule and a single new strand *[1 mark]*.

Page 35 — Protein Synthesis

1   Maximum of 2 marks available.
A codon is a triplet of bases found on a mRNA molecule *[1 mark]*.
An anticodon is a triplet of bases found on a tRNA molecule *[1 mark]*.
This question is only worth two marks so the examiner only expects a brief answer.

2   Maximum of 10 marks available.
Transcription happens inside the nucleus and translation outside in the cytoplasm *[1 mark]*.
A section of DNA is uncoiled by breaking hydrogen bonds *[1 mark]*.
mRNA makes a copy of an uncoiled section of DNA *[1 mark]*.
The mRNA travels outside the nucleus to a ribosome *[1 mark]*.
The codons on the mRNA are paired with anticodons on a molecule of tRNA *[1 mark]*.
The tRNA molecules are carrying amino acids *[1 mark]* which line up and are joined by peptide bonds with an enzyme *[1 mark]*.
You must mention that an enzyme is involved to get this mark.
Specific codons / base triplets code for specific amino acids *[1 mark]*.
A polypeptide chain is formed *[1 mark]* — the primary structure of a protein *[1 mark]*.

Section 6 — Reproduction
Page 37 — The Cell Cycle and Mitosis

1 a) Maximum of 6 marks available.
A = Metaphase *[1 mark]*, because the chromosomes are lining up at the equator *[1 mark]*.
B = Telophase *[1 mark]*, because the cytoplasm is dividing to form two new cells *[1 mark]*.
C = Anaphase *[1 mark]*, because the centromeres have divided and the chromatids are moving to opposite poles *[1 mark]*.
If you've learned the diagrams of what happens at each stage of mitosis, this should be a breeze. That's why it'd be a total disaster if you lost three marks for forgetting to give reasons for your answers. Always read the question properly and do exactly what it tells you to do.
  b) Maximum of 3 marks available:
X = Chromatid *[1 mark]*.
Y = Centromere *[1 mark]*.
Z = Spindle fibre *[1 mark]*.

2 a) Maximum of 2 marks available.
Interphase *[1 mark]*, during the S or Synthesis stage *[1 mark]*.
  b) Maximum of 2 marks available:
Mitosis *[1 mark]*, during the prophase stage *[1 mark]*.
Sometimes you can pick up marks even if you're only half right. You might know spindle fibres are formed during mitosis, but you've forgotten which stage. It's worth mentioning mitosis anyway, and then having a guess. You won't lose marks if your guess is wrong, and even if it was you'd have picked up one mark just for saying mitosis. Better than leaving it blank.

Page 39 — Cloning, Mutation and Cancer

1 a) Maximum of 1 mark available.
This is a substitution / thymine's been substituted by adenine *[1 mark]*.
Make sure you say which base has been changed by the mutation. In this case, Thymine has been substituted by Adenine. You might not get the mark if you just say it's a substitution.
  b) Maximum of 3 marks available.
The different base results in the codon coding for a different amino acid *[1 mark]*.
The new protein formed has a different three-dimensional (tertiary) structure to the original protein *[1 mark]*.
This abnormal protein can't function in the same way as the original *[1 mark]*.

2   Maximum of 2 marks available.
1 mark for any of the points below —
The enzyme that usually catalyses the reaction no longer functions properly *[1 mark]*.
This may be due to a mutation in the allele, which codes for this enzyme *[1 mark]*.
A change in the DNA will result in a protein that has a different shape *[1 mark]* and the enzyme will no longer function, as it can't bind to its active site *[1 mark]*.
Bear in mind an enzyme works by binding to the active site of its substrate. The substrate will have a complementary shape to the enzyme's active site — if the enzyme's shape is altered due to a mutation, the substrate can no longer fit into it.

Page 41 — Meiosis and Sexual Reproduction

1 a) Maximum of 3 marks available.
A = 46 *[1 mark]*.
B = 23 *[1 mark]*.
C = 23 *[1 mark]*.
  b) Maximum of 2 marks available, from any of the points below.
Normal body cells have two copies of each chromosome, which they inherit from their parents *[1 mark]*.
Gametes have to have half the number of chromosomes so that when fertilisation takes place, the resulting embryo will have the correct diploid number *[1 mark]*.
If the gametes had a diploid number, the resulting offspring would have twice the number of chromosomes that it should have *[1 mark]*.

Page 43 — Reproduction in Humans

1 a) Maximum of 2 marks available.
At Y — Primary follicle has developed into a mature Graafian follicle *[1 mark]*.
At Z — Graafian follicle ruptures to release the egg into the fallopian tube — ovulation *[1 mark]*.
  b) Maximum of 3 marks available, from any of the points below.
Primary follicle stimulated to develop by the sex hormone FSH *[1 mark]*.
Follicle matures into a Graafian follicle, which migrates to the surface of the ovary *[1 mark]*.
Luteinising hormone is released into the bloodstream, which causes the follicle to burst *[1 mark]* releasing the egg into the fallopian tube *[1 mark]*.
This is an 'explain' question so needs more detail. To get it right you have to remember the oocyte's fertilised in the oviduct or fallopian tube. Hormones play a crucial role, so must be mentioned in your answer.

Answers

Page 45 — Hormones and the Menstrual Cycle

1 a) Maximum of 2 marks available.
   Oestrogen *[1 mark]*.
   Progesterone *[1 mark]*.
  b) Maximum of 3 marks available.
   These hormones inhibit FSH *[1 mark]*.
   FSH stimulates development of follicles, so inhibiting it means no follicles can mature *[1 mark]*.
   Ovulation can't take place *[1 mark]*.
  c) Maximum of 4 marks available, from any of the following or any other sensible answers.
   Arguments for —
   Allows a woman to have children *[1 mark]* that are genetically related to her *[1 mark]*.
   The method's much cheaper *[1 mark]* and less stressful than IVF *[1 mark]*.
   Arguments against —
   Increasing the amount of FSH could cause ovulation of more than one ovum *[1 mark]*.
   This could lead to multiple pregnancy, which could have health risks for the mother and the children *[1 mark]*.
   Drug could have side effects *[1 mark]*.
   It could cost a lot for taxpayers or for the family — and there's still no guarantee she would get pregnant *[1 mark]*.
   When you're asked to 'Evaluate' something, make sure you discuss both sides of the argument. It's okay to reach a conclusion though, after you've discussed all the pros and cons. There are probably more points to argue about than just those given above, but don't spend too long — this question's only worth 4 marks. Most of it's just common sense, anyway.

Page 47 — Sexual Reproduction in Plants

1 a) Maximum of 4 marks available.
   A = Pollen tube *[1 mark]*.
   B = Embryo sac *[1 mark]*.
   C = Tube nucleus *[1 mark]*.
   D = Micropyle *[1 mark]*.
  b) Maximum of 2 marks available.
   The enzymes digest surrounding cells *[1 mark]*.
   It makes a path through to the ovary *[1 mark]*.

2 Maximum of 2 marks available, from any of the points below:
   It has long filaments and large anthers that stick out *[1 mark]*.
   It has a long, feathery / exposed stigma *[1 mark]*.
   It has no petals *[1 mark]*.
   You wouldn't get a mark for saying it's not scented. You'd be right, but you can't tell that from the diagram. Always read the question properly, and if they ask you to use a diagram make sure you do.

Section 7 — Ecosystems and the Environment
Page 49 — Energy Transfer Through an Ecosystem

1 Maximum of 2 marks available.
   The biomass is measured at a particular point in time, so only the standing crop is measured *[1 mark]*.
   Sometimes there can be a lower standing crop of producers compared to primary consumers if they don't live as long, but have a higher reproductive rate *[1 mark]*.

2 Maximum of 3 marks available.
   100 units passes into the producers *[1 mark]*.
   10 units pass into the primary consumers *[1 mark]*.
   1 unit therefore passes into the secondary consumers *[1 mark]*.
   Don't let daft little details like these 'arbitrary units' put you off. It just means that they're any old units, it doesn't matter what, and this actually makes the question easier for you.

Page 51 — Recycling Nutrients

1 Maximum of 10 marks available, from any of the following:
   If a question asks you to 'give an account,' that means you have to describe what happens in words. But it never hurts to include a diagram, which will make things clearer for the examiner and could help jog your memory.
   Mention the 4 processes that remove nitrogen from the atmosphere:
   Nitrogen fixation by free living bacteria (Azotobacter) *[1 mark]*.
   and those in root nodules (Rhizobium) *[1 mark]*.
   Lightning *[1 mark]*.
   Haber process *[1 mark]*.
   Mention the 4 ways nitrogen enters and leaves the food chain:
   Uptake of ammonium and nitrate ions by plants *[1 mark]*.
   Consumers get nitrogen by feeding on other organisms *[1 mark]*.
   Decomposers release ammonium ions *[1 mark]* when they feed on dead organisms *[1 mark]*.
   2 marks for explaining nitrification:
   Nitrosomonas convert ammonium ions into nitrite *[1 mark]* and Nitrobacter convert nitrite into nitrate *[1 mark]*.
   2 marks for explaining denitrification: Conversion of nitrates to nitrogen gas *[1 mark]* by Pseudomonas and Thiobacillus *[1 mark]*.
   Make sure you know the difference between nitrification and nitrogen fixation, which often get confused. Nitrogen fixation is bacteria turning nitrogen gas into ammonium ions or amino acids. Nitrification is bacteria turning ammonium ions into nitrate.

2 Maximum of 2 marks available, from any of the following:
   Combustion *[1 mark]*.
   Respiration *[1 mark]*.
   Carbon dioxide released by decay of dead organisms *[1 mark]*.

Page 53 — Environmental Adaptations

1 Maximum of 3 marks available.
   Behavioural — buries head in mud with tail pointing upwards. Wiggles tail about to circulate oxygenated water *[1 mark]*.
   Physiological — blood contains haemoglobin to help it absorb oxygen *[1 mark]*.
   Structural — capillaries very close to thin surface at the tail end so that oxygen can diffuse into the worm through the surface *[1 mark]*.

2 Maximum of 5 marks available.
   $10 \, cm^3 l^{-1}$ — fast-flowing river has more oxygen than a pond *[1 mark]* because the movement of water incorporates oxygen *[1 mark]*.
   $210 \, cm^3 l^{-1}$ — terrestrial environment *[1 mark]*. This is 21% oxygen, which is the concentration of oxygen in the atmosphere. More oxygen in terrestrial environments than aquatic. *[1 mark only available, for either or both of these explanations.]*.
   $5 \, cm^3 l^{-1}$ — pond *[1 mark]*.

Page 55 — Modes of Nutrition

1 Maximum of 5 marks available.
   Named parasite: Taenia solium *[1 mark]*.
   4 marks for describing adaptations, from any of the following:
   Hooks and suckers as a means of attaching to the host *[1 mark]*.
   Covered in a cuticle, to resist the defence mechanisms of the host *[1 mark]*.
   Many eggs are produced to increase chance of spreading to another host *[1 mark]*.
   No digestive system— it just absorbs the host's digested products *[1 mark]*.
   Long and thin for a large surface area to absorb nutrients through *[1 mark]*.
   Long and thin shape so that it doesn't block the gut, killing the host *[1 mark]*.

2 Maximum of 4 marks available.
   Rhizopus fungi have thread-like cells called hyphae to penetrate the food *[1 mark]*.
   Enzymes are released from the hyphae to digest the food surrounding them *[1 mark]*.

Answers

Large insoluble molecules are broken down by the enzymes, giving smaller soluble products **[1 mark]**.
These are then absorbed into the hyphae cells **[1 mark]**.

Page 57 — Human Influences on the Environment

1 Maximum of 8 marks available.
Fertilisers increase the nitrate and phosphate levels in rivers and lakes as they are leached into water systems from the soil **[1 mark]**.
This leads to eutrophication **[1 mark]** where the following happens — Algae and other photosynthetic organisms grow faster due to the increase in nitrates and phosphates **[1 mark]**.
These organisms die faster than they can be eaten **[1 mark]**.
This increases the biological oxygen demand (BOD) of the water **[1 mark]** due to the increase in decomposers, which feed on the decaying matter **[1 mark]**.
Their increased respiration depletes the oxygen in the water **[1 mark]**.
The lack of oxygen leads to the death of fish and other organisms in the water **[1 mark]**.
Examiners really like questions about the environment, so make sure you learn these pages extra carefully.

Section 8 — Applications of Biology
Page 59 — Genetic Engineering

1 a) Maximum of 2 marks available.
Extract all the DNA from the cell **[1 mark]**.
Identify the gene and use a restriction endonuclease enzyme to cut it out **[1 mark]**.
  b) Maximum of 2 marks available.
Add the same restriction endonuclease enzyme to bacterial plasmids (the bacterial DNA) **[1 mark]**.
Insert the gene into the treated plasmids and add ligase to attach the gene to bacterial DNA **[1 mark]**.
Don't panic if the question mentions organisms you haven't learnt about. If you read it carefully it will contain familiar ideas. This is the examiners' way of seeing whether you understand the main ideas and if you can apply what you've learnt.

2 a) Restriction endonuclease **[1 mark]**.
  b) Ligase **[1 mark]**.

Page 61 — Genetic Fingerprinting

1 a) Maximum of 1 mark available.
Genetic / DNA fingerprinting **[1 mark]**.
  b) Maximum of 5 marks available.
A blood/semen/sweat/hair/skin sample would be taken from the suspect **[1 mark]**.
The DNA from the sample would be cut into fragments by the specific restriction endonucleases **[1 mark]**.
The DNA fragments from both samples would be separated out by size using electrophoresis **[1 mark]**.
Radioactive gene probes would be used to make the DNA fragment patterns of both samples visible **[1 mark]**.
The bands on the photographic film would be compared to those of DNA samples found at the scene of the crime **[1 mark]**.
'Explain' in an exam question tests your ability to apply your knowledge. You must give your answer in the context of the question. Simply describing the technique of genetic fingerprinting wouldn't get you full marks.

Page 63 — Vectors and Micro-Organisms

1 a) Maximum of 1 mark available.
Replica plating **[1 mark]**.
  b) Maximum of 5 marks available.
Bacteria that have been transformed / have taken up the plasmid contain both the human gene and the gene for antibiotic resistance **[1 mark]**.
After being mixed with plasmids, the bacteria are cultured on an agar plate called the master plate **[1 mark]**.

Then a sterile velvet pad is pressed onto the master plate, which picks up some bacteria from each colony **[1 mark]**.
The pad is pressed onto a fresh agar plate, containing an antibiotic, and some of the bacteria from each colony are transferred onto the agar surface **[1 mark]**.
Only transformed bacteria can grow and reproduce on the replica plate — the others don't contain the antibiotic-resistant gene, so they stop growing **[1 mark]**.

2 Maximum of 3 marks available.
The viral DNA is combined with the useful gene to make recombinant DNA **[1 mark]**.
The virus then infects a bacterium by injecting its DNA strand into it **[1 mark]**.
The viral DNA is then integrated into the bacterium's DNA **[1 mark]**.
You could easily answer this question by drawing the diagram shown on p.62.

Page 65 — Gene Therapy

1 a) Maximum of 4 marks available.
The CFTR protein is a channel protein which allows chloride ions to move out of the cell **[1 mark]**. When there's a mutation in the CFTR gene, the CFTR protein is missing an amino acid which affects its 3D shape **[1 mark]**.
It can't let chloride ions through, so they build up in the cell **[1 mark]**. The build up of ions means that less water moves out of the cell by osmosis **[1 mark]**.
  b) Maximum of 5 marks available.
EITHER — Using liposomes as vectors:
Recombinant DNA technology is used to put healthy CFTR genes into plasmids **[1 mark]**.
The plasmids are wrapped in lipid droplets to form liposomes **[1 mark]**.
These are sprayed into the airways using an aerosol **[1 mark]**.
The liposomes fuse with the cell membranes of the airway epithelial cells, releasing the plasmids into the cells **[1 mark]**.
The human DNA is expressed and normal CFTR is produced **[1 mark]**.
You don't need to go into details about recombinant DNA technology here — the point of the question is how the vector is used.
OR — Using viruses as vectors:
Adenoviruses are treated to make the viral DNA harmless **[1 mark]**.
The inactivated viral DNA and the healthy CFTR gene are joined to form recombinant DNA **[1 mark]**.
The modified viruses are sprayed into the lungs **[1 mark]**.
The viruses inject the airway epithelial cells with their DNA, which also injects the healthy CFTR gene **[1 mark]**.
The CFTR gene is expressed by the epithelial cells in the usual way **[1 mark]**.

2 a) Maximum of 3 marks available.
The human gene coding for production of factor VIII is cloned and combined with a promoter sequence of DNA **[1 mark]**.
Mature eggs are taken from the sheep's ovary, fertilised in vitro and then have the factor VIII gene microinjected into them **[1 mark]**.
The zygotes are cultured in vitro and are implanted into sheep surrogate mothers **[1 mark]**.
Don't be put off just because it's a different protein from the one described on page 65 — the process is exactly the same.
  b) Maximum of 1 mark available, from any of the following:
Less risk of transfer of infectious agents from donor **[1 mark]**.
More protein produced from easily accessible source **[1 mark]**.
Less risk of allergic response from other blood proteins **[1 mark]**.

Answers

Page 67 — Growing Food Commercially

1 Maximum of 4 marks available.
Waterlogged soil has very little oxygen for respiration *[1 mark]* so rice uses anaerobic respiration *[1 mark]*. Anaerobic respiration produces lots of toxic ethanol *[1 mark]*. Rice is tolerant to ethanol and not poisoned by the excess *[1 mark]*.
You don't need to go into loads of details about anaerobic respiration — you just need the details that are relevant to this question about rice plants. You won't get marks for any extra details you put in.

2 Maximum of 4 marks available, from any of the answers below:
Farmers manipulate the environment in carefully controlled greenhouses. They increase light intensity *[1 mark]*, supply carbon dioxide at constant 0.4% *[1 mark]* and keep temperature at 25°C optimum for photosynthesis *[1 mark]*. They supply water *[1 mark]* and fertiliser *[1 mark]* and they control soil pH *[1 mark]*.

Page 69 — Fertilisers and Pesticides

1 Maximum of 4 marks available.
Leaves contain photosynthetic tissue *[1 mark]*.
If leaves are eaten then photosynthesis is reduced *[1 mark]*.
Lower photosynthesis means less food, so respiration decreases *[1 mark]*.
Growth slows and crop yields are lower *[1 mark]*.

Make sure you put in every stage in the sequence of events — so you get the full 4 marks. Don't just assume that a stage is too obvious to mention.

2 Maximum of 4 marks available, from any of the answers below (but at least one advantage and one disadvantage must be mentioned):
Advantages — fewer toxins absorbed by non-target organism *[1 mark]*.
Pests don't build up resistance to biological agents like they do to pesticides *[1 mark]*.
Disadvantages — resurgence of pests *[1 mark]*.
Release of biological agents into environment might damage food chains / webs *[1 mark]*.
Slow to work *[1 mark]*.
It's good to learn some examples of biological agents and pesticides.

Section 9 — Disease and Immunology
Page 71 — Health and Disease

1 Maximum of 4 marks available.
Points you could include in your answer:
Advantages —
Eradication of inherited diseases *[1 mark]*.
Less human suffering / early deaths *[1 mark]*.
Disadvantages —
Religious view of not altering 'God's work' *[1 mark]*.
Choice of 'designer' babies could lead to a change in gender percentage of population *[1 mark]*.
It's hard to draw the line between improving health and changing natural laws *[1 mark]*.
Any other suitable answer referring to ethical/moral issues.
Give a balanced answer — there are two marks available for advantages and two marks for disadvantages.

2 Maximum of 4 marks available. Any of the following points are acceptable.
Many areas of LEDCs have contaminated water supplies *[1 mark]*, poor medical care *[1 mark]*, poor education *[1 mark]*, poor housing *[1 mark]*, and malnutrition *[1 mark]*. Plus any other sensible answer.

Page 73 — A Balanced Diet and Essential Nutrients

1 Maximum of 3 marks available.
Equation EAR = BMR x PAL *[1 mark]*.

EAR = 7.2 x 1.4 = 10.08 (will accept 10.1) *[1 mark]* MJ per day *[1 mark]*.
(One mark for showing the equation / working, one mark for the correct answer (10.8), one mark for including units (MJ per day).
You need to learn the equation for this — they won't give it to you in the exam. Always remember to show your working and put the correct units on at the end or you'll be throwing away easy marks. They've given you the units you need to use in the question (MJ per day), so make sure you use them in your answer.

2 Maximum of 4 marks available.
Essential amino acids can't be made in the body *[1 mark]*, so have to be included in food / diet *[1 mark]*.
Some can be converted into non-essential amino acids *[1 mark]* and all types of amino acids make proteins required in the body *[1 mark]*.

Page 75 — Malnutrition

1 a) Maximum of 2 marks available — 1 mark for correctly naming a disease, 1 mark for giving the correct cause(s):
EITHER: Marasmus *[1 mark]* — cause is PEM / lack of protein and energy *[1 mark]*.
OR: Kwashiorkor *[1 mark]* — cause is PEM / lack of protein and energy *[1 mark]*. Or any other sensible answer.
  b) Maximum of 2 marks available — 1 mark for correctly naming a disease, 1 mark for giving the correct cause(s):
Obesity *[1 mark]* — cause is over-eating / high fat diet / not enough exercise / underactive thyroid gland *[1 mark]*.
Or any other sensible answer.

2 Maximum of 4 marks available.
Vitamin A is needed to make retinoic acid *[1 mark]*, which is needed for fighting pathogens *[1 mark]*.
It's also needed to make rhodopsin in the rod cells in the eyes *[1 mark]*, which is used to help us see in dim light *[1 mark]*.

Page 77 — Prevention and Cure

1 Maximum of 8 marks available.
A bypass operation uses sections of a vein taken from the leg *[1 mark]*. These are attached to the heart *[1 mark]* so that the blood can flow through them and bypass a blocked coronary artery *[1 mark]*. This gives the heart muscle a better supply of oxygen and nutrients so it can function better *[1 mark]*.
Transplant operations can give patients new hearts, but heart donors are in short supply *[1 mark]*. If a patient's symptoms can be eased with a bypass, this leaves donor hearts available for more urgent cases *[1 mark]*. It's best not to do a transplant anyway unless it's absolutely necessary, because the heart might be rejected by the patient's immune system *[1 mark]*, which could kill them *[1 mark]*.
Bear in mind the examiner will give you marks for what you know, not penalise you for mistakes. You won't lose marks if you include something you're not sure about and it turns out to be wrong, but you'll gain them if it's right.

2 Maximum of 4 marks available.
If a patient doesn't take the full prescribed course of antibiotics *[1 mark]* this leads to some of the most resistant bacteria remaining and reproducing *[1 mark]*. Bacteria reproduce asexually *[1 mark]* so offspring will be clones and therefore resistant to the antibiotic *[1 mark]*.

Page 79 — Effects of Smoking

1 Maximum of 4 marks available.
Passive smoking has been shown to be responsible for smoking related deaths and poor health *[1 mark]*. Give examples of diseases caused by tobacco smoke *[1 mark for each]*. Acceptable examples include lung cancer, bronchitis, emphysema, arteriosclerosis, coronary heart disease, strokes, thrombosis.
For a question like this it would be a good idea to briefly say how inhaling tobacco smoke causes these diseases, e.g. 'some of the toxic chemicals

Answers

from the tar in tobacco smoke are carcinogenic, so can cause lung cancer when inhaled.' Note that this question is not asking you to argue for and against banning smoking in public places.

2   Maximum of 4 marks available.
Chemicals in tobacco smoke destroy fibrous elastin tissue in alveoli *[1 mark]*. This means the alveoli can't expand as air enters the lungs *[1 mark]*. The smoke also increases the number of protein-eating phagocyte cells, which digest the alveolar tissue *[1 mark]*. This reduces the surface area for gas exchange *[1 mark]*.

Page 81 — Cholera, Malaria, TB and AIDS

1   Maximum of 3 marks available.
Contact tracing enables quick identification of those people with an infectious disease who might have caught it from an infected person or passed it onto them originally *[1 mark]*. Preventative measures can be taken more quickly *[1 mark]*, so the disease is not transmitted *[1 mark]*.

2   Maximum of 4 marks available. Any of the following are acceptable.
Unprotected sex *[1 mark]* / mixing body fluids, like sweat and blood *[1 mark]* / sharing needles for drug use *[1 mark]* / across the placenta from mother to baby / in breast milk from mother the baby *[1 mark]*. Any other sensible answer.

Page 83 — The Immune System

1   Maximum of 8 marks available.
The cellular response involves the T-lymphocytes *[1 mark]*. T-lymphocytes recognise 'foreign' antigens on the surface of pathogens, like bacteria, which cause disease *[1 mark]*. Cytotoxic / killer T cells stick to these antigens and secrete substances that kill the pathogen *[1 mark]*. Helper T-cells help plasma B-cells make antibodies and attract macrophages which destroy the pathogen *[1 mark]*. Memory T-cells have the ability to recognise an antigen in the future if it re-enters the body *[1 mark]*. This enables a quicker response the second time round *[1 mark]*. Suppressor T-cells stop activity of killer T-cells and B-cells when antigens have been destroyed *[1 mark]*. The cellular response also triggers the humoral response *[1 mark]*.
This question has a lot of marks available. Don't worry if your answer is organised differently to the one above (as long as you've included most of the same points) but do make sure it has a sensible structure.

2   Maximum of 6 marks available.
Antibodies are produced by B-lymphocytes *[1 mark]* and are specific to one antigen *[1 mark]*. They bind to the antigen *[1 mark]* forming antigen-antibody complexes *[1 mark]* which can be disposed of by macrophages *[1 mark]*. They can also rupture cells themselves, and neutralise toxins *[1 mark]*.
Don't fall into the trap of thinking both parts of a question must always be worth equal marks. Most of the marks for this question are for describing the function of the antibodies.

Page 85 — Immunity and Vaccinations

1   Maximum of 7 marks available.
People of blood group A have type A antigens on their red blood cells *[1 mark]* and type B antibodies in their plasma *[1 mark]*. People of blood group B have type B antigens on their red blood cells *[1 mark]* and type A antibodies in their blood plasma *[1 mark]*. If these two blood groups are mixed in one person after a transfusion, agglutination occurs *[1 mark]*. Type A antibodies bind to type A antigens in the foreign blood, and type B antibodies bind to the type B antigens in the foreign blood *[1 mark]*. This can be dangerous as it leads to clumping of blood cells, which can block arteries *[1 mark]*.

2   Maximum of 6 marks available.
The disease is caused by an infectious bacterium *[1 mark]*. Pathogens are killed or weakened for use in vaccines, but it might be possible for some dangerous bacteria to remain *[1 mark]*. Genetic

engineering can reduce the danger by using restriction endonucleases to extract just the antigen genes from the pathogen's DNA *[1 mark]*. These genes can be inserted in plasmids in harmless bacteria *[1 mark]* to produce large amounts of the antigen *[1 mark]*. This can then be injected to give the immune response needed *[1 mark]*.
Exam questions often link in bits from other areas of biology. As long as you've revised everything properly, that shouldn't be a problem. For this one you need to know about genetic engineering as well as the immune system, but it's OK because you'll never be tested on anything not covered by your syllabus.

Section 10 — Exchange and Transport in Animals
Page 87 — Nutrient and Gaseous Exchange

1   Maximum of 4 marks available.
The gills consist of thin lamellae *[1 mark]* which provide a large surface area for exchange *[1 mark]*.
The counter-current system, where blood and water flow in opposite directions, makes diffusion more efficient *[1 mark]*.
Blood is always flowing towards water containing lots of oxygen, which maintains a steep concentration gradient *[1 mark]*.

2   Maximum of 4 marks available.
Humans are large multicellular organisms *[1 mark]*.
The surface area : volume ratio is small in large organisms *[1 mark]*, which makes diffusion too slow *[1 mark]*.
Humans need specialised organs with a large enough surface area to keep all their cells supplied with enough oxygen and to remove CO_2 *[1 mark]*.

Page 89 — Ventilation and Cardiac Output

1   Maximum of 4 marks available.
Blood flow increases in skeletal muscle and heart because demand for oxygen during aerobic respiration increases *[1 mark]*.
Blood flow decreases in the digestive system because demand for nutrients is lower than demand for oxygen *[1 mark]*.
It remains the same in the brain and kidneys because the brain needs a constant supply of oxygen *[1 mark]*, and blood must be continuously cleaned as it travels through the kidneys *[1 mark]*.
As this question shows, it's not always 1 mark for each point you make. In this case you have to say what happens and why to get just one mark. So don't make 4 points and decide you've done enough — make sure you've actually answered the question.

2   Maximum of 3 marks available.
With hypertension, blood pressure is too high *[1 mark]*.
This puts extra strain on the ventricular muscle and causes heart damage *[1 mark]*.
Blood travels at higher pressure through arteries so they are constantly expanding, and this can lead to strokes *[1 mark]*.

3   Maximum of 5 marks available.
Pulmonary ventilation would go up *[1 mark]* because breathing rate would increase *[1 mark]* and so would tidal volume *[1 mark]*. This is because of the increased demand for oxygen for aerobic respiration *[1 mark]* and decrease in pH due to extra CO_2 in the blood *[1 mark]*.

Page 91 — Energy Sources and Exercise

1   Maximum of 4 marks available.
Vigorous exercise means oxygen demand exceeds supply and the body's skeletal muscles begin to respire anaerobically *[1 mark]*. This produces lactic acid, which increases the toxicity in blood *[1 mark]*. Removal of lactic acid by oxidisation to pyruvate requires oxygen *[1 mark]* — when exercise stops this oxygen debt can be repaid *[1 mark]*.

2   Maximum of 5 marks available, from any of the answers below:
Improved heart *[1 mark]* or lung *[1 mark]* function.
Resistance to disease *[1 mark]*.
Reduces excess weight *[1 mark]* and decreases cholesterol *[1 mark]*.
Improved posture *[1 mark]*.

Answers

Improved mental faculties [1 mark].
Better muscle tone/less likely to strain muscles [1 mark].
Loads of marks to choose from here — a lot of the time it's easy to drop one, but with questions like this you need to make the most of it and grab them all. Don't start putting down all the reasons you know, five will do thanks, but if you couldn't think of five then you definitely need to go over the page again. (If the way the question was phrased put you off, I forgive you and you'll know for next time).

Page 93 — Transport Systems

1   Maximum of 4 marks available:
Alveoli [1 mark] and villi [1 mark].
Both are small so have high surface area : volume ratio [1 mark], both have thin membranes and are close to capillaries so there's a short diffusion pathway for exchange of substances [1 mark].
Surface area to volume ratio again. It comes up everywhere — if in doubt, just put surface area to volume ratio. Best if you know what you're talking about though, so make sure you really understand the idea behind those magic words. Have another look at page 86 if you haven't quite got it yet.

2   Maximum of 6 marks available:
Diffusion alone wouldn't be fast enough to carry out enough exchange of materials [1 mark]. This is because larger organisms tend to have a tough outer surface, so it's harder for substances to enter that way [1 mark]. Once the substances were inside they would need to travel too far to reach the cells deepest inside the body in time [1 mark]. Larger organisms have a low surface area to volume ratio [1 mark] and need a large quantity of substances [1 mark] (multicellular animals have greater demand due to a higher metabolic rate) [1 mark].

Page 95 — Blood, Tissue Fluid and Lymph

1   Maximum of 5 marks available.
Tissue fluid moves out of capillaries by pressure filtration / hydrostatic pressure [1 mark].
At the arteriole end, pressure in capillary beds is greater than pressure in tissue fluid outside capillaries [1 mark].
This means fluid from blood is forced out of the capillaries [1 mark].
Fluid loss means the water potential of blood capillaries is lower than that of tissue fluid [1 mark].
So fluid moves into the capillaries at the venule end by osmosis [1 mark].

2   Maximum of 3 marks available.
Phagocytes engulf pathogens / microorganisms and digest them [1 mark].
They contain many lysosomes to aid digestion [1 mark].
They have elongated nuclei, and fluid cytoplasm so they can squeeze through gaps to reach the site of infection [1 mark].
Exam questions relating to structure and function are a favourite. Find a way (cartoons, poems, tables) to remember the name, structure and function all together to avoid confusion.

Page 97 — Haemoglobin and Oxygen Transport

1   Maximum of 3 marks available.
The foetus relies on oxygen diffused from the mother's blood [1 mark].
If the haemoglobin of the foetal and mother's blood had the same affinity for oxygen they'd be competing for oxygen and diffusion wouldn't happen [1 mark].
So foetal haemoglobin has a higher affinity for oxygen than its mother's blood [1 mark].

2   Maximum of 4 marks available.
When tissues are active, cells respire more quickly [1 mark].
Oxygen is used up faster, creating a low pO_2 [1 mark].
Also, more CO_2 is released by cells, giving a higher pCO_2 [1 mark].
Both factors mean oxygen unloading from oxyhaemoglobin is increased [1 mark].
Make sure you mention both pO_2 and pCO_2 in questions about the Bohr effect.

Page 99 — Circulation , the Heart and the Cardiac Cycle

1   Maximum of 3 marks available.
Pressure increases in atria during atrial systole and in ventricles during ventricular systole [1 mark].
Pressure decreases in atria during atrial diastole and in the ventricles during ventricular diastole [1 mark].
There is always more pressure on the left side of the heart due to extra muscle tissue producing more force [1 mark].
This question doesn't ask you to describe the cardiac cycle — it specifically asks you to describe the pressure changes in diastole and systole. Make sure you mention both atria and ventricles in your answer.

2   Maximum of 6 marks available.
The valves only open one way [1 mark].
Whether they open or close depends on the relative pressure of the heart chambers [1 mark].
If the pressure is greater behind a valve (i.e. there's blood in the chamber behind it) [1 mark], it's forced open, to let the blood travel in the right direction [1 mark].
When the blood goes through the valve, the pressure is greater above the valve [1 mark], which forces it shut, preventing blood from flowing back into the chamber [1 mark].
Here you need to explain how valves function in relation to blood flow, rather than just in relation to relative pressures.

Page 101 — Control of Heartbeat

1   Maximum of 4 marks available.
The low blood pressure would be detected by pressure receptors in the arteries [1 mark].
The pressure receptors would send impulses to the cardiovascular centre in the medulla in the brain [1 mark].
The cardiovascular centre would then send impulses to the SAN to speed up the heart rate [1 mark].
This would cause blood pressure to increase [1 mark].
Make sure you've said that speeding up the heart rate is done to increase blood pressure. It might seem a bit obvious, but you should still write it to show you understand the whole process.

2   Maximum of 6 marks available.
The SAN produces a stimulus [1 mark] which causes the left and right atrial muscle to contract [1 mark].
The AVN picks up the stimulus [1 mark] and sends impulses through the Bundle of His [1 mark] and on to the Purkyne tissue in the ventricle walls [1 mark], which enable the left and right ventricles to contract [1 mark].
Examiners hate the use of 'messages' or 'signals' for nerve impulses — use the correct terms so you don't throw away easy marks.

Page 103 — Digestion and Absorption

1   Maximum of 4 marks available, from any of the 8 points below.
Polypeptides are broken down by peptidases [1 mark] to form amino acids [1 mark] when peptide bonds are hydrolysed [1 mark].
Exopeptidases hydrolyse peptide bonds between amino acids on the outside [1 mark] of the polypeptide chain. Endopeptidases hydrolyse peptide bonds between amino acids on the inside [1 mark] of the polypeptide chain. Peptidases are released into the acidic conditions of the stomach in gastric juice [1 mark] and in the duodenum from pancreatic juice [1 mark] and from the epithelial cells lining the small intestine [1 mark].

2   Maximum of 4 marks available.
Small, soluble products of digestion (e.g. glucose, amino acids, fatty acids) [1 mark] are absorbed into the body through microvilli lining the gut wall [1 mark]. Absorption is through diffusion, facilitated diffusion and active transport [1 mark if all 3 methods are mentioned].

Answers

Section 11 — Exchange and Transport in Plants
Page 105 — Exchange and Transport in Plants

1   Maximum of 6 marks available:
Potassium ions are pumped into the guard cells [1 mark] by active transport [1 mark].
Starch in the chloroplasts is converted into malate [1 mark].
This increases the solute concentration / decreases the water potential of the cell sap [1 mark].
Water flows into the cell by osmosis [1 mark].
Due to the different thicknesses of the guard cell's cell walls, the guard cell bulges outwards, opening the stoma [1 mark].
Any of the marks above could be obtained by drawing an annotated diagram. Using a diagram could save time in the exam, and make it easier to remember all six points.

2   Maximum of 8 marks available.
Up to 4 marks for correctly naming each factor. Up to 4 marks for explaining the effect of each one.
Light [1 mark].
The stomata close in the dark, so transpiration cannot happen [1 mark].
Temperature [1 mark].
Increasing temperature speeds up the movement of the water molecules [1 mark].
Humidity [1 mark].
Increasing humidity reduces the diffusion gradient between the leaf and the air, so transpiration slows down (or reverse argument for decreasing humidity) [1 mark].
Air movement/wind [1 mark].
Dispersion of the water molecules in the air around the stomata maintains the diffusion gradient [1 mark].

3   Maximum of 4 marks available.
Leaf is curled [1 mark].
Stomata are in pits [1 mark].
'Hairs' on the epidermis [1 mark].
Thick cuticle [1 mark].

Page 107 — Xylem and Phloem

1   Maximum of 10 marks available:
Distribution can be explained in words or by diagrams, whichever you find easier. In either case, these are the key points:
In the stem —
Xylem and phloem towards the outside, with the phloem outside the xylem [1 mark].
In the root —
The xylem and phloem in the centre, with the phloem outside the xylem [1 mark].
In the leaf —
Main vein in the midrib, smaller veins in the rest of the leaf, with xylem above the phloem [1 mark].
Function of xylem — to transport water and minerals [1 mark] and to provide support [1 mark].
Stem is subjected to bending forces [1 mark].
This is best resisted by strengthening around the outside [1 mark].
Root is subjected to crushing forces [1 mark].
This is best resisted by strengthening in the centre [1 mark].
The leaf is thin and needs support throughout the tissue [1 mark].

2   Maximum of 12 marks available:
Only 1 mark for correctly naming all 4 cell types — vessel elements, tracheids, parenchyma cells, fibre cells [1 mark].
Vessels — Up to 2 marks for correctly naming features, from any of the following:
Thickened and lignified walls [1 mark].
No cytoplasm / dead cells [1 mark].
No end walls [1 mark].
Functions — transport of water / mineral ions and support [1 mark]. Both functions needed for mark.

Tracheids —
Thickened and lignified walls [1 mark].
No cytoplasm/dead cells [1 mark]
Functions — transport of water and support [1 mark].
Both functions needed for mark.
Parenchyma —
Living cells [1 mark].
Unthickened walls [1 mark].
Function — food storage/radial transport [1 mark].
Fibres —
Very thick walls [1 mark].
Narrow lumen [1 mark].
Function — support [1 mark].
Pay attention to how much you need to know about each type of cell. There's more to remember about the structure of vessels than about the structure of fibres, so make sure you spend more time learning it.

Page 109 — Water Transport

1   Maximum of 6 marks available:
a) *Dissolved mineral ions pass through the cell walls en route to the xylem [1 mark].*
   This is the apoplast pathway [1 mark].
b) *Each endodermis cell has a waxy Casparian strip in its cell wall that water can't penetrate [1 mark].*
   This blocks the apoplast pathway and allows selective absorption through the cell membrane [1 mark].
c) *Plasmodesmata connect the cytoplasm of adjacent cells so dissolved ions can travel from cell to cell through them [1 mark].*
   This is the symplast pathway [1 mark].

2   Maximum of 4 marks available:
Loss of water from the leaves due to transpiration pulls more water in from xylem [1 mark].
There are cohesive forces between water molecules [1 mark].
These cause water to be pulled up the xylem [1 mark].
Removing leaves means no transpiration occurs, so no water is pulled up the xylem [1 mark].
It's pretty obvious (because there are 4 marks to get) that it's not enough just to say removing the leaves stops transpiration. You also need to explain why transpiration is so important in moving water through the xylem. It's always worth checking how many marks a question is worth — this gives you a clue about how long your answer should be, and how many details you need to include.

Page 111 — Translocation

1   Maximum of 2 marks available:
Greatest radioactivity would be seen in growing areas of the plant (e.g. young leaves, the growing point of the stem and the growing points in the roots) [1 mark]. These areas would receive most sugar because they are where most energy is needed for growth [1 mark].

2   Maximum of 4 marks available:
Sugars are actively transported into the sieve tubes at the source end [1 mark].
This decreases the water potential of the sieve tubes [1 mark].
This causes water to flow in by osmosis [1 mark].
This means pressure is increased inside the sieve tubes at the source end [1 mark].
I think this is a pretty nasty question. If you got it all right first time you're probably a genius. If you didn't, you're probably not totally clear yet about the pressure gradient idea. It's just that when a cell fills with fluid, the molecules inside are under more and more pressure. If there's a high concentration of sugar in a cell, this draws in water by osmosis, and so increases the pressure inside the cell.

Index

Index

Index

Index

Index